✕ INSIGHT CITY GUIDE

TORONTO

Part of the Langenscheidt Publishing Group

✹INSIGHT GUIDE
TORONTO

Editor
Lesley Gordon
Art Director
Klaus Geisler
Picture Editor
Hilary Genin
Cartography Editor
Zoë Goodwin
Production
Kenneth Chan
Editorial Director
Brian Bell

Distribution

United States
Langenscheidt Publishers, Inc.
36–36 33rd Street 4th Floor
Long Island City, NY 11106
Fax: (1) 718 784-0640

UK & Ireland
GeoCenter International Ltd
The Viables Centre, Harrow Way
Basingstoke, Hants RG22 4BJ
Fax: (44) 1256-817988

Australia
Universal Publishers
1 Waterloo Road
Macquarie Park, NSW 2113
Fax: (61) 2 9888 9074

New Zealand
Hema Maps New Zealand Ltd (HNZ)
Unit D, 24 Ra ORA Drive
East Tamaki, Auckland
Fax: (64) 9 273 6479

Worldwide
Apa Publications GmbH & Co.
Verlag KG (Singapore branch)
38 Joo Koon Road, Singapore 628990
Tel: (65) 6865-1600. Fax: (65) 6861-6438

Printing

Insight Print Services (Pte) Ltd
38 Joo Koon Road, Singapore 628990
Tel: (65) 6865-1600. Fax: (65) 6861-6438

ABOUT THIS BOOK

The first Insight Guide pioneered the use of creative full-colour photography in guidebooks in 1970. Since then, we have expanded our range to cater for our readers' need not only for reliable information about their chosen destination but also for a real understanding of that destination. Now, when the internet can supply inexhaustible (but not always reliable) facts, our books marry text and pictures to provide that much more elusive quality: knowledge. To achieve this, they rely heavily on the authority of locally based writers and photographers.

How to use this book

The book is carefully structured both to convey an understanding of the city and its culture and to guide readers through its sights and activities:

◆ To understand Toronto today, you need to know something of its past. The first section covers the city's history and culture in lively, authoritative essays written by specialists.

◆ The main Places section provides a full run-down of all the attractions worth seeing. The main places of interest are coordinated by number with full-colour maps.

◆ The Travel Tips listings section provides a point of reference for information on travel, hotels, restaurants, shops and festivals. Information may be located quickly by using the index printed on the back cover flap – and the flaps are designed to serve as bookmarks.

◆ Photographs are chosen not only to illustrate geography and buildings but also to convey the moods of the city and the life of its people.

The contributors

This book was created by **Lesley Gordon**, an Insight Guides editor who commissioned a team of writers who were either based in Toronto or who had close links with, and an intimate knowledge of, the city.

The principal author was **Joanna Ebbutt**, an experienced writer and editor, who also produced *Insight Pocket Guide: Toronto* and *Quebec*. Ebbutt has lived in downtown Toronto for over two decades. Her chapters include *Downtown Waterfront*, *Old Toronto*, *Scarborough Bluffs*, *The West End*, *Around Toronto*, and also text on The Elgin and Winter Garden Theatre complex, festivals, the introduction to Places and a run-down of the best places to go in Toronto.

Also on the writing team was **Mimi Tompkins**, a Toronto-born and bred journalist living in New York. Tompkins took to writing about her home with enthusiasm, providing chapters about *The Beaches*, *The Entertainment District and Downtown West*, and the *Financial District*. She also wrote text about people, shopping, the city's comedy clubs, famous Torontonians and the choice of ethnic restaurants.

Penny Phenix, a writer, editor and a frequent Insight Guide contributor, provided several chapters, including text about the CN Tower, the artists known as the Group of Seven, the Art Gallery of Ontario, and chapters about the *Toronto Islands*, *Neighbourhoods*, and *University and The Annex*. Phenix also helped to edit the original text and compiled the index.

Lucy Waverman, a food and drink writer and newspaper columnist, wrote about the Toronto food scene and provided the comprehensive restaurant listings. She was assisted in her research by **Nancy Won**.

Other contributors include **Jo Phenix**, who wrote text for *Art and Culture*, *First Nations*, *Around Toronto*, sport and Toronto's donut shops. **Rebecca Marks** provided additional bar and café suggestions.

Globe and Mail journalist **Brian Milner** wrote an authoritative and colourful account of Toronto's history, while **Sarah Hood** compiled an exhaustive Travel Tips section.

Caroline Radula-Scott proofread the text, and the main photography was provided by a father and daughter team: **Richard** and **Daniella Nowitz**.

CONTACTING THE EDITORS

We would appreciate it if readers would alert us to errors or outdated information by writing to:

Insight Guides, P.O. Box 7910, London SE1 1WE, England. Fax: (44) 20 7403-0290. email: insight@apaguide.co.uk

www.insightguides.com
In North America:
www.insighttravelguides.com

Contents

Travel Tips

THE BEST OF TORONTO

Setting priorities, saving money, unique attractions...
here, at a glance, are our recommendations, plus some
tips and tricks even Torontonians won't always know

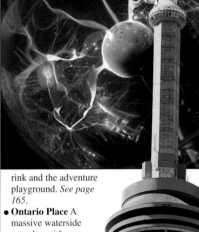

TORONTO FOR FAMILIES

These attractions are popular with children, but not
all will suit every age group.

● **Black Creek Pioneer Village** Life in rural Ontario in the mid 1800s is vividly and authentically portrayed by artisans in period costume. *See page 191.*

● **Casa Loma** A turreted, 98-room folly, designed by E.J. Lennox (of Old City Hall fame), for a riches-to-rags industrialist, Sir Henry

Pellatt. Complete with underground tunnels, secret passageways and huge stables. *See page 159.*

● **CN Tower** The world's tallest building. Spectacular views from the observation gallery with its famous glass-floor – to Rochester, New York and Niagara Falls on a fine day. *See page 123.*

● **Fort York** Established as a garrison in 1793. Guided tours and musket, drill and music demonstrations bring the fort's role in the city to life. *See page 116.*

● **Hockey Hall of Fame** Dedicated to Canada's favourite sport, with memorabilia that includes the beloved Stanley Cup, as well as flashy displays and interactive games. *See page 97.*

● **High Park** Loads to do, from the 25-minute scenic ride on the trackless train (seasonal) to the animal paddocks, the duck ponds, an ice

rink and the adventure playground. *See page 165.*

● **Ontario Place** A massive waterside complex with more than 30 rides and attractions including Soak City and a Cinesphere IMAX theatre. *See page 83.*

● **Ontario Science Centre** Explore what's hot in science and technology. Exhibitions include a scientific Times Square and daily real-world challengers to consider. *See page 192.*

● **Riverdale Farm** Meet the cows, horses, donkeys, sheep and goats on this 19th-century-style farm in the middle of the city. *See page 181.*

BEST SHOPPING

- **Aritzia** A hip Vancouver-based chain whose clothing by West Coast designers has won the hearts of women across the country; Eaton Centre. *See page 102.*
- **Black Market Vintage Clothing** A must for anyone seriously into vintage clothing. Perfect for fashion-savvy people who love to hunt through racks and bins; Kensington Market. *See page 121.*
- **The Guild Shop** A showcase of the Ontario Crafts Council. Worth checking for jewellery, hand-blown glass and wood objects, native and Inuit prints; Yorkville. *See page 65.*

- **Holt Renfrew** From selling hats in Quebec City in 1837, Holt Renfrew is now one of Canada's – and the world's – top peddlers of haute couture for men and women, along with accessories, cosmetics and home décor; Yorkville. *See page 156.*
- **David Mirvish Books** Superb collection of new and out-of-print artbooks. Wide price range; Mirvish Village. *See page 229.*
- **Lululemon** Yoga-inspired gear that has become a major fashion hit, for its comfortable apparel worn beyond the yoga studio; Queen St West. *See page 156.*

BEST FESTIVALS AND EVENTS

- **Caribana** This is the largest street festival of Caribbean music in North America. *See page 86.*
- **Dragon Boat Race** Over 200 teams compete in 100 races in two days. *See page 38.*
- **Cavalcade of Lights** Dazzling light displays and fireworks feature in this month-long event. *See page 38.*

- **Jazz Festivals** There is a wealth of traditional and contemporary jazz festivals throughout the summer. *See page 39.*

BEST SPAS

- **The Elmwood Spa**, 18 Elm Street. Centrally located in a historic landmark building (1890), this unpretentious spa has a wide selection of spa services. Sample the tasty cuisine. *See page 233.*

- **The Old Mill Inn and Spa**, 21 Old Mill Road. Beside the Humber River in the city's West End, a luxurious spa in a picturesque English setting. A place to unwind and rejuvenate. *See page 233.*

TORONTO'S MARKETS

- **Kensington Market** A multicultural enclave where shops sell food from Europe, the Caribbean, and Asia, alongside vintage clothing stores. Daily. *See page 121.*
- **Chinatown** The sights and sounds of Asia at Dundas West and Spadina Avenue, in an ever-expanding selection of oriental shops, fruit markets and restaurants. Daily. *See page 121.*

- **St Lawrence Market** Home to a market since 1803, serious foodies come at the crack of dawn on Saturdays, to get the best of the weekly farmers' market. Tues–Sat. *See page 131.*

- **Roots** A Canadian chain, known for its stylish casual indoor and outdoor wear for all age groups. Always a favourite with visiting celebrities; Yorkville. *See page 156.*

- **The Paisley Shop** Remarkable antiques from around the globe; Yorkville. *See page 65.*
- **Teatro Verde** Accessories for elegant homes; Yorkville. *See page 156.*

ARCHITECTURAL HIGHLIGHTS

- **Art Gallery of Ontario** Undergoing a dramatic redesign and expansion, by Toronto-born architect Frank Gehry. The gallery remains open. *See page 49.*
- **BCE Place** A stunning steel and glass structure designed by Spanish architect Santiago Calatrava, with a cathedral-like, glass-covered galleria. *See page 97.*
- **Fairmont Royal York Hotel** Built by Canadian Pacific Railways, a Toronto landmark since 1929, with its green copper, château-style roof. *See page 96.*
- **Flatiron Building** This wedge-shaped building, with its *trompe l'oeil* mural at the western end, is one of the city's most photographed landmarks. *See page 130.*
- **New City Hall** The 1965 design by Finnish architect Viljo Revell – of two curved towers around the domed council chamber with a large outdoor square in front – remains a well-used and well-liked civic centre. *See page 101.*

- **Old City Hall** A castle-like pile, Toronto's third city hall was built in 1899. Architect E J Lennox incorporated an intricately detailed frieze with caricatures of councillors who had annoyed him on the front façade. *See page 101.*
- **Ontario College of Art's Sharpe Centre for Design** A black-and-white box on coloured stilts, Will Alsop's award-winning design is a love-it or hate-it addition to the Toronto scene. *See page 121.*
- **Royal Bank Plaza** Eye-catching at all times, but especially when the sun reflects in its 14,000 windows tinted with real gold. *See page 98.*
- **Union Station** The cavernous and opulent Beaux-Arts-style 1920s building is the city's busiest transportation hub. *See page 96.*

TORONTO FOR BIRDERS

- **High Park** Hawk Hill is a great draw during the south-bound autumn raptor migration. *See page 165.*
- **Leslie Street Spit** Cited by BirdLife International as an important birding area for several large colonies of ring-billed bull, and Caspian terns. *See page 79.*
- **Scarborough Bluffs** From Bluffers Park east, there is great birding much of the

year, including Northern mocking birds, red-necked grebes, warblers, pileated woodpeckers and great horned owls. *See page 173.*

SCARBOROUGH BLUFF

The layers of sand and clay exposed in these bluffs di a remarkable geological record of the last stages of the Ice Age. Unique in North America they have attracted wide scientific interest. The first 46 metres (150 f sediments contain fossil plants and animals that w posited in a large river delta during the first adva the Wisconsin glacier some 70,000 years ago. T covered by 61 metres (200 feet) of boulder clay ar in alternating layers left by four subsequent advan retreats of the ice. The final withdrawal of the occurred some 12,000 years ago.

TORONTO FOR FREE (OR ALMOST FREE)

- **The Distillery District** The city's latest happening spot – a pedestrian-only arts and entertainment centre. *See page 135.*
- **Harbourfront Centre** Tons of free family activities and events, especially from mid-June

to early-September. It has become a great venue for festivals. *See page 79.*
- **Toronto Music Garden** A lovely waterfront garden designed to reflect, in nature, Bach's Suite No. 1 for Unaccompanied Cello. *See page 82.*
- **Toronto Necropolis** One of the city's oldest cemeteries, renowned for its High Victorian Gothic architecture and the final resting place for some of Toronto's most prominent citizens. *See page 181.*

BEST SIGHTSEEING TOURS

- **Harbour Tours**
Discover Toronto
Harbour and the
Islands by boat. No
need to book, just turn
up at the Harbourfront.
See page 231.

- **Hop-on, Hop-off City
Tour** Narrated tours
on a double-decker or
trolley bus, with the
option to get off and
explore further, along
the way. *See page 231.*

BEST WALKING TOURS – FREE

- **Discovery Walks**
Self-guided walks
through the city and
neighbourhoods. *See
page 232.*

- **ROMwalks** Excellent
tours led by volun-
teers from the Royal
Ontario Museum,
from early May to

mid-October. *See
page 232.*

- **University of
Toronto campus
tours** Capably led by
U of T students, the
tours include stops at
the school's seven
colleges. *See page
153.*

BEST ROOFTOP BAR AND PATIOS

- **Hemingway's** Three
rooftop patios, two
(heated) open all year
round. Great prices in
the heart of Yorkville.
See page 163.

- **Pur Supper Club**
A three-floor bar with
outdoor patios on the
first two floors and a
bamboo-themed
roof deck with
superb views.
*See page
124.*

- **Paupers** In the heart of
the Annex, a cabana-
styled rooftop patio
above a popular pub.
See page 163.

- **Roof Lounge, Park
Hyatt Toronto**
Beloved by Canada's
intelligentsia, with
great views. *See page
220.*

TORONTO FOR GAYS AND LESBIANS

- Home of the famous
Pride celebrations,
which culminate in
the annual show-
stopping parade that
attracts more than
250,000 people from
around the world. *See
page 236.*

- **Buddies in Bad
Times Theatre**
A leading professional

theatre, dedicated
to presenting gay,
lesbian and queer
(bisexual and trans-
gender) themes. *See
page 43.*

- For those wishing to
tie the knot, Ontario
law now permits
same-sex marriages,
through civil wed-
dings. *See page 236.*

MONEY-SAVING TIPS

A **CityPass** is an inexpensive way to visit six of Toronto's most popular attractions – the Art Gallery of Ontario, CN Tower, Royal Ontario Museum, Toronto Zoo, Ontario Science Centre and Casa Loma. It is approximately half price, costing $47.00 for adults and $29.75 for youths (4–12). Purchases in US dollars can be made online at www.citypass.com/city/toronto.html or in Canadian dollars at the ticket office of any of the attractions. The pass must be used within nine days of purchase.

Discounted, same-day **theatre tick-ets** can be purchased at **T.O.Tix**, either online at www.totix.ca or at their booth in Yonge-Dundas Square, Tues–Sat, noon–6:30pm.

Toronto has a good downtown hostel, Toronto Global Village Backpackers at 460 King Street West; tel: 1-888-344 7875; info@globalbackpackers.com. For **low-cost accommodation** in the summer, you can stay in the university dorms for very reasonable prices.

CITY LIVING

Toronto has been called "the city that works" and has long been regarded as a good place to live. But now the word is getting around: it's also a great place to visit

Give Toronto a persona and it would be a twenty-something who has emerged from a sometimes difficult childhood to become a sensible adult with a well-developed sense of fun. At an age when it is gaining a degree of sophistication, it would still enjoy clubbing until dawn and zipping around on rollerblades. It would be lively, good-humoured, politically correct, environmentally aware, immensely likeable and very good looking – the kind of person anyone would enjoy hanging out with.

People who have never been to Toronto often see it as a place their friends go to visit relatives – it seems everyone knows someone with family in Toronto, which in itself is an indication of its charms. They may listen with some scepticism to stories of how great it is: a big city that's cleaner than most, safer than most and very friendly? With world-class nightlife and spectacular scenery close by? A multicultural society with few racial tensions? Wonderful shopping at favourable prices and a high standard of international cuisine? Superb cultural attractions and a packed schedule of festivals and events? Doesn't it all seem too good to be true?

Toronto has all of this and more. And it's not just a place people like to visit – it's also a great place to live. The trend of moving out to the suburbs that prevailed in past decades is reversing, as Torontonians see the benefits of living within such a vibrant city, avoiding the daily commute and having so much to enjoy right on their doorstep. There's an excellent transport network and lovely residential areas: in chic apartments with magnificent lake views, in peaceful leafy streets of century-old homes and within walking distance of verdant parks and sandy beaches.

There's something special about a city that's enjoyed by its own citizens. It makes for a great atmosphere in downtown streets that don't die when the working day ends, in colourful markets full of locals shopping for their daily needs and on streetside restaurant patios where friends meet up on warm summer evenings. In winter, too, you can have fun here, skating alongside Torontonians at one of the open-air rinks, or keeping out of the cold in the PATH underground shopping network. Even if you don't have relatives here, Toronto is a great place to visit. ❑

PRECEDING PAGES: a ferry crosses from the Islands to the city; Toronto at night.
LEFT: Rogers Centre and the CN Tower are well-known symbols of Toronto

THE MAKING OF TORONTO

A young city, by European standards, Toronto has developed from a tiny trading post and sometimes-lawless pioneer town into a thriving modern metropolis that, in many respects, sets an example to the rest of the world

Toronto is widely held up today as a shining model for the rest of world when it comes to racial harmony, social stability, religious tolerance and respect for minorities. Visitors also marvel at the cleanliness, order and high level of civility in a city of such size, complexity and diversity. It has been called simply, and with some justification, "the city that works". But a look back at Toronto's history tells a different story, and shows how far this modern metropolis has progressed from its raw, rough-and-tumble origins and how much it has learned along the way.

Early rivalry

The first humans to reach the area – at least those who left any trace of their existence – arrived about 10,000 years ago, when the last ice age was a fading geological memory. It had left behind a massive lake, with its northern shoreline once reaching the middle of the modern-day city. As the climate became more temperate and the land recovered from glacier shock, nomadic hunter-gatherers set up camp on the Scarborough Bluffs overlooking a smaller Lake Ontario. It would be several thousand years before anyone settled down to stay. By the time the Romans held sway over the Old World, two major First Nations, the Algonquin and Iroquois, had planted roots in this densely forested part of the New World.

When the first Europeans arrived in the 17th century, they found tribes formed into

LEFT: a family from the Iroquois First Nations tribe.
RIGHT: French explorer, Samuel de Champlain.

various alliances and rivalries, spread over a large, thinly populated area. Both the French, who came first, and the British, who followed, were happy to exploit any natural enmity for their own imperial ambitions. And the natives did the same with the European rivals. In 1615 French explorer Samuel de Champlain was eager to establish a foothold in the strategically located peninsula west of his Quebec base. To win the support of the Huron, an Iroquois tribe in control of beaver-rich central Ontario, he agreed to help them fend off a rival Iroquois confederacy – a bad move, as it turned out. They lost the battle, making any foray into the lower Great Lakes treacherous.

First Nations

Huron and Neutral tribes occupied the north shore of Lake Ontario until the mid-17th century, when bands of Seneca, the most powerful tribe of the Iroquois Confederation, moved northwards across Lake Ontario. The villages they founded at the mouths of the Humber and Rouge rivers commanded the only two portage routes for the fur trade between Montreal and the upper Great Lakes via Lake Simcoe and Georgian Bay. Consequently, they became important meeting

and trading places, and laid the early foundations for the city of Toronto.

The incredibly valuable trade in beaver founded the economy upon which Canada was built. It also led to a struggle for control, and for the European trade-goods and weapons it provided. By the early 18th century, Mississauga Indians of the powerful Ojibwe Nation from further north and west had moved into the region. The colder weather north of the lakes gave the beaver thicker coats, resulting in higher quality fur. In the rivalry for control of the continent, the Ojibwe allied with the French and the Iroquois sided with the British.

Once European control of North America was established, aboriginal nations independently entered into treaties – some of dubious legality and many still in dispute today – that established land reserves. Today, about 58 percent of Canada's Status Indians live on reserves, each governed by its own elected chief and band council. These bands make up 52 nations, each with its own distinct language and unique culture.

To experience native culture first hand, you can attend one of the pow wows that are held at reserves most weekends from spring to autumn (see page 200). These colourful spectacles include traditional drumming, dancing and storytelling, and there are foods to sample and quality arts and crafts. The highlight, though, is the Canadian Aboriginal Festival (www.canab. com), held in late November at the Rogers Centre (see page 115), which includes the Canadian Aboriginal Music Awards. It's the largest event of its kind in North America.

Another event, held in October, is the Curve Lake First Nation Traditional Pow Wow near Peterborough, in the scenic Kawartha Lakes region, which offers the opportunity to call in at the Whetung Gallery to see some fine art and excellent quill and bead work. For information on pow wow dates, locations and tours, or the Great Indian Bus Tour, call the Native Canadian Centre (tel: 416-964 9087).

Mass-produced art and crafts are available in department stores and gift shops, but you will find the most authentic and highest quality items in shops specialising in native culture. For prints, carvings, moccasins, clothing, bead and quill work, jewellery, and masks visit the Cedar Basket Gift Shop at the Native Canadian Centre (16 Spadina Road), the Algonquians Sweet Grass Gallery (668 Queen Street West), Native Stone Art (4 McCaul Street) or The Guild Shop at the Ontario Crafts Council (170 Bedford Road). The Bay of Spirits Gallery (156 Front Street West) specialises in totem poles, masks and art of the Pacific North West. ❑

LEFT: the chief of a Mohawk Iroquois tribe.

It was not until 1676 that half a dozen traders braved the trek to a fortified Iroquois village called Teiaiagon in what is now Toronto's west end. Intrepid missionaries had been there before, but these were the first French seeking to conduct business. Among their gifts were kegs of brandy. Men, women and children got drunk for three days, brawls broke out among the natives and the traders met a nasty end. (With no sense of irony, residents of this very part of Toronto three centuries later refused to allow the sale or public consumption of alcohol for decades after prohibition ended in 1927. The ban was only lifted in 1999.) In 1720, after the Iroquois had been supplanted by the Mississauga, the French built a small outpost near the Humber River that came to be known as Fort Toronto.

The Toronto Purchase

Toronto had more strategic than commercial value as the French sought to counter English expansion and safeguard their trading routes. By the time Britain gained complete sovereignty over Canada at the end of the Seven Years War in 1763, the French were convinced that the territory would never be as valuable as their Caribbean holdings. The British thought otherwise, particularly after losing their American colonies. In 1787, they paid £1,700 in cash, a few pots and pans and some ammunition to the Mississauga for a piece of land that stretched over 20 km (12½ miles) along the lake and almost 45 km (28 miles) inland.

It wasn't only the Dutch in Manhattan who knew a bargain when they saw one. But even at the time, the deal known as the Toronto Purchase wasn't considered above board. The deed was blank, there was no description of what the Mississauga were giving up and no signatures on the original document. In 1805, when the town was starting to take shape, worried officials asked the Mississauga to sign a new agreement confirming the sale, for the sum of 10 shillings. Their descendants, who claim the tribal elders thought they were only being paid for helping the British during the American Revolution, have waged a legal battle for years to get proper compensation.

RIGHT: an 18th-century engraving of a First Nations' beaver hunt.

John Graves Simcoe, first lieutenant-governor of the young colony of Upper Canada, cleared part of the oak and maple forest for his headquarters in 1793. It was not his first choice, but, at a time when an American invasion seemed imminent, other sites were too close to the border or too difficult to defend. Simcoe, a British commander during the revolutionary war, was determined to set up a "superior, more happy and more polished form of government" that would lure immigrants to the sparsely populated colony and show Americans that they had made a mistake by abandoning British rule. This certainly appealed to most of Upper Canada's popula-

tion of about 12,000, largely former American colonists who had opposed the revolution.

Simcoe mapped out a settlement of 10 blocks and doled out land grants based on rank and influence. Discarding the tribal name used by the French, he called it York, in honour of the Duke of York, second son of George III. Kingston to the east remained the colony's commercial hub and Simcoe's sliver of civilization in the wilderness grew slowly. When an American fleet crossed Lake Ontario during the War of 1812 and landed 1,700 troops, fewer than 1,000 people called the colonial capital home. The Americans overwhelmed the local garrison in a bloody battle, looted the town, set fire to the government buildings and stole the mace. The British later torched the White House in retaliation.

Once the war ended and Napoleon met his defeat at Waterloo in 1815, the colony experienced its first wave of immigration. Toronto has long attracted a disproportionate share of Canada's newcomers from all parts of the world, which accounts for its modern rise as a multicultural mecca. But those early immigrants were virtual clones of the soldiers, government officials and farmers who already lived there: British to the core, firmly Protestant and staunchly loyal to the Crown. Indeed, they were welcomed as a bulwark against

possible future American attacks. From then on, the town developed as a trading centre and port for the growing number of immigrants clearing the surrounding forests for farms. The transformation was hastened by the extension of new roads into the countryside and the arrival of steamships on Lake Ontario in 1816.

The bishop and the firebrand

The colony was already in the tight grip of a clique of Anglican business leaders and officials who controlled the levers of power, and they were encouraged to do so by the colonial administration, which saw such a stable ruling class as a safeguard against the democratic mania that had swept the American colonies. The most influential among them was John Strachan, a Scottish minister and educator who became something of a folk hero for standing up to the Americans during the sacking of York. As the far from humble voice of the Church of England in the young community, Strachan didn't hesitate to wield his enormous clout to further his own interests, and those of his friends and religion. In early Toronto there was no separation of church and state. Strachan became a bishop while acting as a key political adviser and amassing a fortune.

His arch-enemy was William Lyon Mackenzie, another Scottish immigrant who had arrived in 1820 at the age of 25. Four years later, he started a newspaper, the *Colonial Advocate*, which provided a platform for his caustic attacks on the powerful. He dubbed Strachan and his Tory friends "the Family Compact", a derisive name that stuck. When Strachan built a brick mansion for the then huge cost of £6,000, Mackenzie called it "John Strachan's palace", and wrote that "it adds to the pleasures, mean and grovelling as they are, of such a man as Doctor Strachan, to have a hundred poor miserable wretches humbly attending at his gate or in his 'soup kitchen' begging for a morsel". Mackenzie was a small entrepreneur who didn't actually care much about the working poor; but he did resent the cronyism, nepotism and corrosive influence of Family Compact members.

Late one June afternoon in 1826, 15 men whose wealthy families had been pilloried in print struck back. They trashed Mackenzie's office and destroyed his printing press in what became known as the "Types Riot". It was the first incident of its kind in the supposedly peaceful community. Ordinary townsfolk rallied behind Mackenzie, launching the little firebrand with the flaming red wig on a political career that would take him to the provincial assembly and later into open rebellion against the government.

In 1834, the town was incorporated as the city of Toronto, restoring the Iroquois name by which the area had been known for a century, with an elective municipal government. The borders were also greatly expanded, north to what is now Bloor Street, east to the Don River and west to Dufferin Street. Mackenzie handily won a seat on the first city council as part of a reform majority and was elected by his fellow members as the first mayor.

The time of cholera

It turned out to be a bad year to be a municipal politician. The new city of about 9,200 inhabitants needed money to pay off debts, including the cost of a new market, and to add such vital improvements as sewers and boardwalks. But the citizenry objected to a doubling of the property tax rate to two pence. Protestors stamped their feet so hard during an angry meeting at St Lawrence Market that an overcrowded gallery collapsed, tipping them onto the market stalls below, where several were impaled on butchers' hooks and a dozen others were injured. Then, in mid-summer, cholera struck. At its height, the disease claimed more than 25 lives a day, and the final death toll exceeded 500.

In those days, Toronto would not have won any accolades for cleanliness. There was no sanitation or public water supply. The poor lived in shanty towns, pigs rooted through rubbish piled on every lane, wells were contaminated and outside toilets fouled the air and the soil. After rains, the dirt roads turned into a sea of mud, giving the town its hated nickname, Muddy York, and in the hot summers its lowland swamps were a breeding ground for mosquitoes. A visitor in 1832 wrote that York was "one huge pigsty". A tripling of the population in just three years made things worse, and those who could afford it began looking uphill and to west and east for their new homes. This outward migration, which still continues, began as an escape from the health hazards of the era.

Another cholera outbreak in the 1860s led to the first refuse pickup service, which launched Toronto on the road to its eventual reputation as one of the world's cleanest big cities. How clean would it become? A US movie producer was once using Toronto as a stand-in for New York, a frequent occurrence. But the street where he was filming was far too clean to be taken for any New York location, so the crew spread rubbish before going to lunch. By the time they returned it was gone.

That might not happen today – lax 1990s administrations and budget cuts allowed the urban scourge of litter, grime and graffiti to creep into the city – but the current mildly reformist mayor, David Miller, is working to reclaim Toronto's hard-won reputation.

Back in 1834, Mackenzie, who was himself stricken with cholera, was equally upset about the condition of his city. But he could do little about it amid the constant bickering on the council, the severe shortage of funds and opposition from the Family Compact. In 1835, a council without a single reform member finally began building the first sewer system.

The rebellion

After his Reform Party was defeated in the provincial election of 1836, Mackenzie gave up on electoral politics. He was convinced that the only way to break the power of the Family Compact was the violent overthrow of the colonial government. Anger was also boiling over in Lower Canada (Quebec), and in 1837, both provinces were roiled by uprisings. Mackenzie marched down Yonge Street, Toronto's main artery, with a band of 500 untrained, badly armed and disorganised farmers, artisans and labourers. They were easily dispersed by a citizens' militia that was three times their size. To escape hanging, Mackenzie fled south of the

LEFT: the winters were harsh for the settlers.
RIGHT: Mackenzie, newspaperman and politician.

border disguised as a woman, and remained in exile until an amnesty in 1849. Eight years earlier, Upper and Lower Canada had been combined into the single province with an elected parliament, which had been one of the goals of the rebellion. Soon after his return, Mackenzie donned his politician's cloak for the last time and won a parliamentary seat by defeating another Scottish reformist, George Brown, founder of the *Toronto Globe* and a passionate advocate for escaped enslaved Americans, many of whom took refuge in the city via the Underground Railroad *(see page 200)*.

In the year of Mackenzie's return, the worst fire in the city's early history started in a stable

and quickly spread throughout the downtown area. Businesses hurried to rebuild, and such impressive edifices as St James Cathedral rose from the ashes. The city imposed more stringent building codes, but they proved to be not strict enough. In 1904, a blaze broke out in the shoddily built wholesale district near the waterfront and destroyed more than 100 buildings. One of the few that survived in the business district was the elegant 1853 post office on Toronto Street, which subsequently became the headquarters of the business empire of one-time press baron Conrad Black.

On a visit in 1842 author Charles Dickens described the city as "full of life and motion, bustle, business and improvement". He should have seen it a few years later. By the 1850s, a genuine boom would be under way, triggered by the coming of the railway. Investment capital flowed in, industries flourished and the Toronto Stock Exchange opened in 1852. Financiers realised that rail services would extend Toronto's commercial reach deep into the hinterland. More by luck than design, the city, with its protected harbour, turned out to be perfectly situated to profit from the transport revolution. Rail, for example, opened up Northern Ontario to mining, and Toronto eventually became the world's leading centre of finance for the mining industry, bringing huge profits to its banking institutions.

The new nation

In 1867, Confederation brought a wealth of new opportunities. Suddenly, Toronto was no longer the No. 2 city (after Montreal) in a British colony, but the capital and business hub of the most populous province in a vast new nation. Restrictive tariffs on imports and westward expansion, culminating in the completion of the transcontinental Canadian Pacific Railway in 1885, would open a national market to Toronto's manufacturers and financiers. The wealthiest among them built sumptuous mansions along Jarvis Street and began cultivating an interest in culture and the arts. The 1870s brought an opera house and the city's first symphony orchestra. In 1894, farm machinery magnate Hart Massey built the concert hall that bears his family name to foster "an interest in music, education, temperance, industry, good citizenship, patriotism, philanthropy and religion".

The industrial expansion also triggered labour strife, the inevitable result of low wages and dreadful working conditions. In the early 1850s Toronto was hit by more than a dozen strikes of varying magnitude. In 1872 printers walked out for two months in a fight for a shorter working week. A judge ruled that the walkout was an illegal conspiracy, but the public uproar prompted the government to legalise unions. A decade later, children under the age of 10 were still clocking 12-hour days for 20 cents. Commentators of the day blamed some disruptions on Irish troublemakers, a popular scapegoat.

Large numbers of Irish Catholic immigrants arrived in Toronto in the 1840s, fleeing the potato famine. By 1853, 14,000 had settled in the city, accounting for a third of the entire population. Many lived in small terraced houses in an area east of downtown that became known as Cabbagetown because of the vegetables they grew in the postage-stamp-sized front gardens. Despite their dire circumstances and the need for a greater workforce, the newcomers' welcome was not warm, particularly from members of the Protestant Orange Order, whose number included a who's who of Toronto.

George Brown, the influential publisher and one of the fathers of Confederation, wrote that "Irish beggars are to be met everywhere, and they are as ignorant and vicious as they are poor". Not surprisingly, Toronto suffered at least half a dozen sectarian riots in the 1850s. The religious animosity was rekindled in 1866 when Irish-American veterans of the US Civil War, known as Fenians, launched raids on Canada in a bizarre attempt to provoke a military crisis that would weaken Britain's grip on Ireland. Between 1867 and 1892, Catholics and Protestants clashed more than 20 times on Toronto streets, typically on St Patrick's Day or during the annual Orange Parade, the celebration of William of Orange's victory over the Irish in 1690.

When other ethnic groups began settling in large numbers, they too were greeted with suspicion, fear and occasionally violence. Signs posted as recently as the 1950s at east-end beaches warned Jews, blacks and dogs to keep out. The slurs and taunts finally bubbled over one sultry night in August 1933, when some of the ugliest ethnic violence in the city's history engulfed about 10,000 people. It was the height of the Great Depression and tensions were running high because of the heat, frustration and a police crackdown on meetings of protesters. After a baseball game involving a largely Jewish playground team, a group of young Nazi sympathisers unfurled a swastika. The ensuing six-hour riot brought Jews together with Italians and other immigrant youths against their common tormentors, many of them steeped in Orange beliefs.

Orange sunset

For years it was almost impossible to win an election in Toronto without being a loyal Orangeman or gaining the order's endorsement. The last of the Orange mayors, Leslie Saunders, went down to defeat in 1955. His opponent, Nathan Phillips, tapped into the growing electoral clout of the city's numerous ethnic communities and became the city's first Jewish mayor. The "mayor of all the people", as he billed himself during his eight-year tenure, helped drag the city into a more cosmopolitan and tolerant era.

It was in his first term that an international architectural competition for a new city hall

THE CIRCUS RIOT

The 1850s were turbulent, with sectarian riots, militant labour strikes and growing crime, but the strangest event was the Circus Riot of 1855. An American circus came to town, and that night the clowns headed to a brothel on King Street, where they got into a fight with local patrons. Two of the injured were volunteer city firemen, and next day, joined by an angry crowd, they tore down the circus tent and set fire to the wagons. The clowns escaped with their lives, no thanks to the police, who refused to intervene. Rioting continued until the mayor called out the army. When 17 rioters faced charges, no constable could verify that the accused had taken part.

LEFT: George Brown, founder of the *Toronto Globe*.
RIGHT: Massey Hall c.1890.

was launched, selecting an ultra-modern design of two curved towers that outraged traditionalists but redefined the city's image. Toronto's stodgy past still reappeared with regularity, though. Mayor Philip Givens was defeated at the polls in 1966 over his decision to place an abstract Henry Moore sculpture in the new city hall square. The British sculptor was so impressed by the mayor's stand against the philistines that he donated his large personal collection to the city *(see page 51)*.

From Toronto's halting first steps under British rule, immigration had been openly encouraged. But throughout the 19th century and the first half of the 20th, the bulk of new-

comers came, by design, from the British Isles. By 1901, only about one in 12 Torontonians were neither British nor Irish in origin. These included close to 7,000 Germans, more than 1,000 Italians and 3,000 European Jews. They must have found life stifling in late Victorian Toronto, a conservative provincial British town with a fairly rigid class structure and a moralistic fervour that would have pleased any puritan.

Not for nothing was it called "Toronto the Good". Another apt tag was the "City of Churches", both for the abundance of houses of worship and the restrictive Sabbath laws that lasted into the 1960s.

Blue laws

When meatpacker Joseph Flavelle, whose huge bacon business would soon give Toronto its "Hogtown" nickname, first moved to the city in 1887, he told his wife to pray that they would make it "better and purer than when we came, because we have walked in righteousness and truth".

Where other cities created vice squads to crack down on illegal gambling, drinking and prostitution, Toronto had its morality officers, the brainchild of William Howland, a wealthy teetotaller and zealous Christian who was elected mayor in 1886 on a platform of temperance, religion and anti-corruption. He was the first city politician to seek support from women, who had just won the right to vote in municipal elections. Howland failed to marshal the political support to close down the taverns, but he did succeed in enforcing strict laws governing behaviour and dress. These "blue laws" barred all forms of leisure, culture and entertainment on Sundays. Theatres and bars had to close; fishing, hunting, playing cards and even public bathing were prohibited, as well as sports of any kind. Department stores covered their display windows; bakeries could not sell sweets; and playground swings were chained up to keep children out. Kids faced fines for playing ball, but a group of golfers got off when the judge equated their pastime with a Sunday walk, which was legal.

It was not until 1950 that Allan Lamport, a sports-loving city politician, led a public campaign to lift the ban on Sunday sports. Lamport, who became mayor despite the vocal opposition of church leaders and newspaper editorials, was known for his Yogi Berra-like turns of phrase. He once declared: "I deny the allegations and I defy the alligators". At heart, though, he was a died-in-the-wool conservative who made no effort to tackle other blue laws. Cinemas would not open on Sundays until 1960. And it was 1968 before a small Italian restaurant was allowed to serve customers on a patio – provided there was a hedge to protect passers by from the sight of people imbibing alcohol.

Slowly but surely, Toronto was shedding its preachy, mostly white provincialism and becoming the urbane, cosmopolitan, multi-hued city we see today.

The newcomers

By the eve of World War I, the city had reluctantly embraced thousands of new immigrants without any ties to Britain or the mother tongue. Pre-war Toronto had a Chinatown, a Little Italy, a thriving community of Jews from Eastern Europe and industrial areas that were chock full of foreign workers. But the newcomers remained outsiders in the heavily British city of more than 400,000, largely confined to the fringes of society, many of them living in slum conditions. Because of their circumstances, they were particularly vulnerable when the flu pandemic reached Toronto in 1918 and infected half the population.

The Great Depression stopped a building boom in its tracks. Grandiose plans for the construction of broad, Paris-style avenues were shelved and thousands of immigrant labourers who had worked on entire blocks of new housing and on such iconic buildings as the Royal York Hotel joined native Torontonians on the bread lines. By 1933 almost a third of the city's residents were out of work.

Toronto's industrial fortunes revived during World War II, with many factories converted for war work, and in 1943 planning began for what would become a long post-war expansion, and it soon became obvious that more immigrants would be needed to meet the demands of the growing economy. After the war, Toronto again took in a large number of British immigrants, plus newcomers from continental Europe, many of them refugees. Then came the Italians. Between 1950 – when Canada lifted its ban on immigrants from countries that fought against the Allies – and 1970 Toronto's Italian population shot up by more than 200,000. No other city outside Italy had as many first-generation Italians. Portuguese and Greeks also came in large numbers, but the gates did not creak open for non-whites until 1962, when the last discriminatory rules were finally ditched. Large numbers of Asians were not admitted until the late 1960s, when Canada brought in the most liberal rules of any Western country and permanently changed the face of Toronto.

Peace and preservation

This was a time of considerable social and cultural change, as Toronto became a haven for US draft dodgers and academics opposed to the Vietnam War. Old-fashioned, conservative Toronto was no match for the energy, enthusiasm and relaxed sexual mores of a new generation determined to change the world.

While talented young Canadians like folk singer Joni Mitchell were turning the now chic shopping area of Yorkville into Toronto's version of Greenwich Village, others were changing the political, social and environmental landscape. They fought to preserve historic buildings from the wreckers' ball and

old neighbourhoods from massive redevelopment. In 1971, they halted construction of the Spadina Expressway, which would have cut through the heart of the city. The following year, a group of reformers won control of the city council.

The new mayor, David Crombie, imposed height restrictions on all new buildings and emphasised the necessity of the construction of multi-income housing to avoid the isolation of the poor in public projects, which had so blighted major US cities.

Toronto's skyline changed dramatically in the 1960s and 1970s, with the rise of impressive skyscapers. The austere steel-and-glass

LEFT: Toronto in the 1930s.
RIGHT: Canadian military men demobbed and returning home after serving in World War II.

Toronto-Dominion Centre and the city hall, completed in 1965, signalled a new, uncharacteristic brashness. A city that had never been known for flamboyance suddenly had a desire to showcase its considerable attributes. A decade later, the CN Tower would soar 553 metres (1,815 ft) above Front Street, becoming the world's tallest building and the most distinctive feature of the skyline.

Changing colours

This new confidence coincided with a major shift in the ethnic mix. By 1969, half of Toronto's residents claimed non-British origins. Today close to 70 percent have no

English, French or aboriginal ties. More than a dozen nationalities are represented by at least 100,000 people each, including the largest urban population of Caribbeans outside Kingston, Jamaica, and 192,000 first-generation Chinese, most of whom came from Hong Kong in the late 1960s or in a second wave in the mid-1980s prior to Britain handing back the colony to China. In all, Toronto is home to more than 75 cultures with at least 1,000 people each. More than one in three Torontonians belong to visible minorities, compared with one in nine nationally. All have contributed to Toronto's evolution into one of the world's most harmonious and livable cities.

THE NAME

Several theories have been advanced for the origin of the name of Toronto. The French thought it was a Huron word for their tribal land. Some historians later asserted that it meant "meeting place", from the Huron word *Toronton*. Others equally unfamiliar with tribal vocabulary translated it as "land of abundance" or "lake opening". One even surmised that it was named after an Italian engineer called Tarento. But scholars have concluded that the name actually stems from the Mohawk Iroquois *Tkaronto*, meaning "where there are trees standing in the water". The "trees" were stakes used for fish weirs placed at a point where Lake Simcoe empties into Lake Couchiching, 125 km (80 miles)

north of Toronto. In French maps of the late 17th century, Simcoe was known as Taronto and the canoe route running south to Lake Ontario was Passage de Taronto. When the French built a trading post near the mouth of what they called Rivière Taronto (today's Humber River), it appeared on maps as Fort Toronto, in a further spelling modification. When John Graves Simcoe took over in 1792, he discarded most of the native names, including Toronto, and renamed his new capital York. But it was constantly confused with the many other places called York and had attracted such nicknames as Little York and Muddy York. When it officially became a city, the residents won the right to restore the native name.

Many of the newer, better-off immigrants have headed straight to the suburbs, part of an unusual reversal of population flow. Like all big North American cities, Toronto experienced a flight to new suburbs in the 1950s. But unlike comparable American cities, Toronto's older inner-city neighbourhoods remained healthy, largely thanks to throngs of immigrants.

By the late 1960s, suburbanites or their grown children were moving back into the city, lured by the urban lifestyle and the city's transformation into a vibrant centre of arts, culture and social life. More recently, they have been buying the townhouses and apartments shooting up in every part of Toronto, and turning the formerly industrialised waterfront into prized residential property.

The megacity

On the political front, amalgamation in 1953 brought Toronto together with 12 other municipalities under the umbrella of a single metropolitan government to bring badly needed planning, order and discipline to the haphazard development of housing, roads and services. However, the municipalities retained their own governments, school boards and other services, leading to needless duplication and conflict. In 1998, the metro structure was scrapped and Toronto became a megacity with a single layer of government. So far, this has not made it more efficient or better run, but the future looks more promising.

Scandal, corruption and cronyism in the bureaucracy have prompted tougher oversight, and the city's chronic shortage of money, worsened by the soaring costs of social services, is finally being addressed. Both federal and provincial governments appear committed to the revitalisation of Canada's most important city after years of neglect and the municipal government may finally get the financial and other powers it needs to run a city that is costlier and more complex than most provinces.

Problems still exist. Toronto is not free of grime or crime, including growing gun violence by youth gangs, largely against members of their own ethnic communities. And resources are often stretched to the limit, such as during the SARS (Sudden Acute Respiratory Syndrome) crisis of 2003. The worst outbreak outside of the Far East, which caught officials off guard and highlighted the vulnerability of a city with such a diverse population in the age of global travel. The virus, brought back by a Chinese immigrant returning from Hong Kong, killed 44 people, caused a panic that wreaked havoc in the tourism industry and overtaxed Toronto's considerable medical resources. But the city showed its resilience and rallied in support of Chinese businesses, hurt by a sharp decline in traffic as a result.

Toronto is not a melting pot, and its multiple ethnic communities retain strong cultural identities within a flexible Canadian framework, with access to medical, educational and social services that are the envy of other cities the world over. Like all Canadians, Torontonians prize their public safety net, prefer order and stability to personal freedom and inherently dislike extremes. These are products of a difficult birth in a remote land. Anglo-Saxons are now a minority in the place their ancestors founded, but their best values live on in a vibrant, cosmopolitan community that the early settlers could not have imagined in their wildest dreams. ❏

LEFT: the City Hall building outraged traditionalists.
RIGHT: Toronto residents are a cosmopolitan group.

Decisive Dates

1615 French explorer Etienne Brûlé is the first European to reach the territory, but doesn't linger.

1676 French traders arrive at a Seneca Indian village bearing brandy, with unfortunate results.

1720 The French build Fort Toronto just east of the Humber River.

1723 Mississauga Indians sell the site of present-day Toronto to the French.

1763 British rule begins, after victory over France in the Seven Years War.

1787 British governor, Lord Dorchester,

acquires more than 100,000 hectares (250,000 acres) from the Mississauga at a cost of £1,700 and a few trade goods.

1793 John Graves Simcoe, the first Lieutenant-Governor of the colony of Upper Canada, lays out a 10-block town as his new headquarters and names it York, in honour of the Duke of York.

1813 During the War of 1812, American troops seize the garrison, loot the town and destroy public buildings.

1815 After the war and Napoleon's defeat in Europe, a wave of British immigrants settles in the sparsely populated area.

1821 The Bank of Upper Canada becomes the first banking institution in what would one day be Canada's financial capital.

1826 A charter is granted for the University of King's College at Toronto.

1832 Cholera outbreak hits a quarter of the population.

1834 York's name is changed to Toronto, which is incorporated as a city with 9,200 residents and 78 taverns.

1837 Rebellion in Upper and Lower Canada. In Toronto, rebel leader William Lyon Mackenzie is defeated by a citizens' militia.

1841 The first gas street lamps appear.

1849 The downtown area is gutted by the first "Great Fire".

1850 Population grows to 30,000, boosted by Irish Catholic immigrants fleeing the potato famine. They are not welcomed by the English Protestant majority. Major sectarian riots result.

1852 The Toronto Stock Exchange opens.

1853 The first rail service carries passengers north to Lake Simcoe, following the original First Nations route along what was known as the Toronto Passage.

1860 The first streetcars appear, pulled by horses. They are electrified in 1892, but there is no Sunday service until 1897.

1866 Irish-American Fenians launch unsuccessful raids on Canada, triggering renewed sectarian clashes in Toronto.

1867 Canada becomes a dominion within the British Empire. Toronto becomes the capital of the new province of Ontario.

1873 John Howard, the city's first professional architect, donates his large rural estate, High Park, for public use.

1880 Dr Emily Stowe becomes Toronto's first licensed female physician, after practising without a licence since 1867.

1886 Reformist teetotaler William Howland is elected mayor and vows to tackle the problems of alcohol and prostitution. He appoints Toronto's first morality officer.

1892 Women win elective office for the first time, claiming three seats on the board of education.

1899 The imposing Romanesque city hall is built, reflecting the city's strong Victorian influence.

1904 The second "Great Fire" destroys the wholesale district.

1907 The Royal Alexandra Theatre opens.

1911 Casa Loma is completed by the eccentric multimillionaire Sir Henry Pellatt at a cost of $3 million. He would die broke in 1939.

1914 Royal Ontario Museum opens.

1916 Prohibition comes to Ontario. The sale of alcohol is banned in West Toronto until 1999, 72 years after the prohibition era officially ends.

1918 Spanish flu affects half the population. The health crisis is exacerbated by a shortage of heating fuel and economic hardship at the end of World War I.

1920 The first exhibition by Toronto-based landscape painters calling themselves the Group of Seven, who spark an uproar among critics and launch a revolution in Canadian art.

1921 Insulin is discovered by Frederick Banting, Charles Best and James Collip at the University of Toronto.

1923 Young *Toronto Star* reporter Ernest Hemingway quits to write fiction in Paris.

1929 The Royal York opens as largest hotel in the British Empire, with 1,048 rooms.

1931 Maple Leaf Gardens, destined to become a Canadian hockey shrine, opens. The Canadian Bank of Commerce constructs the tallest building in the British Empire, at 34 storeys.

1932 The Toronto Stock Exchange reaches bottom during the Great Depression. Canadian government sets up relief camps for single, unemployed men.

1933 The worst ethnic rioting in the city's history erupts when a pro-Nazi gang waves a swastika during an amateur baseball game featuring a mainly Jewish team.

1939 Canada joins the Allies in declaring war on Germany, but waits for a week after Britain to demonstrate its independence.

1949 Fire destroys the cruise ship *Noronic* in Toronto harbour, killing 118 passengers and prompting tougher standards that all but end the luxury cruise business on the Great Lakes.

1950 Sports events can be held on Sundays for the first time, but only after church services are over.

1954 Toronto gets its first subway line.

1964 Construction begins on the landmark Toronto-Dominion Centre, ushering in the city's modern architectural era.

1965 Finnish modernist Viljo Revell builds a strikingly original city hall after winning an international design competition.

1975 Completion of the CN Tower, still the world's tallest free-standing structure at 553 metres (1,815 ft).

1976 Toronto becomes Canada's biggest metropolis, surpassing Montreal.

1989 The world's first domed sports stadium with a retractable roof opens at a cost of $500 million.

1998 Toronto and 12 neighbouring municipalities are amalgamated into a single municipal government. The expanded city's population becomes the fifth biggest in North America.

2001 Census figures show that 51.2 percent of Toronto's 2½ million residents were born outside Canada.

2003 The worst SARS (sudden acute respiratory syndrome) outbreak outside of the Far East kills 44 people.

2005 The Liberal government led by Paul Martin is ousted by a vote of no confidence, ending more than 12 years of Liberal rule.

2006 The Conservative party win the general election, party leader Stephen Harper heads a minority government. The Canadian Opera Company and National Ballet move into their first permanent home, a purpose-built performing arts centre. ❑

LEFT: trading on credit.
RIGHT: the aftermath of the Great Fire in 1904 .

CHANGING FACES

Toronto has been in the grip of a remarkable transformation over the past few decades, changing from its British-based character into one of the world's most varied, multicultural and dynamic cities

A t the Second City comedy club in Toronto, the opening sketch of their show, *Reloaded*, features two characters in a taxi cab locked in mock debate over who is more legitimately Canadian – the taxi driver is a Sikh with a Scottish accent and the passenger is a Caucasian of Irish heritage born in India. The comedians successfully put their finger on what it's like to live in Toronto today, one of the world's most multicultural cities where 40 percent of people speak a foreign language at home, and where nearly half the population of the city was born outside the country.

Ethnically diverse

There are more startling statistics: one in five of this city's population of about 2½ million arrived here after 1991; one in four children in the city is an immigrant. The United Nations calls Toronto one of the most ethnically diverse cities in the world, having more than 100 languages and dialects, and with immigrants hailing from 170 different countries. In addition, Statistics Canada projects that by the year 2012, more than 50 percent of Toronto's population will be from a visible minority.

It wasn't always like this. For nearly two centuries Toronto was deeply and profoundly Anglo-Saxon in nature. The city was founded as a British colonial outpost in 1793, and by 1850, only three percent of the city's popula-

---

PRECEDING PAGES: Torontonians of Asian heritage.
LEFT: a Canadian vendor in Chinatown.
RIGHT: a local girl.

tion of about 31,000 did not claim origins from the United Kingdom. By 1901, when the population had exploded to about 220,000, only eight percent of the city's population was not of British extraction. The minorities who did slip in were mostly Germans, Italians and European Jews. By 1941, when the city's population had more than tripled to about 670,000, the non-British in extraction accounted for just 22 percent of all Torontonians.

By design, the city's forefathers favoured a policy that supported immigration from Great Britain but, by World War II, rapid economic growth forced them to open the doors to new Torontonians a little wider. Chinese and Italian labourers began to arrive along with other immigrants from Western and Eastern Europe, giving birth to the city's Chinatown, Little Italy, and a growing community of European Jews who settled in Kensington Market. Most of the homes found today in the downtown core below Bloor Street were built around this time to house people who came to work in nearby factories. Today, most of the factories are closed and the buildings are being converted into high-priced condominium lofts.

After World War II, the city accepted many refugees, and in 1950 when Canada lifted its ban on immigrants from countries that fought against the allies, Italians arrived *en masse*,

along with many Portuguese and Greeks. By the mid-1960s, it's said that Toronto had more Italians living in the city than in any other city outside Rome.

The current multicultural era began in the mid-1960s, when remaining restrictive immigration laws were thrown out, and the federal government put in place the most liberal immigration policy of any Western country. Toronto would accept waves of immigrants from South Asia, China and Africa, and by 1969, half of the city's residents were not from Britain. Today, close to 70 percent of all Torontonians have no ties to Britain, France or native Canadians. Despite the fact that French is Canada's second

official language, only 1.4 percent of Torontonians actually speak it. The largest and fastest growing immigrant groups are now Chinese (currently 10.6 percent of the population) and South Asian (10.3 percent). They are followed by Africans and Jamaicans (8.3 percent), and Filipino (3.5 percent). Most Torontonians today are Roman Catholic or part of the Anglican Church, but the city also has large Muslim, Hindu, Jewish, Buddhist and Sikh communities.

"Toronto the Good"

Despite this massive influx of foreign nationalities over the past decades and how it's changing the cultural make-up of the city, the majority of Torontonians still claim their origins from the British Isles. And for the time being, the value system of this group remains at the core of the city's psyche, largely thanks to more than 200 years of being in power.

New Canadians seem to respect the fundamental qualities on which Torontonians and Canadians pride themselves: politeness, deference to authority and maintaining an essentially low-key nature. (A popular joke asks: "How do you get 50 Canadians out of a swimming pool?" Answer: "Just clap your hands and say, 'Time to go everybody!'")

In the United States, it's the words "life, liberty and the pursuit of happiness" that are at the heart of the country's constitution. In contrast, Canadians signed up for the phrase "peace, order and good government", which helps explain the general feeling of politeness and reserve in Toronto, even among immigrants and their children.

For example, the atmosphere and mood in a crowded bus or subway can be subdued compared to most big cities; pedestrians in Toronto rarely cross a street on a red light, even with no approaching cars in sight; and respect for personal space means larger distances between people extracting cash from bank machines and those waiting behind them than you'd find in other cities and countries.

About the only place you'll see people being openly aggressive and boisterous is in the hockey arena, whether on the ice or in the bleachers. This is thought to be part of the explanation why hockey is so popular in Canada – it's one of the few places where aggression, confrontation and even violence are socially sanctioned. Torontonians, like most of their compatriots, have almost a phobia against conflict, a characteristic that separates Canadians from Americans, who tend to thrive on confrontation and competition.

Toronto has been called one of the most civilised cities in the world, and its fundamental respect for law and order has helped it earn one of its nicknames, "Toronto the Good". That moniker is for the moment still firmly in place, even while the city is undergoing rapid change in the ethnic and social composition of its population. Toronto government statistics show the city is one of the safest in North America, with levels of

the past few years, there has been a growing number of shootings in the Greater Toronto Area and a small spike in the crime rate. For the most part, the violence is taking place within ethnic groups in isolated parts of the city such as what is known as the Jane-Finch corridor in the northwestern area of Toronto, or in the eastern suburb of Scarborough.

Positive Welcome

On the whole, Torontonians and Canadians are accepting of the newcomers. A recent poll by the Centre for Research and Information on Canada shows that an overwhelming majority of Canadians feel multiculturalism is

violent crime lower than in any major metropolitan area in the United States, and among the lowest in Canada.

Filmmaker Michael Moore, in his documentary *Bowling For Columbine*, about the culture of guns and violence in the United States, walks up to homes in the central core of a Canadian city and shows how front doors are often left unlocked. It's an exaggeration, staged for the camera, but it does accurately get the point across that strict gun control in Canada means less fear and violence. Nevertheless, in

having a positive effect on the Canadian identity. It can be seen in Toronto: the city is more animated than it was a decade or so ago.

Thousands of ethnic restaurants represent cuisines from around the world; cafés and outdoor restaurants abound where they did not previously exist. The ethnic enclaves, such as Little Italy, Little India, Chinatown and Koreatown draw in people from all over the city. There are nearly 80 different ethnic publications in the city, as well as several important ethnic radio and television stations, and a considerable number of people from visible minorities are being hired as reporters and newsreaders in the mainstream media.

LEFT: anything is possible on the city's streets.
ABOVE: warm smiles.

The government-funded lakefront cultural centre, Harbourfront, which frequently showcases events celebrating ethnic arts and foods, is a huge success. The annual Caribbean parade, Caribana, draws in tens of thousands of people from all over the region and worldwide, with relatively few incidents of violence.

While the older generation of established Torontonians of British stock is known to express discomfort about the number of new immigrants living in Toronto, the tolerance by the majority is perhaps a result of the Canadian sense of liberalism that is prized by Torontonians more than in any other region (a 2004 poll showed that Canadians, had they been able to vote in the last US presidential election, would have voted overwhelmingly for the Democratic candidate John Kerry over Republican George W. Bush).

Toronto is a city in favour of gay marriage and nude sunbathing, did not support sending Canadian troops to Iraq, and has an active employment policy about hiring minorities. Toronto has one of the most comprehensive recycling programmes in North America, and has so many bicycle riders and bike paths that *Bicycling* magazine hails the city as the greatest place to cycle in North America – quite a title considering winters here can be long and bitter cold, with snow for several months of the year.

FAMOUS TORONTONIANS

Canadians, unlike Americans, have the compulsion when travelling abroad to point out famous compatriots. This need comes from the fact Canadians are only subtly distinguishable from Americans, and from the economic truth that most Canadian actors, musicians, scientists and journalists generally need to go to the larger US market to make it big.

Canadians have a love-hate relationship with celebrity and disdain the grandiosity that comes with fame. Generally it's only when a Canadian becomes famous abroad that they are appreciated and applauded at home.

But there is talent in this country and a system that nurtures it. Canada is educated, wealthy and culturally diverse, with government grants that support developing writers, artists and researchers.

Toronto, as the country's largest city and its media and cultural capital, has produced famous and respected actors, directors, writers, artists, thinkers and comedians. Some of the biggest names in their fields were born and raised in Toronto, including Roberston Davies, Dan Aykroyd, Keanu Reeves, Glenn Gould, Oscar Peterson, Dr Frederick Banting, Frank Gehry and Linda Evangelista.

All this liberalism marches hand-in-hand with a British-style stiff upper lip, alcohol laws that are still restrictive (its sale is allowed only in province-run shops, which can be hard to find and have limited hours) and a reserved nature that can border on coldness.

It's this interesting mix of European and international influences, British heritage and the impact of having the powerful United States next door that has helped shape the social demeanour of the average Torontonian. Toronto web-blogger Craig Space refers to it as a blend of "Scandinavian liberalism, peace-and-order British persnickediness, and a healthy North American respect for individual rights and freedoms".

A desirable city

Toronto is a desirable city to live in, which is why it's drawing in people from across the country, not just internationally. People in Toronto are educated and literate: more than 62 percent of homes and 98 percent of businesses have high-speed internet. The Toronto Public Library has the highest circulation rate in North America, and about 60 percent of the city's workforce is employed in knowledge-based businesses. The population and the economy are booming. The Greater Toronto Area (estimated population 5.2 million) is the fifth largest and now fastest growing metropolitan region in North American. City officials estimate GDP growth at five percent annually, with about one-sixth of all jobs in the country located in the Greater Toronto Area. The median income here is 25 percent higher than in other parts of Canada. Toronto ranks above Seattle or Boston in the US for a lower cost of living, despite the fact that housing prices have jumped 75 percent since 1996.

Toronto is Canada's financial centre and economic engine, as well as one of the country's most important centres for culture, art and health services. It is home to many of Canada's most important writers, including Margaret Atwood and Michael Ondaatje, and filmmakers David Cronenberg and Norman Jewison, and has been home to important intellectuals such as the late media critic Marshall McLuhan and literary critic Northrop Frye. The city is in the throes of a cultural boom, actively promoted by its dynamic mayor, with such developments as the new Opera House and extensions to major museums. And the number of tourists coming to the city is growing too. About 18 million people visited Toronto in 2004, and city officials estimate that figure will jump to around 21 million in the coming decade; recent figures indicate an even greater potential.

Toronto is, quite frankly, a very pleasant place to live and to visit, filled with leafy neighbourhoods of houses with front and back gardens, as well as interesting ethnic enclaves.

Unlike US cities of similar sizes, Toronto did not experience a mass migration to the suburbs during the 1960s and 1970s, or any dramatic urban decay, largely thanks to good city planning and such social services as quality public schools. Toronto's transit system is the second largest in North America after New York City and has won awards for its high quality service. As a result, the central core is populated by a lively mix of Canadian and immigrant families and students.

Toronto has come a long way from its repressive British puritanical roots and is still a city in transition, perhaps more than any other place of its size in North America. ❑

LEFT: Toronto is good for cyclists.
RIGHT: hockey fans celebrate in the street.

FEASTING ON FESTIVALS

Toronto's annual celebrations bring the city's streets to life

Whether it's due to the city's climactic extremes, multicultural makeup, or simply an honest-to-goodness desire to celebrate everything that its citizens are passionate about, there's virtually a year-round roster of major festivals in Toronto.

Winters can be harsh, so to beat the February blues, the 14-day WinterCity Festival captivates the crowds with fireworks, extravaganzas, fire dancers and stilt walkers, while inside, arts organisations have post-performance talks, free ballet classes and behind-the-scene tours.

During Winterlicious more than 100 top restaurants have amazingly-priced *prix fixe* menus. Its popularity spawned a warm weather version, Summerlicious, in July. The month-long Cavalcade of Lights in December begins with the First Lighting Celebration – of 100,000 lights – in Nathan Phillips Square, and continues with skating parties, fireworks, circus acts, live music and tours of beautifully lit neighbourhoods.

ABOVE: The Toronto International Dragon Boat Race Festival is the largest of its kind outside Asia. More than 200 teams from around the world participate, paddling their huge, brightly coloured canoes during non-stop races over two days of festivities in June.

LEFT: The annual 10-day fFIDA International Dance Festival in August showcases the work of independent choreographers and dance companies, such as Malgorzata Nowacka's Chimera Project. Performances of mostly avant-garde works are held in the theatre and studio spaces at the Distillery District.

RIGHT: An exciting street race held in July, the Grand Prix of Toronto (formerly Molson Indy) is part of the American Champ Car World Series for single seater (open wheel) cars. The 2.8-km (1.7-mile) course around Exhibition Park, south west of the city near Ontario Place, winds around Princes' Boulevard and along Lakeshore Boulevard.

ABOVE: The Canadian International Air Show has aerial displays over Lake Ontario on Labour Day weekend (September). The best views are from the waterfront, Canadian National Exhibition and Ontario Place.

RIGHT: Caribana is an exuberant two-week bacchanalia in July, which is rooted in the carnival traditions of the Caribbean and Latin America. The finale of the festival is a parade, with more than one million people dancing to calypso, steel pan and soca music as floats with brightly-costumed dancers and calypso bands roll along Lake Shore Boulevard.

FESTIVAL HIGHLIGHTS

All that Jazz

Toronto has a wealth of summer jazz festivals including the Distillery Jazz Festival in May, the Toronto Downtown Jazz Festival in June, and in July the week long Beaches International Jazz Festival. All have an enticing line-up of renowned performers playing everything from traditional to contemporary jazz music.

Canadian Aboriginal Festival

For three days in November, this life-affirming event brings together the best of Canadian Aboriginal talents. You can meet First Nations elders and healers, watch a showcase of Aboriginal fashions, and purchase Aboriginal art, crafts and foods. One of the highlights is the traditional Pow Wow – during its spectacular finale, around 1,000 native dancers and drum-singing groups gather en masse, within the Pow Wow's sacred circle.

Doors Open Toronto

During this citywide celebration on the last weekend in May, locals and visitors line up to visit the city's most outstanding historical and architecturally significant buildings (150 in all). Most are not usually open to the public and include modern landmarks and national historic sites, from private schools to artists' homes.

International Festival of Authors

This October fest is one of the world's pre-eminent literary events, attracting novelists, poets, biographers and playwrights from almost 50 countries.

Pride Week

Canada's largest gay population struts its stuff in the last week of June. Pride Toronto, one of the biggest celebrations of gay culture in the world, has a three-day street fair, family events, all-night parties and a Dyke March. The week climaxes with the high-spirited and flashy Pride Parade, when crowds up to six deep line the downtown route.

Woofstock

Dog owners and their pets flock to the Distillery District, over the first weekend in June, to browse stalls with everything for a pampered pooch, and to watch a beauty pageant, a canine fashion show and a stupid dog trick competition.

ART AND CULTURE

Toronto has an extraordinarily rich cultural life that places it third in world rankings, close behind New York and London. Superb theatres, concert halls and art galleries draw the cream of international talent and have nurtured Canadian performers and artists who have taken the world by storm

Cultural life in Toronto is quite astonishing. In performance arts, you can enjoy the best in opera, ballet and classical music, Broadway-style shows, experimental drama, intimate jazz, folk and blues clubs, and stadium mega-concerts. Visual arts are represented in stunning public and private galleries, and sculptures, statues, monuments and murals dot the city streets. And there's a huge calendar of festivals celebrating every branch of the arts, including film – the Toronto Film Festival is one of the most prestigious cinema events on the continent *(see page 126)*.

Theatre

From international, large-budget blockbusters to smaller companies offering perennial favourites, world premieres and cutting-edge experimental drama, the Toronto theatre scene has something for every taste. And here, music, dance and the spoken word reflect the city's multicultural society, adding an extra dimension to the cultural atmosphere.

The growth of Toronto's theatre district into one of the world's largest and most dynamic during the last quarter of the 20th century was nothing short of phenomenal, growing from two professional theatres in the 1960s to over 40 today. Only London and New York sell more theatre tickets in a year. This explosion owes much to one man with a vision. Ed Mirvish is a legendary figure in Toronto, patriarch of the family that has been instrumental

in transforming Toronto's theatre scene. When the Royal Alexandra Theatre on King Street was scheduled for demolition, Ed bought it for a song, then revived it to its 1907 glory, opening it to great acclaim in 1963. It was pronounced a national monument in 1987. One of the first to see that theatres and restaurants complemented one another, he opened several restaurants along the street. Other businesses related to entertainment and hospitality grew nearby, and Ed's creation became a "theatre district", contributing to the pavement culture developing in downtown Toronto.

In 1993, almost next door to the "Royal Alex", Ed and son David built the Princess of

LEFT: the Princess of Wales Theatre, West King Street.
RIGHT: Ed Mirvish transformed the city's theatre scene.

Wales Theatre, the first privately owned and financed theatre built in Canada since 1907, and the first in North America in 30 years. With one of the widest and deepest stages in North America, and state-of-the art technical facilities built to accommodate *Miss Saigon*, the theatre melds the best in traditional and innovative theatre design, creating a 2,000-seat auditorium that is surprisingly intimate. The interior features the work of dozens of artists, notably the murals and reliefs of Frank Stella, which attracts visitors as much for the art as for the theatre performances.

Mirvish Productions also operates The Canon Theatre on Yonge Street. Built in the

taneous gathering of talent that has prospered despite a perennial lack of funding. Only recently has there been a movement to raise public and political awareness of the value of the arts, both in forming the character and identity of a city and in enhancing economic benefits through cultural tourism. The Toronto Arts Council Foundation, backed by Ed Mirvish and Karen Kain, has launched an initiative known as Great Arts/Great City. The goal is to generate more corporate support, and encourage attendance in order to eliminate the annual shortfall in revenues.

Typifying the grass-roots movement is Soulpepper, the dream of 12 leading theatre

1920s, the building has experienced life as a vaudeville house and cinema, Canada's largest and most elegant, before being lavishly refurbished and reopened as a venue for *The Phantom of the Opera* in 1989. All three Mirvish theatres feature large-scale, long-running West-End and Broadway-style shows, with the Canon hosting the world premiere of *Lord of the Rings* in 2006. (For the Mirvish box office, tel: 416-872 1212; www.mirvish.com.)

Nearby the Canon, on Yonge Street is the Elgin and Winter Garden Theatre, a beautiful national historic site *(see page 138)*.

The growth of Toronto's theatre scene has been a grass-roots movement, an almost spon-

artists who in 1997 founded a classical repertory theatre in Toronto. These artists benefited in their early careers from theatre mentors and "young company" training, so their aim was to combine the production of classical theatre with training for a new generation of artists, and mentorship programmes for young people using theatre as the vehicle. They have maintained their goal of keeping the artists at the centre of the organisation. Soulpepper performs at the Premiere Dance Theatre and Harbourfront Centre Theatre.

Canadian Stage is Canada's largest not-for-profit theatre company, producing Canadian and international contemporary theatre, and promoting Canadian theatre overseas. CanStage presents productions at the St Lawrence Centre and at two stages at the Berkeley Street Theatre. It also mounts "theatre under the stars" Shakespeare in High Park, called "Dream in High Park", in August and September.

An area of growth since the turn of the millennium has been in summer performances in tourism areas and scenic venues surrounding Toronto. Many companies have made it their focus to develop and produce new Canadian works, and this has given a great boost to native playwrights. Following the lead of Stratford (*see page 197*) and the Shaw Festival in Niagara-on-the-Lake (*see page 204*), a growing number of professional companies provide excellent entertainment value with musicals, dramas, mysteries and high comedy, at prices to suit all budgets, and in theatres ranging from state-of-the-art to restored historic buildings to the great outdoors. Most remarkable has been the success story of Drayton Entertainment. Started in an old town hall in a tiny village, and mobilising local community and corporate support, it made Canadian history by completely selling out its 1993 and 1994 seasons. During the subsequent 10 years it grew to six venues, and is regarded as Canada's most successful summer theatre company (www.summertheatre.org).

Beyond the mainstream

Theatre in Toronto goes far beyond classical and mass-appeal productions. Buddies in Bad Times Theatre is home to a gay and lesbian theatre company, while the Bathurst Street Theatre, Factory Theatre, Tarragon Theatre, and Theatre Passe Muraille all specialise in producing new and experimental scripts, and encouraging new playwrights and directors. Famous Players Dinner Theatre is the world's first dinner theatre dedicated to and performed by people with special needs. Their unique "black light" shows bring out the creative potential in performers with disabilities. The Solar Stage has plays and concerts specially for children, and The Lorraine Kimsa Theatre for Young People presents plays often based on favourite stories from children's literature.

LEFT: the Royal Alexandra Theatre.
RIGHT: gay theatre at Buddies in Bad Times.

The Toronto Fringe Festival follows the formula first created by the Edinburgh Fringe Festival more than 50 years ago, and typically welcomes over 42,000 "Fringers" in 11 venues with more than 120 theatre companies. The concept is simple: to provide artists with an opportunity to produce their plays, no matter the content, style or form, and to make the event affordable. There is a kids' venue, with children's tickets at half price. At least 50 percent of the tickets are available at the door, and they go on sale 30 minutes or one hour before show time. (Cash only at the door, with a limit of four tickets per person. You can get a good deal with Show Passes and Frequent Fringer Passes.)

Comedy giants

Toronto is a fertile breeding ground for stand-up and satirical comedy: Yuk Yuk's, founded by Mark Breslin in 1976, is known as the birthplace of Canadian comedy, and has such famous alumnae as Jim Carrey, Harland Williams and Howie Mandel. This is where visiting comedians like Jerry Seinfeld and Robin Williams can be found performing.

Founded in Chicago in 1959, and opening in Toronto in 1973, The Second City achieved national fame through its successful television series, SCTV. As well as being an audience favourite, Second City has been the training ground for many actors who have become international household names – Mike Myers, Bill Murray, John Candy, Dan Aykroyd, Gilda Radner, Andrea Martin, Eugene Levy and more. The Second City is Toronto's undisputed leader in improv, topical satire and sketch comedy, presented in an intimate performance space. Dinner-theatre packages are available at the famous Wayne Gretzky's Restaurant, which has direct access to the Second City Theatre and reserved seating for ticket holders.

Opera and ballet

The classical performance arts are well represented by the Canadian Opera Company and the National Ballet of Canada. The ballet, with more than 60 dancers and its own orchestra, ranks as one of the world's premier companies. It features a full classical repertoire, but also embraces contemporary works and sponsors the creation of new ballets. In 1972, Rudolf Nureyev staged his spectacular *The Sleeping Beauty* with the company and took New York by storm. The legendary Erik Bruhn, considered one of the greatest classical male dancers of the 20th century, held the post of Artistic Director for 20 years during the 1980s and 1990s, and added many famous ballets to the company's repertoire. Karen Kain, who retired as principal dancer in 1997, has been Artistic Director since 2005, and is

JAZZ FESTIVALS

The Distillery Jazz Festival, taking place over nine days in late May, features a variety of styles from Canadian musicians and visiting artists from the US, with continuous performances on five stages. Together with the dining, shopping and galleries in the Distilleries Historic District, it all combines for a romantic night out. There are five free afternoon concerts, plus five ticketed evening concerts, and you can save money with a Passport. For information tel: 416-872 1212 or visit www.distillery jazz.com.

Accessibility is the key to the TD Canada Trust Toronto Downtown Jazz Festival, as some of the biggest names in jazz play free concerts that command high prices at other festivals. During the festival, 1,500 of the best Canadian and international artists perform styles of jazz that encompass traditional to bebop. In addition to the main stage performances, you can listen to the beat in concert halls, at free indoor and outdoor stages and at more than 30 clubs, hotels and lounges. The festival takes place in late June and early July. For information tel: 416-928 2033 or visit www.tojazz.com.

The Beaches Jazz Festival (www.beachesjazz.com) features free concerts at three venues, including Kew Gardens, in the third week in July.

taking on a leading role as a promoter of the arts in Toronto. The ballet performs spring, summer and winter seasons, with the ever-popular *Nutcracker* each Christmas.

The Canadian Opera Company mounts seven operas in Toronto each season, running for about 24 weeks, then tours Canada and the opera venues of the world. Formerly based at the Hummingbird Centre, the company have a purpose-built home in the Four Seasons Centre for the Performing Arts, opened in the autumn of 2006. Toronto Operetta Theatre presents light opera, Gilbert and Sullivan and music theatre at the St Lawrence Centre.

Major performance venues

The Hummingbird Centre (www.humming birdcentre.com) is Canada's largest perform-ing arts venue, designed to represent the cultural diversity of the city. Formerly the O'Keefe Centre, it gained international fame in 1974 when Mikhail Baryshnikov defected after a performance with the Russian Ballet. Since opening in 1960 with a production of *Camelot*, starring Richard Burton and Julie Andrews, it has presented touring musicals, international stars in concert, comedy and children's shows.

The Hummingbird was also the long-time home of the Canadian Opera Company and the Royal Canadian Ballet, however, both compa-nies are moving to the Four Seasons Centre for the Performing Arts (www.four seasonscen-tre.ca) in late 2006, where the 2,000-seat the-atre will provide state-of-the-art acoustics and four-tier, European-style horseshoe-shaped seating. The centre fills the entire block bounded by University Avenue, Queen, Richmond and York streets. Once the Four Seasons Centre is fully open, the Humming-bird will be downsized to accommodate a smaller theatre, and a 50-storey condominium development designed by Daniel Libeskind.

The historic landmark Massey Hall (www.masseyhall.com) and the newer Roy Thomson Hall are Toronto's two premier concert halls, playing host to top Canadian and international performers. Roy Thomson Hall (www.roythomson.com) underwent an acousti-cal enhancement programme in 2002 and won the Performing Arts Venue of the Year Award in 2005. With opera, jazz, classical, popular and folk music, plus choral ensembles and dance, the two downtown venues provide year-round entertainment.

Torontonians love to gather outdoors for entertainment in the summer months. There is always something happening at Harbourfront (www.harbourfrontcentre.com), an area developed as part of a movement to restore the waterfront to the people. It is home to the Premiere Dance Theatre, the Harbourfront Centre Theatre and several outdoor stages.

Harbourfront hosts music, dance, drama, read-ings and weekly festivals throughout the summer, plus free Sunday family concerts. The Power Plant gallery showcases contem-porary art, while in the craft studios you can watch artists at work in ceramics, glass, metal and textiles. Yonge-Dundas Square, Nathan Phillips Square and Mel Lastman Square have free Sunday concerts all through the summer.

One of the newer entertainment and cultural centres is the Distillery District. The 40 plus buildings of what was once the largest distillery in the British Empire form the best-preserved example of Victorian industrial architecture in North America. The district is

LEFT: the landmark Massey Hall.
RIGHT: *The Nutcracker* is a Christmas tradition with the National Ballet of Canada.

The Group of Seven

In the early 20th century, Canada was still a relatively new country developing at an exciting pace and inspiring enormous patriotism in its burgeoning population. Among these residents was a group of artists who had a passion to portray the spectacularly wild landscapes around them in a uniquely Canadian style, which they achieved with atmospheric images, bold brush strokes and subtle underlying symbolism. These artists came to be known as the Group of Seven.

Though he was not a member, dying tragically before it was formed, no mention of the Group of Seven can be made without reference to Tom Thomson (1877–1917), whose dramatical representations of raw Canadian nature was such an enormous inspiration. Several of the group worked alongside Thomson as commercial artists at the Toronto engraving firm, Grip, and during time off would take sketching trips together into the wilderness. Subsequently, Thomson left Grip to devote more time to painting while working as a guide in Algonquin Park, and his friends would visit him there, discovering both a superb quality of light and spectacular subject matter. Thomson's work can be seen in Toronto at the McMichael Canadian Art Collection *(see page 194)* and at the Art Gallery of Ontario *(see page 51)*; there's also a gallery dedicated to his work at Owen Sound, in his beloved northern Ontario.

The Group of Seven formed in 1920, and their first exhibition was in Toronto in May that year. Founding members were Arthur Lismer, Franklin Carmichael, Lawren Harris, James Edward Hervey MacDonald, A.Y. Jackson, Frank Johnston and Frederick Horsman Varley. Other artists then joined the group, including Edwin Holgate, L.L. Fitzgerald and A.J. Casson.

The group included artists from England (Lismer, MacDonald, Varley) as well as Canadian-born, and all had worked through such influences as Impressionism, Post Impressionism and European landscape art – not to mention their commercial draughting training – to achieve their own unique style. Some were not entirely devoted to landscapes, producing portraits, still lifes, abstract works and townscapes, and the variations of style is marked. Compare Thomson's powerful *The West Wind*, for instance, with Carmichael's gentle *Jackfish Village* and MacDonald's *Mist Fantasy, Sand River* and *Algoma*.

Together these artists eventually overcame the prejudices of the art world, which at that time held the widespread opinion that European art was always better and that the Canadian wilderness was not a suitable subject. How fortunate for us that they had the vision, determination and mutual encouragement to maintain their new direction and provide today's art world with such a wonderful legacy. The group disbanded in 1931, forming in its place the Canadian Group of Painters in order to encompass a larger, more widely representative number of artists, but the Group of Seven will always occupy a special place in the hearts of Canadian and international art lovers. ❏

LEFT: *Black Spruce in Autumn*, c.1916, by Tom Thomson.

located near "Hollywood North", the major studios of the Toronto film industry and location for over 800 films, notably *Chicago* and *X-Men*. The area is now a pedestrian village devoted to arts, culture and entertainment, with galleries, artists' studios, restaurants and live entertainment, and hosts festivals and special events throughout the year.

Music

The Toronto Symphony Orchestra (tel: 416-598 3375; www.tso.ca) is Canada's foremost symphonic ensemble, under the dynamic leadership of Musical Director Peter Oundjian. The orchestra plays a varied programme at Roy Thomson Hall throughout the season featuring top international guest artists.

A highlight of the year each May is the Last Night of the Proms, modelled on the famous Promenade Concerts at London's Royal Albert Hall, including flag-waving and audience participation.

Tafelmusik (www.tafelmusik.org) performs baroque music on period instruments, or faithfully designed modern replicas, and has achieved international recognition for its concerts and recordings. The 18 core members, expanded as needed, are all specialists in historical performance. Complemented by the Tafelmusik Chamber Choir, the orchestra performs over 50 concerts each season.

Founded in 1894, The Toronto Mendelssohn Choir (tel: 416-872 4255; www.tmchoir.org) is a world-renowned ensemble comprising 160 volunteer choristers and 20 professionals, performing the finest choral repertoire. Also part of the choir family are the Toronto Mendelssohn Youth Choir and the Toronto Mendelssohn Singers. The choir is heard regularly on CBC radio and television, tours the great concert halls of the world, and performs at Roy Thomson Hall and other venues, presenting *The Messiah* each Christmas season.

The Nathaniel Dett Chorale (tel: 416-340 7000; www.nathanieldettchorale.org) is Canada's first professional choral group dedicated to Afrocentric music. Their repertoire consists of many styles, including classical, spiritual, gospel, jazz, folk and blues.

RIGHT: the Toronto Symphony Orchestra is Canada's foremost symphonic ensemble.

Cultural Festivals

Annual festivals reflect Toronto's multicultural nature. Caribana (last two weeks of July; tel: 416-466 0321; www.caribana.ca.) is North America's largest street festival, a celebration of Caribbean music, dance, arts and crafts, fashion and food that attracts over a million people each year. The highlight is the Caribana Parade, with thousands of brilliantly-costumed masqueraders and dozens of bands filling the streets with the sounds of soca, calypso, reggae and salsa. Other events include the King and Queen of the Bands Competition, the two-day Olympic Island Caribbean Arts Festival, dances and concerts.

Caravan (last week in June; tel: 416-977 0466; www.caravan-org.com) is a nine-day cultural event with national pavilions throughout the city, each offering pageantry, shows, and food. Canada Day, 1 July, sees festivals and parades throughout the country, with food, entertainment and fireworks. The Celebrate Toronto Street Festival (second week of July. tel: 416-338 0338; www.city.toronto.on.ca) runs for three days with 90 bands and hundreds of performers on 10 stages. Toronto WinterCity Festival (tel: 416-395 7329), held the second week of February, attracts 400,000 people to three sites presenting 850 performers, including an ice-skating show. Among other attractions, you can enjoy rides, ice-sculptures and pancake breakfasts. The Canadian Aboriginal Festival is Canada's largest First Nations event, held at the Rogers Centre in late November. Here you can experience traditional teachings, art, music, food, pow wow dancing, lacrosse and a vendors market.

Pride Week (third week of June; www. pridetoronto.com), originally started to raise public awareness of gays and lesbians, has become a dynamic arts and culture festival, with a community fair and marketplace, entertainment, awards banquets and the Dykes March, and culminates in a joyful, spectacular parade that attracts 750,000 spectators.

Visual arts

In a country that was mostly wilderness, perhaps it was natural that landscape painting should so dominate Canadian art in the 19th and early 20th centuries, typified by the Group of Seven *(see page 46)*. No other group of artists has made such a deep and lasting impression on the people of Canada. They were among the first to capture the spirit of the country, what Northrop Frye characterised as not so much a question of "Who am I?" but of "Where is here?" Their work reflected a growing Canadian nationalism, a belief that art must flourish before the country could be a real home for its people. After their triumphant 1931 exhibition, other painters

INFORMATION AND TICKETS

Some useful websites to find out what's on include www.toronto.com and www.torontolife.com; www.showmetoronto.com has gallery and theatre listings. The free weeklies, *Now* and *Eye*, available on newsstands and in bookstores and cafés, have up-to-the-minute listings and reviews. Most tickets can be purchased from Ticketmaster, tel: 416-870 8000, but there's a service charge on every ticket. It is usually cheaper to call each venue's box office. The TO Tix booth in Yonge-Dundas Square sells half-price day-of-performance tickets (Tues–Sat noon–7.30pm; purchase Sun and Mon tickets on Sat; tel: 416-536 6468).

complained of being ignored and formed support groups such as the Canadian Group of Painters, who began to stage annual exhibitions, and the Beaver Hall group, a collective of largely female artists in Montreal, who developed figurative rather than landscape art.

After 1945, Canadian artists began to look to the world outside and saw how limited was the scope of Canadian art. Dynamic developments were taking place in New York, and Canadian artists could not fail to be stimulated by it. Perhaps national identity was not to be found in the wilderness, but rather in depictions of everyday life and people. The 1950s and 1960s saw an explosion of abstract art, and a fight for recognition against the conservatism of galleries and colleges. Albert Franck and William Ronald led the growth of independent galleries willing to display new and different works. Toronto department stores like Eatons and Simpsons were persuaded to set up room settings in which artists could display their work. A group including Harold Town, Jack Bush and Jock Macdonald formed the hugely influential Painters Eleven, which mounted touring exhibitions. Much of the new work was deeply shocking to the public, but the strength of the opposition served to draw attention to the new works.

Official support for the arts came in 1957

many artists were influenced by the mythic and spiritual nature of Indian and Inuit art.

The very size and range of Toronto's art community defies categorisation. There is a strong school of abstract colour-field painting, typified by Harold Feist. If there is a modern Toronto "look", according to Barrie Hale of the former *Toronto Telegram*, it is characterised by the painterliness, figuration and zany humour of John MacGregor, Alex Cameron and Paul Hutner. Recent figurative painters like Rae Johnson, Oliver Girling, Brian Burnett and Andy Fabo use the imagery of TV and mass media to address issues of urban conflict and the seamier side of city life.

with the founding of the Canada Council, and art in Canada experienced unprecedented growth. Commercial galleries proliferated in Toronto. The 1960s saw the growth of the hippie and artist colony of Yorkville, now unrecognisably fashionable. The complexity of Toronto art was deepened by the groundbreaking work of artists such as Michael Snow, Dennis Burton, Joyce Wieland, Graham Coughtry, and Gordon Raynor. From Emily Carr to Jack Shadbolt,

LEFT: First Nations art on a blanket.
ABOVE: a showcase of the work of Henry Moore.
RIGHT: an exhibit of Dhritarashtra Buddhist Guardian King of the East at the Royal Ontario Museum.

Art Galleries

The Art Gallery of Ontario (AGO) shows Canadian works by the Group of Seven and others, old European masters and the largest collection of Henry Moore sculptures outside England. Many commercial art galleries are clustered in two areas: Yorkville Avenue and Hazelton Street, and Queen Street West between Bathurst Street and Roncesvalles Avenue. Art at 80 has 11 galleries in one historic building at 80 Spadina Avenue. The Thomson Gallery has over 300 works from the private collection of Kenneth Thomson, including Group of Seven, Paul Kane, and Cornelius Kreighoff, notably the famous *Toll*

Gate, at the Hudson Bay store, 176 Yonge Street. The Museum of Contemporary Canadian Art (5040 Yonge Street; free; tel: 416-395 7430) features paintings, sculptures and photographs. The pre-eminent centre for ceramics in North America, the Gardiner Museum of Ceramic Art *(see page 155)* houses a remarkable collection of ancient American artefacts, and one of the world's most noted collections of European pottery and porcelain of the 15th and 16th centuries.

Several of Toronto's arts institutions are undergoing major structural changes, reflecting the best and often the most controversial in contemporary design. Internationally

Literature

For a celebration of literature, the Harbourfront Reading Series (www.readings.org; www.artbar.org) presents the Annual International Festival of Authors in late October, showcasing the best in Canadian and international contemporary writing, with readings by authors. At The Word on the Street (Queen's Park; free; last Sunday in September; tel: 416-504 7241; www.thewordonthestreet.ca) writers, booksellers, journalists, and TV personalities come together in this "literary theme park" to celebrate the printed word with displays, panel discussions, book awards, author-readings, signings, advice for aspiring

known Torontonian architect, Frank Gehry, has transformed the AGO *(see opposite)*. Almost next door on McCaul Street, the addition to the Ontario College of Art and Design takes the form of a huge rectangular box perched on stilts above the existing building, and has been described as whimsical, breezy, inspired and just sheer fun. Daniel Libeskind's crystal design for the Royal Ontario Museum *(see page 153)* creates a luminous public space extending into Bloor Street, drawing passers-by into the museum experience without them having to cross the threshold. The crystal will allow every major ROM collection to have a permanent home.

writers, sales and special promotions, activities for children, and musical performances.

To enjoy the spoken word, drop in on the Victory Café poetry readings in the Art Bar every Tuesday, or visit Celtic Jam, which has music every Thursday (581 Markham Street; free; tel: 416-461 5657). Members of the Storytellers School of Toronto appear regularly at the Harbourfront Centre, presenting colourful stories from different countries and cultures (tel: 416-973 2948). ❏

LEFT: Roberston Davies keeps an eye on literature.
ABOVE: the striking Ontario College of Art and Design building is hard to miss.

The Art Gallery of Ontario

One of the largest art galleries in North America – eighth largest to be exact – the AGO *(see page 120)* is currently in the throes of a huge construction project that will expand it even further. The scheme, aptly called Transformation AGO, will dramatically increase its exhibition space and give the entire Dundas Street facade an exciting new look.

Internationally renowned Toronto-born architect Frank Gehry has designed the new façade, an entire city block long, featuring curving windows that sweep up from street level to create a lofty exhibition space full of natural light. Contemporary artworks will be visible from the street, creating an appealing link between the gallery and the world outside. A restaurant, café, bar and gallery shop will also be invitingly located here, alongside the new entrance (there's currently a temporary entrance on McCaul Street). Inside, the expansion will give the Canadian historical section more than 160 percent more space, the photographic galleries will expand by more than 250 percent and contemporary art will get an additional 40 percent. The project will also make room for the 2,000 works of art recently donated to the gallery by Kenneth Thompson.

The transformed building will be completely open in 2008. In the meantime, much of it is closed, but there is certainly enough on show to make a visit worthwhile. Some notion of the wealth and scope of the permanent collections can be gained in *Favourites: Your Choices from Our Collection*. Gallery-goers and celebrities were invited to nominate their favourite works of art, and the most popular ones have been plucked from storage and put on show. These include the fun *Dick N' Mao* (Richard Nixon and Mao Tse Tung) by Joanne Todd, Kazuo Nakamura's *Inner Structure*, *The Peasant's Wedding* by Breughel and a wonderful whalebone sculpture, *Shaman*, by Markosce Karpik. One of the most powerful works is Joseph Légaré's *The Fire in the Saint-Jean Quartier Seen*

Looking Westward, and there are works by Cezanne, Tom Thomson *(see page 46)*, Rodin and Otto Dix, to name but a few.

The Group of Seven *(see page 46)* is currently represented by an exhibition of works by Arthur Lismer, alongside a display relating to the Gallery Art School that he founded in 1930. Further galleries on this floor contain contemporary works and innovative media art, while the Transformative Power of Art exhibition features works of many different eras and genres, including the atmospheric *Charing Cross Bridge, Fog 1902* by Claude Monet and Canadian Jean-Paul Riopelle's wonderful *Composition* (1952).

Return to the entrance area then climb the ramp to the Henry Moore Sculpture Gallery, one of the glories of the AGO. The English sculptor had a particular fondness for the city of Toronto, ever since he was commissioned to create a piece for the new City Hall. The bronze by Moore outside the AGO is somewhat obscured by contractor's fencing, but up here there is a superb collection of his plasters (forms from which the bronzes are cast), which he donated to the gallery. Telephone-style information points in the gallery include excerpts from an interview with Henry Moore in which he discusses his work and his love for Toronto. ❏

RIGHT: a design eye view of the AGO facade.

THE ANCIENT ART OF THE INUIT COMES OF AGE

Canada's galleries and museums are giving due recognition to the country's rich heritage of native art, dating back to the Dorset peoples of 600 BC

Traditionally, there was no word for "art" in the Inuktitut language. Early carvings tended to be functional – tools, weapons and utensils – or they were used for spiritual purposes, such as amulets and masks. The sculptures of creatures and human figures simply represented daily life.

The first people to produce what we recognise now as "art" belonged to the Dorset culture (*circa* 600 BC–AD 1000). They used ivory, bone and wood, keeping closely to the original shape of the material. The items were often small and smooth.

ABOVE: Decorative necklace with a carved pendant figure. Carvings were often made to be given as good-luck charms.

Inuit ancestors

Thule people from northern Alaska, the ancestors of today's Inuit, replaced the Dorset inhabitants around AD 1000. Their art was more feminine and less ritualistic, consisting of decorated items such as combs and needlecases. In the 16th and 17th centuries, European exploration provided the Inuit with customers for their carvings.

ABOVE: Amulets, such as this Thule culture example in the form of a fish, were one of the most common items of carving.

In the 1940s, the federal government realised that the development of Inuit art would bring an income to their isolated communities. So with the help of the Hudson's Bay Company and the Canadian Handicrafts Guild, Inuit-owned co-operatives were set up across the Arctic. Today, contemporary Inuit art has international status.

RIGHT: This miniature ivory mask is representative of the early Dorset culture in the Hudson Strait region, when carvings generally had spiritual connotations. It was probably one of the many items used in shamanic rituals.

CONTEMPORARY ARTISTS AT WORK

Inuit art comprises a great number of regional styles determined by tradition, available materials and the artists themselves. Many of today's artists have experienced life away from their communities, and combine the various cultural influences in their work. Most keep in close touch with their roots.

Prominent Inuit sculptor David Ruben Piqtoukun is renowned for his stone sculptures which are inspired by his concern for the loss of his culture, and the spiritual beliefs of his ancestors. The artist's work has been exhibited widely. He was born in 1950 north of the Mackenzie River Delta, where his father was a hunter and trapper. At the age of five, Piqtoukun, like so many of his generation, was sent away to school and forced to come to terms with an English culture. As a result, while his work has a strong spiritual element, it also explores the impact of outside influences on his culture. He lives in Toronto and regularly returns to his home community of Paulatuk.

Ovilu Tunnillie also experienced life in an alien world, which is reflected in her carving. She was born on Baffin Island in 1949, just 10 years before the first Inuit artists' co-operative was set up on the island. As a child she contracted tuberculosis and spent three years in hospitals in Manitoba. On her return she had to relearn both her language and way of life. Taught by her father, Tunnillie began carving in 1972. She lives in Cape Dorset, a large art community, and her sculptures are exhibited worldwide.

LEFT: This comb (*circa* AD 1000) is carved in the shape of a female figure. It is an excellent example of decorative Thule culture.

RIGHT: A comb incised with an archer standing over a man and animals, *c.*500 BC. Dorset hunters are thought to have brought bows and arrows to North America from Asia. Their ancestors found their prey on the sea ice in the Bering Strait and Arctic Ocean to stalk, but the Dorset peoples moved south to hunt the caribou.

BELOW: *My Mother and Myself*, in dark-green stone by Ovilu Tunnillie (1990).

THE FOOD SCENE

As Toronto's population became more ethnically diverse,
so did its restaurants. The resulting vibrancy attracted
talented star chefs. The result: world-class gastronomy

Toronto has around 7,000 restaurants and though this number includes all of the suburban fast food joints and take-away counters, there's a huge number of really great places to eat. The variety is enormous, too, covering many cuisines from every continent. The city has come a long way since the 1950s and 1960s, when it was a white bread town, influenced mostly by British immigrants. It was all rather dreary, with nowhere to have a gastronomic adventure.

Now, there are many adventures awaiting, and you'd need a lengthy stay to explore all Toronto has to offer. Savvy diners are seeking out the growing number of talented and creative chefs who are consistently exceeding culinary expectations.

A food revolution

The transformation initially began in quite a small way, with a few places offering French or Italian food, but the most notable change took place in the late 1970s when George Minden, a man with a vision, opened the Three Small Rooms at the Windsor Arms Hotel. Each of the rooms served a different kind of cuisine, and this soon became *the* place to see and be seen. The Courtyard Café here is still one of the best places to eat in Toronto, and the Windsor is a honeypot attracting visiting celebrities during the Toronto Film Festival.

Minden hired Michael Bonnancini (Canoe,

Biffs, Jump), a protégé of the world-renowned master chef Anton Mossiman. Bonnancini produced food that simply knocked Torontonians back on their heels.

Bursting on to the scene at the same time was a group of young chefs who had the imagination and the skill to produce exciting food that teamed the best local produce with accomplished techniques. Two of them had worked together at Scaramouche, still one of Toronto's best restaurants – Jamie Kennedy (JK Wine Bar) and Michael Stadtlander, of Eigensen Farm near Collingwood, the finest Ontario restaurant, which has also been voted one of the top restaurants in the world.

LEFT: spicy, hot peppers add flavour and colour.
RIGHT: delicious dessert and coffee at Accents.

Another was Mark McEwan (North 44, Bymark), and between them they enticed the city with their innovative approach and exciting preparations.

Multicultural cuisine

As the new breed of chefs raised the standard of gourmet cooking, the city's ethnic restaurants began to introduce more authentic flavours, rather than the watered down versions that they had previously believed would be more acceptable to Canadians. Chinese and Italian restaurants began to flourish and dining out became an event, going hand-in-hand with the growing cultural and theatre scene.

Today the restaurant scene is booming, chefs are creating world class food and the cultural mosaic is stronger than ever. There is nowhere better to explore this feast of exotic flavours than in Toronto's neighbourhoods – Little Italy and Corso Italia for authentic wood-oven pizzas, freshly made pasta and many other Italian specialities; the three Chinatowns for the best Chinese food outside of China; Little India for richly flavoured birianis and curry dishes; Koreatown for delicious specialities of Korea; Greektown on the Danforth for souvlaki and succulent roast lamb; Portugal Village for sardines and piri piri dishes. While the Eastern European

MUCH MORE THAN DONUTS

The donut is not a Canadian invention, but the nation has certainly taken it to its heart. Canada has more donut shops per capita than any other country. The largest chain, Tim Hortons, with more than 2,300 stores nationwide, and other franchises are pinpointed on *The Doughnut Map of Canada*. Wherever you go, there is always a donut shop around the corner.

Donut shops have built their reputation on the quality of their coffee as much as on the baked goods. Local wit claims that if you want a police officer, call the nearest donut shop; the police know where to find the best coffee in town.

Along with dozens of different styles and flavours of donut, you can find a great variety of croissants, muffins, tea biscuits, cakes and cookies. Most places have lunch menus, with soup and sandwiches made to order on rolls freshly baked on the premises. Many locations also have drive-up windows, for take away orders. For a coffee and snack at any time of the day and late into the night, or lunch served in minutes, you cannot beat the value of the donut shop.

To sound like a local, order a "double double" (coffee with double cream and double sugar) or a "double double twin", which will get you double cream and a sugar substitute. Not for weight watchers, but enjoyable.

enclaves out in the West End produce some of the best comfort food to be had anywhere. It's like a World's Fair of Food permanently sited in one large city.

Gourmet dining

Classic Continental cuisine tends to dominate the upper strata of Toronto's gourmet scene, with the multi-award-winning Truffles restaurant at the Four Seasons Hotel in Yorkville still at the pinnacle of fine dining (it's the only restaurant in Canada to have the maximum five-diamond rating from the AAA).

Other stand-outs include the gorgeous Auberge du Pommier at 4150 Yonge Street; other cuisines too. The city is renowned for the quality of its Oriental restaurants, which extend far beyond the confines of the Chinatowns. Some that consistently hit the gastronomic heights with their authentic and inventive concoctions include Lai Wah Heen, on Chestnut Street, just north of Nathan Phillips Square; Rain, at 19 Mercer Street (the restaurant of TV chef Guy Rubino); and the superb Edo Japanese restaurant on Eglinton Avenue West, which serves exemplary sushi and other Japanese favourites.

Torontonians have also developed a particular liking for Thai food, and there are probably in excess of 30 Thai restaurants in

Annona in the Park Hyatt hotel on Avenue Road; Susur, on King Street, just east of Bathurst; and the elegant Canoe, up on the 54th floor of the Toronto Dominion tower *(see page 100)*. Surprisingly, the 360 Restaurant in the CN Tower *(see page 117)*, is not the tourist trap it might have been, but is a classy restaurant serving top-notch food and has some excellent wines.

Regardless of the high-end bias, Toronto wouldn't be Toronto if the scope was that narrow, and there are outstanding examples of

LEFT: an Ethiopian restaurant sign.
ABOVE: out for a bite in Greektown.

TORONTO EATING EXPERIENCES

● **360 Restaurant**, at the CN Tower, for superb food and wonderful views.
● **Bistro 990** for good bistro fare and celebrity-spotting.
● **Omonia**, for patio dining in exuberant Greektown, specially good at festival time.
● **Patriot**, to discover Canadian cuisine and wines.
● **St Lawrence Market**, to breakfast on a peameal bacon sandwich from the Carousel Bakery.
● **Shopsy's Deli**, for one of their famous hot dogs.
● **Sightlines Club**, at the Rogers Centre, for great open-air dining while watching a baseball game.
● **Tim Horton's**, for exceptionally good donuts.

the city. Golden Thai, on Church Street, is consistently rated the best.

Affordable Feasts

You don't have to pay top dollar to enjoy good food in Toronto, and there's a huge selection of mid- and low-priced restaurants that provide a rewarding dining experience. The Entertainment District is particularly well served with places to enjoy a pre- or post-theatre dinner, and the stiff competition ensures that quality and value are maintained.

The Financial District is where you'll find big-ticket restaurants full of business movers and shakers, but you don't have to break the

an Italian Jew from Uruguay. The menu includes a vast selection of tapas. Elsewhere along Bloor West you'll find international choices, such as Italian, Thai, Mediterranean and French, and if it's burgers you want, drop in at the Yellow Griffin pub (No. 2202), where there are more than 30 varieties.

Trendsetting Toronto

Torontonians have led the way in Canadian food trends for a long time. They were eating healthily when the rest of the nation was still boosting their cholesterol levels, so there are a number of long-established vegetarian restaurants too. The Vegetarian at 2849 Dundas

bank to eat here. Just east of the financial core, on Church Street, you'll find the Jamie Kennedy Wine Bar, owned by one of the city's star chefs, with a reasonably priced "tasting" menu of creative dishes. Romagna Mia, at 106 Front Street East, is another small place with more heart than many downtown spots.

One of the best places to head for when you are hungry is Bloor Street West, including Bloor West Village, where there's an enticing range of restaurants, bistros, pubs and bars. At one Bloor West restaurant (No. 2980, in Etobicoke) you can get a taste of Toronto's multiculturalism in one location: Casa Barcelona is a great Spanish restaurant run by

Street West in Etobicoke has a terrific choice of meat-free dishes. Trendy Queen Street West has a few good options (including two of the Fresh juice bar chain), while Le Commensal at 655 Bay Street has a tempting buffet, where you help yourself then pay by the weight of food on your plate.

To find out what the latest trend is, one of the best places to go is the hip Ultra Supper Club at 314 Queen Street. Here, in summer you can eat on the lovely rooftop patio and enjoy the imaginative fusion cuisine while surveying this undeniably foodie city. ❑

ABOVE: catching up in the Distillery District.

Ethnic Eateries

One of the great advantages of Toronto's multiculturalism is the city's wide choice of ethnic restaurants. Here are some of the tastiest in town:

Chinese: A standout in Chinatown is Bright Pearl Seafood, serving delicious dim sum all day long. (346–8 Spadina Avenue at Dundas Street West, tel: 416-979 3988). For some of the best Cantonese food in North America, try upscale Lai Wah Heen (Metropolitan Hotel, 108 Chestnut Street, tel: 416-977 9899).

Ethiopian: Cosy and comfortable Ethiopian House (4 Irwin Avenue, tel: 416-923 5438) serves traditional spicy stews of meat, pulses and vegetables the Ethiopian way – using a piece of *injera* (sourdough flatbread) in place of cutlery.

French: Gamelle (468 College Street, tel: 416-923 6254), serves creative dishes with Canadian ingredients such as lamb and foie gras from Quebec. Uptown you can get a top-notch meal at elegant Scaramouche (1 Benvenuto Place, tel: 416-961 8011).

Greek: Greektown on the Danforth has dozens of Greek restaurants. One standout is Mezes (456 Danforth Avenue, tel: 416-778 5150) serving small plates of dishes such as grilled octopus. Find hearty fare at Penelope (225 King Street West, tel: 416-351 9393).

Indian: For good service in a pretty Victorian house, try The Host (14 Prince Arthur Avenue, tel: 416-962 4678). Nataraj (394 Bloor Street, tel: 416-928 2925) is more casual, but also serves delicious, above-average Indian fare.

Italian: Visiting celebrities enjoy stylish Trattoria Giancarlo (41 Clinton Street, tel: 416-533 9619) for its superb Northern Italian food and great wine list.. For delicious light fare try John's Italian Caffe and Pizza (27 Baldwin Street, tel: 416-596 8848).

Jamaican: The Real Jerk (709 Queen Street East, tel: 416-463 6055) is a favourite for its spicy jerk chicken and shrimp creole, its casual atmosphere and reggae beats.

Japanese: Nami (55 Adelaide Street East, tel: 416-362 7373) serves elegant sushi in a hushed atmosphere. Tempo (596 College Street, tel: 416-531 2822) is a hip, fusion restaurant.

Korean: Buk Chang Dong Soon To Fu (691 Bloor Street, tel: 416-537 0972), in Koreatown serves a popular dish of Seoul: a delicious, spicy stew-like soup with silken tofu, vegetables, seafood or beef.

Middle-Eastern: Critics love 93 Harbord Street (at Spadina, tel: 416-922 5914).for its stylish décor and creative Mediterranean-inspired dishes such as beef-wrapped asparagus over a tamarind marinade.

Pan-Asian/Thai: East! (240 Queen Street West, tel: 416-351 3278) is popular for its sleek modern decor, and wide choice of delicious and inexpensive curries, pad thai and sushi.

Portuguese: Elegant and romantic Chiado (864 College Street, tel: 416-538 1910) is one of the city's best restaurants. Or try the relaxed warmth of Leao d'Ouro (356 College Street, tel: 416-926 9899).

Spanish: Lively and colourful Segovia (5 St Nicolas Street, tel: 416-960 1010), is tucked away on a nice little alley. It is a city favourite, offering delicious Paella and a great lunch deal. ❑

RIGHT: traditional dim sum can't be beaten.

SHOPPING IN THE CITY

With an almost limitless choice of things to buy, plenty
of interesting little independents as well as the big
chain stores and a number of attractive shopping
enclaves, Toronto makes it easy to spend money

Toronto is a great place to shop. It's a city where major streets are lined with small shops and boutiques, many of which are independently owned (thanks largely to property prices that are lower than in cities such as New York, London or Paris), and the handful of department stores here have a good selection of products, both domestic and imported.

But it's not only what you can buy that makes it so good – favourable exchange rates provide great bargains for many foreign visitors, with some unexpected bargains, and even with the addition of the 15 percent tax at the till (beware: it's not included on the price tags), you may still find you are paying half the price the same item would cost at home. Remember, too, that you can get some of that tax back on certain items when you leave the country. Many shops and all tourist offices have leaflets explaining the process, so pick one up and keep all your receipts.

Yonge Street and the Eaton Centre

Yonge Street is the main north–south artery of the city, with some parts of the street more salubrious than others, and it's lined with shops, from discount electronics and music stores to fashion retailers and sports shops.

On the block between Dundas and Queen Streets you'll find the famous Eaton Centre, a massive complex housing nearly 300 stores within a glittering multi-level galleria, topped by three soaring office towers. It's served by

two convenient subway stations (Dundas and Queen) that lead right into the centre, making it exceptionally convenient for a downtown mall. The Eaton Centre is one of the major tourist attractions in the city, pulling in more than a million people every week. Surprisingly, it only really gets an overcrowded feeling down in the food court on weekday lunchtimes, and it's far less claustrophobic than most shopping centres. This is particularly true of the upper levels, where the higher-end shops are.

You'll be able to find absolutely anything you need here, from tennis shoes to drill bits, and the centre is open seven days a week. The

LEFT: the shopping in Yorkville is upscale.
RIGHT: Yonge Street in the heart of downtown.

northern (Dundas) end of the complex is anchored by the American-owned department store Sears, who bought out the much-loved Canadian chain, Eatons, when it hit financial difficulties in the late 1990s. A decision was taken to retain the name for the centre, though.

Another Canadian-owned shopping icon is The Bay, the city's oldest department store, which can be reached from the Eaton Centre by an upper-level footbridge across Queen Street. The Bay is the modern incarnation of the historic Hudson's Bay Company, which was crucial to the exploration and development of trade in Canada from the earliest pioneer days.

Just north of the Eaton Centre, across Dundas Street, is the cool and rather less frantic Atrium on Bay, with around 50 shops, restaurants and banks. Fashion retailers here include the massive Guess (with regular in-store fashion shows) and a Tall Girl shop, fitting out taller than average ladies in style.

The PATH

Toronto has the biggest underground shopping complex in the world, a vast network of store-lined walkways that connects all the major shopping centres, office blocks, entertainment venues, subway stations and some hotels. Known as the PATH, it is a fantastic asset in a city that can be stiflingly hot at the height of summer (when air quality can at times be poor) and bitingly cold in winter. With access to five subway stations, the Union Station transport hub, 20 car parks and some 1,200 shops, the 27 km (16 miles) of corridors stretch from the coach terminal at Dundas and Queen in the north to the Toronto Convention Centre in the south.

Bloor Street West and Yorkville

The stretch of Bloor Street between Yonge Street and Avenue Road provides classy shopping, with such stores as Chanel, Gucci and Hermes, as well as the country's most up-market department store, Holt Renfrew and the Canadian sportswear retailer, Roots.

Also along this stretch of Bloor, you'll find fine china and silver from around the world at Ashley's, quality jewellery and silver at Birks and a number of shops selling mid-priced cutting-edge women's and men's fashion. US-owned Pottery Barn has a store here, full of gorgeous housewares, and you can rummage for price-slashed fashion at Winners.

The narrow streets just north of the Bloor strip form an area known as Yorkville, where there's a distinct air of affluence, both in the type of shopping and the style of shopper. Wealthy Torontonians mingle with the visiting jet-set and celebs as they amble between fashion design houses, spas, tanning salons and bijou restaurants. Even if the prices are a little too rich for you, it's one of the best places for a stroll and window-shopping, stopping, perhaps, for a spot of lunch or a coffee at one of the pavement cafés on Yorkville's leafy Victorian streets.

Queen Street West

One of the more vibrant and creative shopping areas in the city is along Queen Street West from University to Bathurst, and the continuation of the area referred to as West Queen West, running from Bathurst to beyond Ossington. The first part of the stretch is a busy one, anchored by the headquarters of the Chum Television network at John Street, and is lined with quirky fashion boutiques, bars and restaurants, and bigger stores such as the music chain HMV and the Canadian housewares firm Caban.

Further west, beyond Spadina Avenue and Bathurst Street, you'll find where the creative energy is thriving in the city right now, especially in the independent art galleries and fashion boutiques. For Canadian fashion designs go to Annie Thompson at No. 674, Comrags at No. 654, Preloved at No. 613 and Peach Berserk at No. 507. Here you'll also find cutting edge furniture and houseware shops such as Morba at No. 665, scrumptious homemade chocolates at js bonbon, at No. 881, and an extraordinary selection of beautiful Japanese paper at No. 887.

Art galleries representing Canadian artists line the north side of Queen between Crawford and Dovercourt. Young Canadian designers are popping up on nearby Dundas Street West. Of note are Skirt at No. 903, and men's cutting-edge fashion at Model Citizen, at No. 913.

Uptown shopping

If you prefer a peaceful shopping experience in a residential neighbourhood, you will enjoy strolling up Yonge Street north of Eglinton between Roehampton and Strathgowan below Lawrence. This is a stretch of small, interesting boutiques and cafés catering mostly to well-heeled locals. Much of what's for sale here can generally be found elsewhere in the city, but what makes shopping appealing here is its High Street, residential feel.

Some of the city's best sports shops are on this part of Yonge: yoga and stylish sportswear at Higher Ground, at No. 2488, and an extensive selection of sporting goods and fashion at Sporting Life at No. 2665. Pastries and flowers are sold at Dufflet, at No. 2638, and Just Cuz, at No. 2624, has a fun assortment of jewellery and accessories. Alex Farm Products on Yonge sells a good selection of cheeses, and The Butcher at No. 2636 sells organic meat. This area is worth exploring on a nice day to see how a comfortable Toronto neighbourhood leads its life.

Individual highlights

In addition to these main shopping areas, there are some stand-out places that provide a rewarding retail experience. Down on the lake

shore, Queen's Quay Terminal is a splendid conversion of an old warehouse in a fabulous location, where acres of shining glass enclose about 30 high class shops, including quality arts and crafts, designer fashions and home decor, with several waterside restaurants.

Further east in the Distillery Historic District, there's a great range of shops with an upmarket, individualistic style – designer furnishings, jewellery, ceramics, Segway scooters, contemporary art galleries and even a fashion boutique for dogs (Mona's Dog Boutique), with designer knits and jackets to keep your pooch warm in winter. The Auto Grotto specialises in car-related items,

including model cars, posters, signs, badges, books, pictures and clothing.

Toronto's markets

Contrasting with Toronto's ultra-modern shops selling a range of international goods are it's terrific markets, full of inviting aromas and the sound of shoppers interacting with the friendly vendors. St Lawrence Market, at Front and Jarvis streets, high on the list of places you should not miss, is ranked among the top 25 markets in the world. Occupying three buildings, it's the South Market that houses the Tuesday to Saturday food market, with 50 stalls piled high with fresh fruit and

LEFT: find art and one-offs in the Distillery District.
RIGHT: Roots stocks goods produced at home.

vegetables, prepared food, organic produce, meat and seafood, gourmet teas and coffees, confectionery and other goods. The North Market has a long-established farmers' market on Saturdays, when Ontario growers bring their produce to town, and on Sundays there's an antiques market, with more than 80 stalls.

Kensington Market, between Dundas and College, is more of a street scene, blending a hip, counter-culture atmosphere with traditional stalls of fresh produce and colourful shops spilling out onto the pavements. This is also a great place to look for vintage clothing. It's noisy and vibrant and fun, with buskers and events.

Where to find Canadiana

Visitors like to pick up something that's uniquely Canadian, and there are plenty of places to find top quality souvenirs that go beyond the standard maple-leaf emblazoned items. First Nations crafts are showcased in a number of galleries. Down on the harbourfront at Queen's Quay you'll find the excellent Arctic Nunavut (207 Queen's Quay, tel: 416-203 7889) with an award-winning gallery and a superb range of carvings, clothing, jewellery, books and gifts. Nearby, at 12 Queen's Quay West (between Yonge and Bay streets) is the Eskimo Gallery (tel: 416-366 3000), an elegant space displaying a huge selection of sleek

THE SPA TREATMENT

When shopping fatigue sets in, treat yourself to a massage, facial, pedicure or manicure at one of the many top-quality spas in Toronto. Here's a pick of three of the city's favourites:

Jeanet Spa and Salon: Visiting celebrities and uptown mavens swear by this long-running spa and salon that's consistently voted one of the best in the city for its service and high standards. The atmosphere is friendly, but quarters are a little tight and somewhat noisy. (140 Yorkville Avenue, tel: 416-921 2996; www.jeanetspa.com).

The Spa at the Windsor Arms: For more tranquil old-world comfort, The Spa located on the 4th floor of the gracious Windsor Arms hotel offers spa and salon services to drop-in clients as well as hotel guests. After your treatment, enjoy a sauna or a peaceful dip in the hotel's intimate swimming pool lit by its own wood-burning fireplace. (18 St Thomas Street, tel: 416-971 9666; www.windsorarmshotel.com).

Civello: A small chain of highly successful hair salons and spas that cater to stylish urban professionals, with a general philosophy of natural wellness. The atmosphere is hip and serene, with gentler prices than its more upscale counterparts. (269 Queen Street West, tel: 416-977 7755; www.civello.com. Three other locations).

soapstone carvings. Native Stone Art, at 4 McCaul Street (tel: 416-593 0924) has a fine range of First Nations crafts, including Navajo jewellery, Inuit and West Coast cedar carvings and Cowichan sweaters.

The non-profit Guild Shop in Yorkville (118 Cumberland Street, tel: 416-925 4222) is the showcase of the Ontario Crafts Council, and has one of the city's best selections of Inuit art and sculptures, plus work by Ontario crafts-people, including pottery, leatherwork, sculpture, jewellery and prints. Comestible souvenirs include chocolates from Laura Secord (several stores around the city), or some maple syrup, maple sugar candies and smoked salmon.

below Eglinton. The Toronto Antique Centre at 276 King Street West (at Duncan Street) houses more than two dozen antiques dealers, and some of the city's best antiques shops are along the stretch of Yonge Street between Rosedale and Summerhill subway stations.

Reading and music matters

For a lasting souvenir of Toronto there are some excellent bookshops. The national chain is Indigo and Chapters, selling books, music, small gadgets and coffee. There are four in central Toronto. Book City is a small chain of independent bookstores with five city locations. Nicolas Hoare (45 Front Street East at

Antiques Hunting

For a good selection of antiques shops, take the Queen Street streetcar eastbound and walk the north side of up-and-coming, trendy Leslieville between Pape and Greenwood. Many of these shops, such as Mugsy's at 1162 Queen Street East and Jaws Antiques at 1374 Queen Street East rent to nearby film studios.

For quality pieces, try Canada's oldest antique shop, the Paisley Shop (77 Yorkville at Bellair). There are a handful of shops selling quality antiques on Mount Pleasant Road

LEFT: uptown style and fashion in Yorkville.
ABOVE: CDs and DVDs at Sam the Record Man.

Church) is considered one of the finest in the country, thanks to its selection of fiction, biography and art book titles. It's relaxing and inviting, with a fireplace and comfortable furniture. Pages Books and Magazines (256 Queen Street) has the city's best selection of academic works, fiction and books on art and cinema, along with art and design magazines from around the world.

And for musical entertainment Sam the Record Man, on the stretch of Yonge Street between Dundas and Wellesley has the widest selection of new CDs and DVDs, but if you're looking for something less mainstream try Soundscapes at 572 College Street. ❑

PLACES

A detailed guide to the city with the
principal sites clearly cross-referenced
by number to the maps

Toronto, with its high ratio of foreign-born citizens, frequently surprises first-time visitors. It is home to people from more than 200 countries, and whether you're exploring the waterfront, the galleries in Yorkville, the shops in the Eaton Centre or the clubs on Richmond Street West, the city's multiracial makeup is an obvious driving force. Torontonians' willingness to embrace its differences underlies its passion for global cuisines *(see page 55–9)*, its celebration of festivals *(see page 38–9)* and its flourishing arts scene. It adds up to a pretty great place to spend time.

The first four chapters in Places focus on downtown Toronto. Beginning on the Waterfront, we take you to Harbourfront Centre, a dynamic cultural centre, to the tranquil Toronto Islands, and along the sparkling necklace of parks, gardens and reclaimed wetlands along Lake Ontario's once-industrial shores. The hard-driving edge of the Financial District is tempered by extraordinary architecture, from Old City Hall to BCE Place, superb shopping along the Underground PATH, the avant-garde Design Exchange and the very Canadian Hockey Hall of Fame.

Downtown West takes in some well-known icons – the CN Tower and Rogers Centre (formerly SkyDome) – along with the Entertainment District and the Fashion District, and ends at Historic Fort York. Then we look at Old Toronto, from the 10-blocks of the original town to the St Lawrence Market and the revamped Distillery Historic District.

The ensuing chapters take you out of the centre to enjoy the chilled-out vibe of The Beaches and Queen Street East's funky boutiques and eateries; to the University and Annex areas – home to two reborn museums – and to eccentric Casa Loma; to the urban wilderness of High Park in the West End; and to cliff-top trails and beaches along Scarborough Bluffs. A detailed primer *(pages 179–87)* then guides you through the neighbourhoods, from ritzy Rosedale to exuberant Greektown. The final chapter *(pages 191–209)* heads out to attractions on the city fringes, and to such easy-to-reach highlights as Niagara Falls, Stratford, the Six Nations Reserve, Ontario's wine country and Prince Edward County.   ❏

PRECEDING PAGES: mural art in Kensington Market; a monument to multiculturalism stands outside Union Station.
LEFT: traffic travels along Queens Quay West, near the Harbourfront.

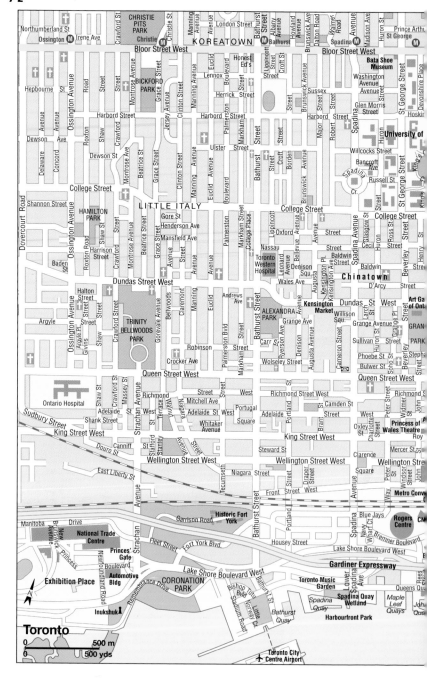

Northumberland St
Ossington Ⓜ Irene Ave

CHRISTIE PITS PARK
Christie Ⓜ

KOREATOWN

Bloor Street West

Honest Ed's

Bata Shoe Museum

Bloor Street West

Bathurst Ⓜ
Spadina Ⓜ
Prince Arthu
St George Ⓜ

Hepbourne St

BICKFORD PARK

Lennox Boulevard

Herrick Street

Washington Avenue
Avenue
Glen Morris Street

Hoski

Harbord Street

Harbord Street

Harbord

Dewson Ave

Dewson St

Ulster Street

University of

Willcocks Street

Bancroft Ave
Russell St

College Street

College Street

College Street

HAMILTON PARK

LITTLE ITALY

Gore St
Henderson Ave
Mansfield Ave
College Place

Oxford Street

Baldwin

Chinatown

Cecil Street

Baldwin

Nassau
Toronto Western Hospital

Wales Ave

D'Arcy

Dundas Street West

Andrews Ave

Dundas St West

Art Ga of Ont.

Kensington Market

ALEXANDRA PARK

TRINITY BELLWOODS PARK

Grange Ave

Willison Squ.

Grange Avenue

GRAN

PARK

Carr St

Robinson Street

Wolseley Street

Sullivan St

Phoebe St

Stepha

Crocker Ave

Bulwer St

Queen Street West

Queen Street West

Ontario Hospital

Richmond

West

Richmond Street West

Richmond

Mitchell Ave

Camden St

Adelaide St

Portugal Square

Adelaide

Portland

West

Shank Street

Whitaker Avenue

King Street West

King Street West

Princess of Wales Theatre

Canniff

Steward St

Roy

Wellington Street West

Wellington Street West

Wellington Stre

East Liberty St

Niagara Street

Front Street West

Metro Conv

Manitoba Drive

Garrison Road

Historic Fort York

Blue Jays

Rogers Centre

CN

National Trade Centre

Princes' Gate

Fleet Street
Fort York Blvd

Housey Street

Lake Shore Boulevard West

Exhibition Place

Automotive Bldg

Lake Shore Boulevard West

Gardiner Expressway

Toronto Music Garden

Queens

CORONATION PARK

Spadina Quay Wetland

Maple Leaf Quays

Inukshuk

Bathurst Quay

Harbourfront Park

Toronto

0 ——— 500 m
0 ——— 500 yds

Toronto City Centre Airport

DOWNTOWN WATERFRONT

An enticing cocktail of natural and cultural
attractions, Toronto's restored Waterfront
is, once again, a playground for
more than 3 million people

There's no other stretch of land in Toronto that is treasured by so many as the Waterfront, on the north shore of Lake Ontario. For centuries past, First Nations enjoyed the sheltered bay – not only as a source of food and water, and a way of getting around, but also for the tranquillity of its lagoons, beaches, woodlands and wetlands. When European settlers first arrived, tall stands of oak trees stretched from Fort York east to the mouth of the Don River. Salmon thrived in the rivers and loons (the bird on the one dollar coin) nested in the rushes bordering the sandy shoreline.

From the 1850s onwards, however, the city's rapid growth as an industrial hub meant that vast amounts of landfill pushed the shoreline from Front Street south to where it is today at Queen's Quay. In between Lake Ontario and downtown, a barrier grew – formed by wharves, railway lines, factories, warehouses and, eventually, expressways. Spending time at the lake inevitably involved what was then a long trek by streetcar out to The Beaches or Sunnyside Park, or by ferry to the Toronto Islands.

Reclamation

With the restoration of Old Toronto in the early 1970s came the desire to take back the Downtown Waterfront from industry and develop its enormous leisure potential. It has been a long, arduous process, but the powerful forces of change are gradually transforming an ugly blot in the heart of the city into a waterfront playground, artfully linked by a string of boardwalks, pathways, beaches, parks and gardens.

As David Crombie, a former city mayor now involved in the regeneration of the Waterfront has said, it is no longer "yesterday's waterfront of

Map
on pages
76–7

LEFT: ferries cross
between The Islands
and the mainland.
BELOW: time to catch
up with the local news.

Air Canada Centre is is not only the home of the city's hockey, basketball and lacrosse teams, it is also a prestigious rock concert venue. The centre is located at the northwest corner of Lakeshore Boulevard.

neglect and decline, but tomorrow's Waterfront, full of bright promise". However, until recently, access to the Waterfront wasn't easy unless you had a car. And while there are parking areas along the downtown section, they are generally exorbitantly expensive. Now it's easier, with various parts of the Waterfront served by the Toronto Transit Commission (TTC; tel: 416-393 4636).

Once you are at the Waterfront, the going is easy, along the 22-km (12½-mile) **Martin Goodman Trail**. This is part of a much longer waterfront trail that runs from Niagara-on-the-Lake to Brockville, in eastern Ontario. The Toronto stretch winds along the Waterfront past lush parks, towering condos, bustling marinas and wide sandy beaches, from the city's western to eastern borders. It is smoothly paved and wide enough to accommodate cyclists, pedestrians, joggers and in-line skaters.

In some areas, those who prefer to meander may do so along a parallel, pedestrians-only trail or boardwalk. It is inevitably busy at weekends, far quieter during the week, or early mornings.

Renaissance of the east

Minutes southeast of downtown, **Cherry Street** divides Toronto's inner and outer harbour, its southernmost point where the Toronto Islands were once connected to the mainland. This was an industrial wasteland for years, but then things began to change. First came **The Docks** (11 Polson Street, tel: 416-469 5655), a vast entertainment complex with three nightclubs, a golf academy, a drive-in cinema, beach volleyball, go-karting and a large octagonal swimming pool.

Then, spanking new docks were built to accommodate a newly launched fast ferry service (tel: 1-877-283 7327; www.catfastferry.

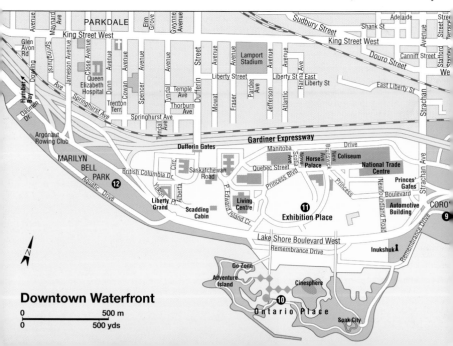

Downtown Waterfront

0 ____ 500 m
0 ____ 500 yds

Map on pages below

com), linking Toronto with Rochester, New York. The *Spirit of Ontario I* (popularly "the Cat") makes the crossing in just 2½ hours, port-to-port.

At the foot of Cherry Street, **Cherry Beach** is a peaceful, less frequented enclave, and one of Toronto's cleanest sandy beaches. Just behind it, the Martin Goodman Trail winds east towards The Beaches, through a pleasantly wooded area, which also provides welcome shade for picnickers.

East of Yonge Street, the huge **Redpath Sugar Refinery ❶** (95 Queens Quay East, tel: 416-366 3561; small charge) is hard to miss. In 1954 Redpath was the first company to relocate to the Toronto Waterfront as a result of the opening of the St Lawrence Seaway. The company had been refining sugar in Montreal since 1854 and continues to receive raw sugar by ship and convert it into granulated and liquid

forms. A small on-site museum provides the lowdown on the history and production of sugar.

The Air Canada Centre

Home of the Toronto Maple Leafs hockey team, Toronto Raptors Basketball Club and the Toronto Rock lacrosse team, the **Air Canada Centre ❷** (40 Bay Street, tel: 416-815 5982; www.theaircanadacentre. com; subway: Union Station) opened in 1999, on the site of the old (1939–1941) Canada Post Delivery Building. During construction of this state-of-the-art sports complex and concert venue, the best elements of the former building's design – which had been heavily influenced by the simplicity of the German Bauhaus architectural movement – were preserved. The original façade, including the polished black granite, fluted pillars, historic windows and detailed bas-reliefs, has been beautifully

Cherry Beach is one of four Toronto beaches – the others are Woodbine, Ward's Island and Hanlan's Point – that have met the high standards set by the international Blue Flags jury, winning the environmental award for clean and safe beaches.

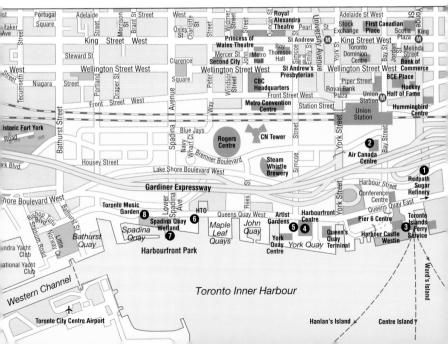

Ferries to the Islands depart from the ferry docks at the foot of Bay Street. The nearest subway station is Union Station, from where you'll need to take either of the street-cars (Nos. 509 or 510). The schedule is complex, depending on the season, but there are ferries at regular intervals throughout the day to Centre Island (no winter service) and Ward's Island.

BELOW: boats dock in Toronto's pretty marina.

restored. Hour-long guided tours (Wed–Sat) offer a glimpse into the centre's inner workings.

Islands ferry

The ferry terminal for the Toronto Islands *(see page 91–5)* is just east of the Westin Harbour Castle Hotel at Bay Street and Queen's Quay. If you are driving, there's a handy place to park to the west of the Westin, beside Captain John's shipboard restaurant, moored opposite the foot of Yonge Street. The **Toronto Islands Ferry Service ❸** (tel: 416-392 8193) to Ward's Island and Centre Island runs regularly during the summer, but between Labour Day (first Monday in September) and the beginning of June, the service is limited. The ferry to the city airport departs from a point further east *(see page 83)*.

A regular ferry service has carried Torontonians over to the Islands since the 1890s, and the 10-minute ride across the harbour – with the soaring city skyline behind, the tree-lined islands ahead, and all manner of boats, from tiny dinghies to huge

ocean-going vessels, on either side – continues to be a favourite part of any island excursion. And it is, for most people, the only way to appreciate – somewhat distantly – the grandeur of the Southern-style clubhouse of the **Royal Canadian Yacht Club** on South Island.

Since Toronto's earliest days, the islands have been a favourite refuge from the heat and clamour of the city. When John Graves Simcoe and his wife Elizabeth first arrived here, they were still part of a long sandy peninsula that extended nearly 9 km (5½ miles) southwest to form a sheltered bay. Deemed ideal for a harbour by Colonel Simcoe, the site was selected for the town of York in the early 1790s.

In 1858, a major storm washed away a section of the peninsula, completely separating it from the mainland. Around this time, city residents began to flock to the islands on paddle steamers, to escape the sweltering summer heat. Tents and shacks soon sprung up beside gracious Victorian homes and, since the early 1900s, a year-round cottage community has thrived on Ward's and Algonquin islands.

Architectural contrasts

Back on Lake Shore Boulevard, just west of Bay Street, the impressive **Toronto Harbour Commission Building** is a 1917 landmark. It was built right on the Waterfront, and large ships could tie up right at its front door. Ironically, the Commissioners' policies – which led to more than a century's dumping of landfill into the bay – resulted in their own building being totally cut off from the water. However, the heavy commuter traffic that now streams by does not lessen the impact of the neoclassical grandeur of its four-storey-high beaux-arts columns. The building is now home to what is considered one of the city's best

steakhouses, so you can enjoy a great meal while surrounded by its traditional opulence.

At the foot of York Street, beside the York Street Slip, is a rather different example of Waterfront architecture. Built in 1907, **Pier 6** is the oldest surviving building on Toronto's Waterfront. A small wooden building with a steep roof and deep eaves, it now performs double duty as an information booth (you can buy tickets for harbour cruises here) and a harbourside coffee shop.

Jewel of the Waterfront

In the early 1970s, the federal government expropriated a stretch of prime waterfront property that extended from York Street to Stadium Road. Over time, the factories, warehouses, railway sidings and wharves were either demolished or superbly converted to create the **Harbourfront Centre ❹** (www. harbourfrontcentre.com; subway: Union Station, then streetcar west) – a dynamic art and culture complex on the revitalised Waterfront that

has proved to be a popular and valuable asset to the city and a splendid venue for a number of festivals and events.

To explore this area, head for the tranquil, under-used boardwalk rather than contend with the constant bustle of Queen's Quay. Dotted with benches, trees for shade and lush green patches, the boardwalk extends from the ferry terminal almost to the western end of Queen's Quay, with easy access to Harbourfront's many attractions.

Queen's Quay Terminal (207 Queens Quay West; tel: 416-203 0510; daily) was an imposing waterfront warehouse built in the mid 1920s. Beautifully restored by architect Eberhard Zeidler, it remains an architectural landmark, home to waterside restaurants and speciality shops, several of which focus on Canadiana. **First Hand Canadian Crafts** sells mostly furnishings made by Canadian artists and craftspeople from across the country, while **Arctic Nunavut** sells Inuit carvings, clothing and jewellery, as well as books about Inuit

Map on pages 76–7

Paddling among the islands, around the Leslie Street Spit or in the Humber River bay is a peaceful way to explore Toronto's Waterfront. Contact the Harbourfront Canoe and Kayak Centre Toronto.

BELOW: keeping an eye on the Waterfront.

A potter at the Harbourfront Centre.

BELOW: modern art in the art gallery at the Harbourfront Centre.

art and life in the Canadian Arctic. On the third floor, the **Premier Dance Theatre** is the only theatre in Canada designed specifically for dance. It was modelled on The Joyce in New York, and no seat in the house is further from the stage than about 23 metres (75 ft).

The **Artist Gardens ⑤** make ingenious use of the space between Queen's Quay Terminal and York Quay Centre. Landscape architects, set designers, craftspeople, visual and performing artists were all brought in to create the 23 intriguingly different gardens. The plants, flowers, shrubs and design elements often underscore complex concepts. Enjoy them on your own, with the help of a map, or check the available guided tours at the information desk in York Quay (tel: 416-973 4000).

Nearer the lake, the **Harbourfront Theatre** (box office tel: 416-973 4000) and the **Power Plant Contemporary Art Gallery** (tel: 416-973 4949; www.thepowerplant.org) are based in a former icehouse and powerhouse building respectively, built in 1926 to house

heating and refrigeration equipment. The sleek, glass-sided theatre is in constant use, by both local and international theatre companies, while the gallery's cutting-edge exhibitions – or installations – are wonderfully backdropped by the simplicity of their surroundings.

Always a hive of activity, **York Quay Centre** (235 Queens Quay West) was a truck warehouse in its previous life. In the old loading bays, complete with roll-up garage doors, is the **Craft Studio** – where you can watch self-employed craftspeople working with ceramics, glass, textiles or metal. Much of what they produce is sold, along with work from other artists across Canada, in the adjacent **Bounty**, a contemporary Canadian craft shop. Nearby, the contemporary photography on the curving walls of the **Photo Passage** can be counted on to provide food for thought.

Harbourfront's calendar ranges from avant-garde theatre to improv comedy, music and performance art. One of York Quay Centre's longest-running events is the year-round

Harbourfront Reading Series and the annual **International Festival of Authors**, where writers from around the world come to participate in discussions and on-stage interviews and, of course, to read from their books. For youngsters, the **Milk International Children's Festival of the Arts** is one of the biggest of its kind in North America.

Cultural magnet

Summer-long, the place is hopping with global sounds, fiery food festivals and Celtic rhythms. Opera, ballet and symphony concerts are presented outside, at one of Toronto's most lovely waterside venues. Another huge draw is the water-orientated events and activities. In addition to three Harbourfront marinas, tall ships and navy vessels come visiting, and sailing (tel: 416-203 3000), kayaking and canoeing (tel: 416-203 2277) and tall ship adventures (tel: 416-596 7117) can be arranged at the **Nautical Centre** (275 Queens Quay West).

At the end of York Quay, the outdoor terrace of **Lakeside Eats** overlooks a pond that alternates as one of Toronto's most popular ice-skating rinks. More than 40,000 people enjoy the free skating and the inspiring views each winter.

West of York Quay, a large lawn around a small stage is another focal point during the summer – and is one of the best spots for people-watching. Crafts from around the world are sold at the **International Marketplace** and tasty fare prepared by a rota of Toronto restaurants is sold in the marquee of the **World Café & Bar.**

A drawbridge over the Simcoe Street Slip leads to **Pier 4** (245 Queen's Quay West), where a couple of nautically themed restaurants occupy another old warehouse. With water on three sides, their outside patios fill up quickly on a summer's night, as people come to enjoy the lakefront action and views across the water to the Toronto Islands.

For some of the best views of the harbour and Toronto Islands, from its restaurant and bar, the **Radisson Plaza Hotel Admiral Toronto – Harbourfront** (249 Queens Quay West; tel: 416-203 3333) is hard to beat. As you continue heading west, look up to your right for an exceptionally fine view of the CN Tower.

As part of the sprucing up of the Waterfront, a new 4-hectare (10-acre) lakeside park, called **HTO ❻**, is being developed on Maple Leaf Quay, just east of Spadina Avenue. Scheduled to open in 2006, it is interestingly described as an urban beach hangout, and will have an "elegant" concrete platform jutting out 10 metres (30 ft) over Lake Ontario, steel-mesh umbrellas and a series of large treed islands.

At the corner of Lower Spadina and Queens Quay, **Spadina Quay Wetland ❼** (479 Queens Quay West) was once a parking area. The first wetland on the downtown Waterfront in more than 80 years, it

Map on pages 76–7

Baseball legend Babe Ruth scored his first home run with the Maple Leafs baseball team at the stadium that once stood on Hanlan's Point. The Maple Leafs team is no more, and the name now belongs well and truly to Toronto's hockey team. Another Islands sporting hero was Edward "Ned" Hanlon, a world-beating rower whose hotel-owning family gave its name to Hanlan's Point.

BELOW: a glass-blowing artist at work.

is home to spawning fish, frogs, toads and marsh birds such as red-winged blackbirds. Meandering trails cross the park, which is fronted by the boardwalk. In the centre, an elaborate birdhouse replicates Toronto's late 19th-century Waterfront, with warehouses, the Italianate bathing palace of Sunny-side Beach, ice cream parlours and boathouses. Beyond the wetland, in the adjacent **Waterfront Children's Garden**, youngsters can try their hand at organic gardening.

Spadina Quay Wetland is a great place to take children.

Toronto Music Garden

One of the most imaginative arrivals on the Waterfront, the **Toronto Music Garden ❽** (475 Queens Quay West, between Bathurst and Spadina; daily, dawn to dusk) was conceived by internationally renowned cellist Yo-Yo Ma. Visualising the garden as "a concert hall without walls", he worked with garden designer Julie Moir Messervy to create a garden inspired by Johann Sebastian Bach's *Suite No. 1 for Unaccompanied Cello.*

BELOW: an inspirational garden.

There are guided tours (tel: 416-338 0338; June–Sept; free) or you can rent a hand-held audio player, with commentary by Yo-Yo Ma and Julie Moir Messervy, from the Marina Quay West office (539 Queens Quay West).

Each of the six dance movements within the suite corresponds to a different section in the garden. **Prelude** reflects a flowing river, bordered by Canadian Shield boulders; **Allemande** offers wandering trails, handpicked boulders and a circle of Dawn redwood trees – these trees existed more than 100 million years ago and were chosen to reflect the age of this ancient German dance. In the exuberant **Courante**, a swirling path winds through a wildflower meadow up to a maypole, while the contemplative **Sarabande** is a poet's corner. In the more formal **Menuett**, small musical ensembles or dance groups can perform in an attractive ornamental pavilion. And twice-weekly concerts are held in **Gigue**, where giant grass steps form a curved amphitheatre around a stone stage, overlooking the water.

Opposite the Toronto Music Garden, **Kings Landing** (480 Queens Quay West) is a spectacular condominium designed by Arthur Erickson, built on the site of a ship-building factory where minesweepers were produced for the Royal Canadian and British Royal navies. The ground level is occupied by the **William Carsen Centre** (tel: 416-345 9686), the former home and rehearsal studios of the National Ballet of Canada.

Bathurst Quay

Up to this point, all of the condominiums along Queens Quay are luxurious and appropriately pricey. At **Bathurst Quay**, however, most of the community consists of attractive yet affordable housing, including a number of housing co-operatives. Here you'll find **Little**

Norway Park, named as a tribute to the Norwegian aviators and air crew that were housed in barracks here while training at the City of Toronto Island Airport on Centre Island during the early days of World War II. The ferry to the airport leaves from the foot of Bathurst Street for the quick 122-metre (400-ft) journey across the Western Channel. Plans to build a bridge link to the airport met with much opposition, on the grounds that traffic and noise pollution would be significantly increased, and were scrapped.

Beyond Stadium Road, named after the Maple Leaf Stadium – a baseball stadium until it was demolished in 1968 – the Martin Goodman Trail turns sharply from a brief stretch along Lake Shore Boulevard West into the forest-like setting of **Coronation Park** ❾.

Inspired by both conservationists and war veterans, the park was officially dedicated on the same day that King George VI was crowned at Westminster Abbey in London in May 1937. A "royal" oak tree surrounded by silver maples represented the king and the countries of the British Empire, while a grove of maple trees commemorate the Canadian troops who fought overseas. In 1995, a dramatic sculpture of two bronze gates forming a ship's prow was unveiled on the 50th anniversary of World War II. The work of John McEwen, it is engraved with descriptions of the European Front and other operations, and the word "Peace" in 50 languages.

Continuing west, you'll see a 9-metre (30-ft) high **Inukshuk** towering over the Waterfront. Primarily found in the Arctic, these stone monuments would guide travellers on land and sea, and are a powerful symbol of a safe harbour. This one was installed in 2002 to honour World Youth Day and the visit of Pope John Paul II.

Ontario Place

A huge, dazzling white geodesic dome is one of the most architecturally distinctive landmarks on the shores of Lake Ontario, and is a sign that you are approaching the children's paradise of **Ontario Place** ❿ (tel: 416-314 9900; www.ontario place.com; May–Sept, daily June–Aug; admission charge; free shuttle bus from Union Station).

Designed by Eberhard Zeidler (of Queens Quay Terminal fame), Ontario Place opened as a showcase for the province in 1971 and straddles three man-made, interconnected islands, largely form the landfill created by excavations when the subway was being built). The site is protected from Lake Ontario's turbulent waters by a seawall, consisting of three large lake freighters that were filled with concrete and sunk.

East of the main entrance, **Market Square** is largely geared towards children under six, with attractions such as mini go-karts and bumper boats. Nearby, **Soak City** is the park's water play area, where a mind-boggling 13,500 litres (3,566

TIP

Streetcar services 509 and 510 head along the same waterfront route from Union Station; 510 heads inland up Spadina Avenue, but the 509 continues along the waterfront as far as Exhibition Place. To venture further west pick up the 501 westbound on Queen Street, which follows the lakeshore way out to Browns Line.

BELOW: inner city living Toronto style.

A heart-warming sight in these energy-deprived times, a windmill – officially known as a wind turbine – at the southwest corner of Exhibition Place, beside Lake Shore Boulevard – produces enough electricity for up to 250 households.

gallons) of water per minute is circulated through the shallow pools, fountains, slides, spouts and Canada's tallest tipping bucket. As the city's only water park, it's the perfect place to be on a hot summer's day. A trio of body-hurling water slides include the Hydrofuge, a 70-degree slide down which people twist and twirl on an eighth of an inch sheet of water, before a dramatic splashdown.

Follow the Waterfront west to the geodesic dome, and you'll find that it houses the **Cinesphere**, the original IMAX, which has a gigantic six-storey screen and one of the world's most powerful digital sound systems. A schedule of dramatic films focuses on subjects that lend themselves to the stunning large-format footage, from the majesty of nature to airborne acrobatics, that really makes the audience feel part of the action.

Go Zone, on the west island, is for older children, with a number of interactive attractions such as a Driving School and the H2O Generation Station – the largest outdoor soft-play climbing structure of its

kind in Canada. At the westernmost point of Ontario Place, on **Adventure Island**, you can get lost in the multi-maze complex of mirrors, lasers and optical illusions, pan for gemstones, get absolutely soaked on the Wilderness Adventure Ride, or zoom to outer space on the Mars simulator ride. From here, close to the pedal boats in Bob's Boatyard, you can board a free water shuttle back to the main entrance – an absolute boon to anyone with exhausted children and aching feet.

Picnic spots

All this activity is bound to engender ravenous appetites and there is no shortage of eating options. In addition to a vast array of fast-food outlets and full-service restaurants (a couple have great waterfront views), there are plenty of grassy slopes – often at the waterside – to enjoy a quiet picnic under the trees, away from the crowds.

The **Molson Amphitheatre** (tel: 416-870 8000) is the main reason that adult Torontonians trek down to Ontario Place each summer; its diverse series of big-name concerts include jazz, rock, pop, blues, country and classical music. There are 5,500 reserved seats under cover, but on a balmy summer's evening concert-goers hunker down on the sloping lawns encircling the stage.

Festival of Fire

The annual fireworks competition is also immensely popular. During the **Canada Dry Festival of Fire**, a magnificent display of dazzling pyrotechnics from different countries is choreographed to music and fired from a lake freighter docked off Ontario Place, creating spectacular reflections to double the effect. These four nights of fireworks are guaranteed to slow down late-night traffic on Lake Shore Boulevard and the Gardiner Expressway. In Ontario

Icons in the Western Beaches

East of Budapest Park, the **Palais Royale** opened in 1920. It became the place for dancing, especially in the Big Band era of the 1930s and 1940s. In its heyday, big-name bands that visited the joint included Duke Ellington and Count Basie. More recently, The Pogues and the Rolling Stones both played here. After showing its age, badly, for years, it is being transformed – sensitively, with the guidance of the local preservation board – into a "high-end" banquet hall. With luck, Torontonians will again be able to kick up their heels beside the lake.

Sunnyside Amusement Park opened in 1922 and was the place – with its roller coaster, merry-go-rounds and dance pavilions – that all age groups flocked to be entertained, for the next 33 years. The only original building, a Roman-style **Bathing Pavilion**, opened in 1925, with what was announced as the world's largest outdoor swimming pool – for bathers who found Lake Ontario too cold! With the closing of the amusement park, the pavilion was under-used for years. However, the pool is still very popular and the pavilion is back in favour as a beachfront restaurant, while its handsome inner courtyard is used for parties and wedding photos.

Place, restaurants and Waterfront grandstand seats (tel: 416-870 8000) should be booked in advance, and the same applies to the lake cruises that carry fireworks viewers from the Harbourfront Centre.

Exhibition Place

On the north side of Lake Shore Boulevard, **Exhibition Place** (tel: 416-263 3600; www.explace. on.ca) is a park with a lot of history, and, since 1879, the official home of the Canadian National Exhibition (CNE or, as it is universally known, The Ex). Easily accessed by TTC from Union Station, Bathurst, Dufferin and Dundas West subway stations, Exhibition Place is also connected by a footbridge to Ontario Place.

The main entrance on Lake Shore is at the magnificent Princes' Gates, built in 1927 and topped by a 7-metre (24-ft) statue, *Winged Victory*, while nine soaring columns, representing the original provinces of the Confederation, flank the gates. Illuminated at night, it is a breathtaking sight for anyone driving west.

More than 4.5 million visitors descend upon the 78-hectare (92-acre) park annually, not only for The Ex, but also for various trade and consumer shows, conventions and many other long-established fixtures on Toronto's calendar.

At any time of year, however, you can explore the grounds, and admire its collection of handsome old buildings – most of which are now used as exhibition space. Close to Princes' Gate, the **Automotive Building** is a unique blend of classical and modern architecture. Built in 1929, it was originally used to showcase the latest cars and trucks each year at The Ex. Behind the recently built National Trade Centre, the **Coliseum** was billed as the largest floor space under one roof anywhere in the world when it was built in 1922. Neighbouring the Coliseum, the **Horse Palace** is a marvellous example of art deco architecture, with a copper cupola and figures of horses portrayed in the exterior masonry. When it was built in 1931, it was considered one of the finest equestrian facilities in Canada.

Beyond the 1936 Bandshell, which is still renowned for its acoustic excellence, you can step back into some much older history. An obelisk marks the spot where the French built **Fort Rouillé** as a trading post in 1750. A cement outline of the fort walls gives you an idea of its original size and shape.

Close by, **Scadding Cabin** is Toronto's oldest home. Built in 1794, on the east bank of the Don River, it was moved here in 1879 to mark the inauguration of the forerunner of the CNE. It was built for John Scadding, who had accompanied Lieutenant-Governor John Graves Simcoe to Upper Canada in 1792.

Of all the buildings of Exhibition Place, the belle of the ball is **Liberty Grand**, a unique triangular structure

The eastern entrance to Exhibition Place is marked by the Princes' Gates.

BELOW: the geodesic dome at Ontario Place.

Map on pages 76–7

TIP

The Molson Indy was renamed the Grand Prix of Toronto in 2005. It is an exciting street race that draws big international crowds every year, so buy your ticket well in advance if you want to watch the race from the stands in Exhibition Place *(see page 38)*. Visit: www.grandprix toronto.com

BELOW: Caribana is an important event on the city's festival calendar.

with an interior courtyard, constructed in the beaux arts style in 1926. A huge dome crowns the main entrance facing the lake, and pairs of cupolas decorate each corner. Look up at the elaborate friezes that portray – rather oddly – emblems of both the Canadian wilderness and Greek mythology.

Some regular fixtures

The **Molson Grand Prix of Toronto** (formerly Molson Indy) is one of Canada's largest sporting events, and takes place every July, when Canadian and international superstars compete through the roadways of Exhibition Place at speeds of up to 320 kph (200 mph). There are various ancillary events to build the excitement.

At the end of July, the highlight of the annual **Caribana Festival** takes place through Exhibition Place and along Lake Shore Boulevard. Steel bands, hundreds of floats and exuberant dancers in elaborate costumes parade in what is touted as the biggest single-day happening and largest Caribbean festival in North America.

Visiting the **Canadian National Exhibition** has become a cherished tradition for generations of Torontonians. It winds up the summer, with a two-week extravaganza of over 500 attractions and more than 60 rides. People come to see butter sculpting, cook-offs, horse shows, lumberjack shows and the stomach-churning three-day air show by Canada's "Snowbirds" air display team. There are nightly fireworks, Mardi Gras-like parades and a full programme of star entertainers.

Every November, a loyal following comes for the ultimate showcase of all things relating to living in the Canadian countryside. The **Royal Agricultural Winter Fair** is the largest indoor agricultural, horticultural, canine and equestrian event in the world, offering urban dwellers a chance to see what modern country life is all about.

Water sports central

Just west of Exhibition Place, the **Marilyn Bell Aquatic Park** ⓬ is named after the intrepid 16-year-old who became the first person to swim across Lake Ontario from New York State in 1954. Battling the cold water and nausea, and against tremendous odds, she managed the 51.5-km (32-mile) crossing in almost 21 hours. In keeping with her competitive spirit, a new 650-metre/yard-long flat-water training site is being built just off the park, in time to host the 2006 International Dragon Boat Federation World Crew Championships.

At the western end of this park are two long-established clubs that date back to the late 19th century – the **Argonaut Rowing Club**, which offers excellent rowing conditions along a breakwater-protected course, and the **Toronto Sailing and Canoe Club**. Beyond this point, the Waterfront turns into Toronto's Western Beaches. ❑

RESTAURANTS, BARS & CAFÉS

Restaurants

Captain John's Harbour Boat Restaurant

1 Queen's Quay West. Tel: 416-363 6062. Open: L & D daily. **$$$**

Something of a novel location, this restaurant is actually aboard a real ship, its prow pointing straight up Yonge Street from its mooring on the lake. It retains its plush wardroom character, with nautical accoutrements, and service by uniformed staff is suitably formal. Seafood is the speciality, and the Alaskan king crab is superb. There are one or two meat dishes on the menu, including a tender and tasty stroganoff. Great views from the bar up on deck.

Gui Rei Japanese Restaurant

600 Queen's Quay West (at Bathurst Street). Tel: 416-977 6111. Open: L & D Mon–Sat, D only Sun. **$$**

One of the Waterfront's hidden gems, the sushi bar at Gui Rei competes with some of the best in the city. The fresh fish and gracious service attract both tourists and Harbourfront residents.

Harbour Sixty Steakhouse

60 Harbour Street (at Bay Street). Tel: 416-777 2111. Open: L & D Mon–Fri, D only Sat–Sun. **$$$$**

This top ranked steakhouse occupies a prime location in the historic Port Commissioner's building by the Lakeshore. US prime bone-in rib and rib-eye are the favourites here. Fish and seafood are also cooked well. Mushroom ragout and Lyonnaise potatoes liven up a list of otherwise traditional side dishes. Excellent (and expensive) local wines, as well as superb international varieties. Service is smooth.

Lago Restaurant Bar

Queen's Quay Terminal, 207 Queen's Quay West (at Harbour Square). Tel: 416-848 0005. Open: L & D daily. **$$**

One of the Il Fornello family of restaurants but with a more upmarket pedigree, Lago offers sophisticated lounge fare and a fabulous floor-to-ceiling view of the lake. Seafood is simple and fresh; try crispy skin striped bass served with light summery greens and oven-cured tomatoes. Snazzy cocktails make up for a moderate wine list. The large patio is great for cool summer lounging by the water.

Pearl Harbourfront

Queen's Quay Terminal, 207 Queen's Quay West (at Harbour Square). Tel: 416-203 1233. Open: L & D daily. **$$**

A sophisticated Chinese restaurant with stunning views of the harbour. Dim sum at lunch is traditional and well prepared. Food carts feature dumplings, crisp deep-fried delicacies and excellent sticky rice in lotus leaves. Dinner showcases typical Cantonese dishes like chicken cubes in a crispy taro basket and stir-fried chicken leaves.

Porticello

370 Queen's Quay West, (at Spadina). Tel: 416-598 2572. Open: L & D daily. **$$–$$$**

A traditional trattoria with delicious seafood specialities, which make up for the cheesy decor.

Bars & Cafés

Boathouse Bar & Grill

207 Queens Quay West. Tel: 416-203 6300

There's a casual atmosphere, with two patios overlooking the harbour.

Lakeside Terrace

235 Queens Quay West (York Quay Centre). Tel: 416-973 3000

A casual place that is part of the Harbourfront Centre, with an outside patio-bar where you can listen to musical performances at nearby Molson Place.

The Jersey Giant

71 Front Street West. Tel: 416-368 4095

One of the best English pubs in town.

PRICE CATEGORIES

Prices for three-course dinner per person with a half-bottle of house wine:
$ = under $25
$$ = $25–50
$$$ = $50–70
$$$$ = more than $70

THE TORONTO ISLANDS

Just a short ferry ride from downtown lies a
recreational paradise of beaches, expansive
parkland, waterways and children's
amusements, where even the nearby
city airport doesn't shatter the peace

t's worth taking the ferry *(see
page 78)* across to the Toronto
Islands just so you can look back
at the picture postcard view of the
city – the dome of the Rogers Centre
(formerly SkyDome) and the CN
Tower take centre stage behind the
deep blue water of the harbour,
framed by the glittering high-rise
lakeshore apartments and downtown offices.

The view is not the only reason
for visiting the Islands, though. The
parks and gardens, sandy beaches
and other attractions make this one
of the most popular places for Torontonians and visitors to relax away
from the bustle of the city streets.
Around 1½ million people visit the
Islands each year, however, on busy
summer weekends on Centre Island,
you might think that they had all
come on the same day, yet there are
still peaceful spots to be found.

The Islands are the result of centuries of silt washing across the lake
and being deposited here, originally
as a long sand spit arcing out from
the mainland. First Nations people
came here to relax long before
European settlers discovered the
area during the 19th century, and
considered it to be a health-giving
place. Then, during a particularly
severe storm in 1858, the lake
waters broke through the Eastern

Channel and the Islands were cast
adrift. The strong Lake Ontario cur-
rents always made the low-lying
land unstable, but various dredging
and shoring up operations over the
past century or so have reduced erosion and the risk of flooding.

Centre Island

The most manicured of all the
islands, with orderly flower beds,
fountains and lagoons, **Centre
Island ❶** is where young families
tend to spend their time.

Map
on page
90

LEFT:
a picture postcard
view of the city from
the Islands.
BELOW:
a balloon vendor
on Centre Island.

Centre Island is the venue for the annual International Dragon Boat Race Festival, with 20-man boats rowing to the beat of a drum and plenty of sideshows. It takes place in late June each year (tel: 416-598 8945).

From the ferry dock, pathways lead in several directions. Turn left for the children's attractions of Centreville and Far Away Farm (*see box, page 92*). The path ahead leads across a bridge that links Centre Island with the great semicircular sweep of land that stretches from Ward's Island in the east to Hanlan's Point in the west. Beyond the bridge is a cooling fountain (stand awhile in the spray on hot summer days) and a wide walkway, bordered by trees and flower beds, that leads to the beach. To the right are vast lawns shaded by trees, with picnic tables and barbecues for anyone who has had the foresight to bring a bag of charcoal and some food to cook (no alcohol, though – it cannot be brought to the island, but must be ordered in advance from Centreville Amusement Park & Catering, tel: 416-203 0405). This is a favourite spot for summer parties, with families celebrating birthdays, students with guitars and African drums, or people just hanging out with friends… and always people throwing frisbees.

The **beach** is a wonderful stretch of fine sand, gently shelving into the

Toronto Islands

0   1000 m

0   1000 yds

waters of the lake and protected at one point by a bank of rocks just off-shore. There's also a pier jutting out across the water at this point, and a beach volleyball court nearby. For those who want to sunbathe or swim there are changing rooms just behind the beach, but don't be fooled by the scorching summer temperatures: the water, frozen solid in winter, takes several months to warm up.

If you take the pathway east from the fountain, you'll find the boat rentals, offering paddle boats, kayaks and canoes for independent exploration of the network of water-ways that thread between the Islands. You can also go on sight-seeing boat trip through the wider channels.

From the boathouse there's a delightful walk through woodland and alongside boat moorings, some of which belong to the Island Yacht Club or the exclusive Royal Canadian Yacht Club. Along the way you'll pass the picturesque white clapboard Anglican church of **St Andrew-by-the-Lake**, built in 1884 (services every Sunday) and now the only surviving remnant of the original cottage community. Every so often along this path the trees thin out to provide a superb view of downtown Toronto across the water, and you will eventually pass residential Algonquin Island and arrive at Ward's Island.

Ward's Island

During the 1950s, the Islands as a whole were designated city park-land, and moves were made to elim-inate all residential developments. Centre Island inhabitants were moved out and their homes burned down to create a purely recreational area. **Ward's Island ❷** residents were not so easy to displace. When eviction notices were handed out, they put up a spirited and eventually successful fight, and an arrangement

was put in place that allowed islanders to lease the land under their mainly cottage-style homes. There now remains a population of more than 500, who enjoy a quiet, traffic free environment.

Not surprisingly, there's no short-age of people wanting to live here, and the waiting list is long and dependent on someone moving out. The only down side of island life is that residents have to do all their shopping on the mainland; on Ward's Island ferry you are likely to see people with adapted bicycles hauling trailers full of groceries.

After the walk from Centre Island there is no more welcome sight than the **Rectory Café** *(see page 95)* with lovely garden and patio seating amid the trees at the rear. Indoors the walls are adorned with original artworks, the food and surroundings are definitely a cut above the cafe-teria-type places on Centre Island, and you'll get a warm welcome, not only from the staff, but also from Hunter, a neighbour's white cat who often strolls in to try to charm guests into parting with a snack.

Map on page 90

The islands are traffic-free, but many Torontonians bring their bicycles across on the ferry. Visitors can rent bicycles and four-person pedal vehicles from a build-ing near the beach; rental is by the hour, and you'll need to leave a deposit.

BELOW: bridges connect the Islands.

*Centreville
Amusement Park
provides a full day
of fun for children.*

RIGHT: the lighthouse
is an island landmark.

Suitably refreshed, you can set out to explore this peaceful little enclave. Lining the narrow streets – here, and on adjoining **Algonquin Island ❸** – is an eclectic assortment of spruced up cottages side by side with their more dilapidated cousins, and some rather jarringly large and recent additions.

An alternative route from Centre Island follows a path west from the bicycle rental building, with a boardwalk that ends at **Ward's Island Beach**, the most peaceful of the Islands' beaches. Bordered by trees and dunes, young families and picnickers enjoy the sand, water and lovely views.

The Ward's Island ferry dock is on the north side of the island, with benches along the waterfront where you can enjoy the splendid view of the city while you wait – or there's a seasonal coffee house offering pleasantly shaded outdoor seating, organic fair trade coffees and vegetarian snacks.

The ferry ride from here has a different atmosphere from the tourist-thronged boats to and from Centre Island. Many of the passengers are Island residents, and you'll travel amidst friendly greetings and small talk.

Hanlan's Point

If you head west from Centre Island along the path that backs **Manitou Beach** you'll arrive at the westernmost island, **Hanlan's Point ❹**. The first part of the Toronto Islands to be settled by a summer cottage community, it is named after a family that settled here in 1862. The most famous member of the family, Edward "Ned" Hanlan, went on to find fame as a rower, becoming the world champion sculler in 1880.

In addition to three hotels, an amusement park was built in 1894 and a baseball stadium with a capacity for 10,000 spectators was added in the early 1900s. The stadium put Toronto into the annals of sporting history as the place where baseball legend Babe Ruth hit his first professional home run, playing for the now defunct Maple Leafs baseball team (the name has, of course, been appropriated by the city's hockey

Specially for Children

Any park is a good place for children, but add to that a fun ferry ride and a clutch of special attractions for children (under about 10 years old) and you really have a winner. Centre Island has the **Centreville Amusement Park** (tel: 416-203 0405 or 234 2345 in winter; www.centreisland.ca; June–early Sept, daily 10.30am–5, 6, 7 or 8pm; weekends May & Sept; admission charge) with more than 30 rides, from an antique carousel to a treetop cable car and a log flume. Close by is **Far Away Farm**, where domestic animals, including horses, donkeys and turkeys, will delight little ones.

In 2004, **Franklin's Children's Garden** opened, based on the *Franklin the Turtle* books by Paulette Bourgeois, with some appealing bronze figures of Franklin and friends, an amphitheatre and a garden where children can get involved with hands-on tasks.

Outside the garden, there's a traditional **playground**, with a climbing frame, see-saws (called teeter-totters here), swings and a paddling pool. Children also love the **swan boats** that can be rented from the boathouse, the maze near the fountain and, of course, just running free in the parkland and digging in the sand.

team). In the 1930s, the amusement park was closed and the stadium demolished, to make room for the **City of Toronto Island Airport** ❺.

In 2003, a citywide controversy over the airport – which is reached by a two-minute ferry ride from the foot of Bathurst Street – led to the decisive election of Mayor David Miller. As a city councillor, Miller had spearheaded opposition to the building of a bridge linking the airport to the mainland, fearing an inevitable increase in air and noise pollution on the city's beloved Waterfront.

As a result, there is minimal disturbance from the executive jets, light aircraft and helicopters that use the airport, approaching and taking off out over the lake to the west. Spectacular sightseeing flights, of nine and 16 minutes' duration, are also available from the airport (tel: 416-203 3280).

The crescent-shaped sand on the western shores of Hanlan's Point is Toronto's only official clothing-optional beach. Just behind the beach, **Gibraltar Point Lighthouse** ❻ is the city's oldest stone structure, and believed to be the oldest lighthouse on the Great Lakes. Built in 1808 with Queenston limestone, it operated until 1907.

Nearby is the **Gibraltar Point Centre for the Arts**, with studios for about 15 resident artists and craftspeople, along with short-term studio rentals, providing local artists with a place to develop their creative ideas and work in a peaceful environment.

Also in the vicinity is the **Island Natural Science School**, to which mainland students from the age of nine to 13 come to experience the wonders of the natural world. Immediately north of the school, eastern cottonwood, dogwood and willows bordering wetland meadows provide shelter to masses of migratory birds.

The Toronto Islands are a wonderful asset to the city, sheltering the inshore waters for recreational boating as well as providing a unique opportunity for rest and relaxation within a stone's throw of the downtown core. ❑

Map on page 90

The southern portion of Hanlan's Point Beach, located on the Toronto Islands near the airport, has been designated as clothing-optional by the City. The Park's Department maintains lifeguard services and other facilities on the beach. Please note that only the designated beach section is clothing-optional. Clothes must be worn in all other areas.

BELOW: bring your own transport to travel around the Islands.

CAFÉS

The Carousel Café
Centre Island
In a waterside setting, this café has indoor seating plus a patio that overlooks the Long Pond. There's a wide variety of menu options, including a kids' menu.

The Rectory Café
Wards Island.
Tel: 416-203 2152
A delightful, arty place that offers an interesting menu, friendly service and seating inside or in the beautiful shady garden and covered patio. In winter, it's the only place on the Islands that's open for food and drinks service.

THE FINANCIAL DISTRICT

Towering bank skyscrapers define the economic and fiscal powerhouse of the nation, but there's much more to explore, from the Old City Hall and the Eaton Centre shops to the hallowed home of the Stanley Cup

As you arrive in the downtown core of Toronto along the shore of Lake Ontario by car or train, you're treated to one of the best and most dramatic views of the city: the massive 1929 beaux-arts Royal York Hotel with it's stone façade and copper-topped roof, framed by soaring modern skyscrapers in silver, black and gold.

This is the Financial District, the heart of the city, perhaps of the country, and home to the nation's most powerful fiscal institutions including the Toronto Stock Exchange, the national head offices of major banks, businesses and law firms, and City Hall. And, of course, home to what some would call the nation's Holy Grail: the Stanley Cup trophy, closely guarded at the Hockey Hall of Fame.

Architectural history

The Financial District is a great place to soak up the architectural and social history of the city. Many of the older buildings were destroyed by the tragic Great Fire of April 1904, which ravaged a large part of the area; other buildings were torn down to make way for skyscrapers, but many beautiful examples of mid to late 18th-century design still stand. They were built at a time when the city was rapidly making the transi-

tion from its beginnings as a colonial fur-trading outpost into a centre of manufacturing and industry. These older structures stand next to examples of ambitious modernism from the 1960s, an era that launched Toronto into its current incarnation as an expanding international, multicultural city.

And there is good news for visitors who are uncomfortable on a sweltering day in summer or a frigid one in winter: you can move through this entire area without

Map
on page
96

LEFT: the Toronto Convention Centre. **BELOW:** a statue stands tall in the financial district.

going outside. Linking most of the major buildings, hotels and subway stations are 27 km (17 miles) of underground passageways – a huge shopping concourse known by tourists as The Underground City, and by Torontonians as the PATH.

Union Station and the Royal York

At the foot of the Financial District, running a full block along Front Street between Bay and Yonge, is the beaux-arts **Union Station ❶**, Toronto's central railway station and a major transport hub. When it was officially opened in 1927 by the then Prince of Wales, Union Station was the largest and most opulent in the nation, designed at a time when a station was the gateway to its city.

The front facade of the building is impressive – 230 metres (755 ft) in length, and featuring 22 limestone columns weighing 75 tons each. Inside, the long Great Hall has a

The grand ceiling in the Great Hall, Union Station.

BELOW: the impressive Fairmont Royal York Hotel.

four-storey vaulted ceiling laid with Gustavino tiles, and carved on the north and south walls are names of the cities the station first served. It's generally calm on this level, with passengers departing for or arriving from long-distance travel, but downstairs it's a different scene altogether – a chaotic, crowded jumble of shops and people in a hurry, as they rush to and from suburban trains and subway, bus and streetcar connections. Plans are underway to restore this part of the station to its former glory, similar to the successful renovations of the Grand Central Terminal in New York City, and Union Station in Washington, DC.

Across the street from Union Station, the **Royal York Hotel ❷** (100 Front Street West; tel: 416-368-2511; www.fairmont.com/royal york; subway: Union Station) still stands, now part of the Fairmont group of luxury hotels. It opened to much fanfare in June 1929 as the largest

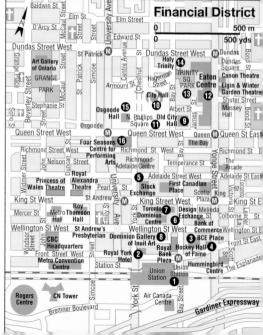

and tallest hotel in the British Empire, boasting 1,945 beds (of which only 245 were double); a hospital clinic complete with an operating room, and a radio station. The hotel's nightclub, The Imperial Room, was for many years a Toronto institution, playing host to such entertainment greats as Tony Bennett and Ella Fitzgerald.

The Royal York fell into disrepair in the 1980s and 1990s, but a multimillion dollar renovation has restored its original dignity (though it couldn't increase the size of the rooms, most of which remain rather small). There's a comprehensive photo exhibition on the mezzanine level of the lobby, detailing the hotel's illustrious history.

BCE Place

Just down the street, at the corner of Front and Yonge streets, is an ornate 1885 building that was originally the Toronto head office for the Bank of Montreal. Today it houses the **Hockey Hall of Fame** ❸ (BCE Place, 30 Yonge Street, tel: 416-360 7765; www.hhof.com; subway: Union Station), and the grandeur of the edifice could be a nod to the great importance Canada places on its sporting obsession – one that's also worth millions of dollars to the economy.

The Hockey Hall of Fame is one of the city's most popular tourist attractions, especially for kids. Inside are 4,600 sq. metres (50,000 sq. ft) of space on two levels dedicated to the sport. There are interactive computer terminals, hockey memorabilia and, of course, the treasured Stanley Cup, on display here when it's not out on tour.

The Hockey Hall of Fame building is part of the sprawling **BCE Place** ❹ office and shopping complex built in 1990 (BCE stands for Bell Canada Enterprises, the country's leading communications network). Not to be missed is the stunning glass-covered Allen Lambert Galleria, designed by renowned Spanish architect Santiago Calatrava. This "crystal cathedral of commerce" as it's been called, is a soaring glass and steel structure that spans an entire block from Bay to Yonge, linked by two office towers.

Two of the most noticeable features of the Toronto skyline: the 51-storey Canada Trust Tower (discernible by the green TD logo on the top of its spire) and the 47-storey Bay Wellington Tower look like giant works of Lego with upper floors inter-cut and squared off. It's a distinctive if not lucrative look, as it gives the buildings' owners as many as 16 corner offices per floor to lease at premium rates.

The 241,500 sq. metre (2.6 million sq. ft) complex incorporates several 19th-century buildings that were left standing after the Great Fire, most of them on the Yonge Street side. Particularly notable is the 1845 facade of the Commercial Bank, cleverly integrated into the ground level of the Galleria. A good place to get a bite to eat and enjoy

Map on page 96

The coveted Stanley Cup trophy is part of the local obsession with hockey. Yet the official national game is actually the ancient sport of lacrosse.

BELOW: stained-glass detail in the Hockey Hall of Fame.

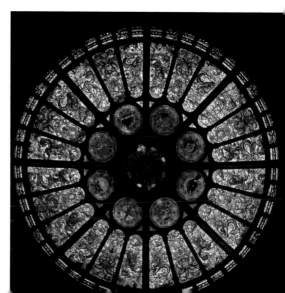

An art deco mural detail at the old Stock Exchange building.

the beauty of the Galleria is the popular Richtree restaurant, near the Yonge and Front street entrance.

Bay Street icons

Leave BCE Place on the west side and you'll be on Bay Street, the symbolic heart of the financial district. This is the Wall Street of Toronto, and it's lined with some of the most impressive skyscrapers in the city. Look up and at 200 Bay Street you'll see the **Royal Bank Plaza** (subway: Union Station), two triangular-shaped towers with gold-tinted windows that refract light at unusual angles no matter what the time of day or the season.

The gold colour is actually a total of 2,500 ounces of gold leaf that's been baked into the building's glass for insulation. Each window contains nearly $100-worth of gold, but it's quite secure – the processing technique makes it nearly impossible to separate the gold from the glass, should anyone think of stealing it.

On the next block, north of Wellington on the east side at 199 Bay Street, is the 57-storey **Commerce Court West** (subway: King). Built in 1973 by the internationally respected architect I.M. Pei (best known for designing the pyramid entrance at the Louvre in Paris), Commerce Court was once the tallest office block in the city, and is still one of the world's largest stainless steel buildings.

Across the street at 234 Bay Street is the former headquarters of the city's stock exchange. Several years ago the **Toronto Stock Exchange ❺** (Exchange Tower, Main Floor, 130 King Street West, corner of York Street; tel: 416-947 4676; www.tsx.com; call for opening hours; subway: King) moved a few blocks away, largely because of the requirements of the new electronic way of doing business, and now has what's considered the largest floor-less trading environment in North America. Visitors can tour the TSE's interactive broadcast centre and learn about the exchange through computer terminals and electronic boards, and occasionally reporters present live TV reports from here.

The art deco trading floor of the old stock exchange lives on as part of the **Design Exchange ❻** (234 Bay Street; tel: 416-363 6121; www. dx.org; subway: King), which promotes awareness of Canadian architecture and commercial design through exhibitions, awards and competitions. The historic trading floor is frequently closed to the public, though, as it's in high demand as a private rental site, so if it's best to check before you go.

Toronto-Dominion Centre

The facade of the old stock exchange, which forms the entrance to the Design Museum, is incorporated into part of the **Toronto-Dominion Centre ❼** (subway: St Andrew), a complex of buildings centring on three structures in bronze-tinted glass and black-

painted steel, designed by world renowned modernist architect Ludwig Mies van der Rohe in the 1960s.

The project was Canada's first foray into the International Style and changed Toronto's skyline for ever, setting the tone for new architecture in the area. Even today, the TD Centre remains one of the most impressive and prestigious sets of buildings in the city, and is considered to be Mies van der Rohe's most refined corporate structure.

The best way to appreciate the TD Centre is to walk down Wellington Street in the Wellington and York area. Explore the lobbies and then take note of the effect as you walk from one building to another – they were designed on a grid so that as you move around them, the views seem to slide open and closed.

Yellow flowers

The sleek TD Centre towers were patterned after the architect's 1958 Seagram building on Park Avenue in New York. The first part of the complex opened in 1966 and, at 56 storeys, the Toronto Dominion Bank Tower would be the tallest tower he ever completed. The second building, which opened in 1968, is the single-storey Banking Pavilion, widely regarded as one of the best public spaces ever designed by Mies van der Rohe. It's interior has been left virtually intact since he supervised the final touches. To this day, yellow flowers sit in fishbowl vases on the service counters, just as Mies had placed them.

He passed away months before the third element, the 46-storey Royal Trust Tower, was completed in 1969. Since then, four more towers by other architects have been built.

The Mies Van Der Rohe towers are centred on a granite-paved pedestrian plaza, with manicured lawns and public sculptures. The plaza was named after Canadian jazz legend Oscar Peterson in 2004, and it is a favourite spot for lunch to listen to jazz concerts in the spring and summer.

There is no observation deck in the towers, but to enjoy the view and an excellent restaurant, you can reserve a table at **Canoe** on the 54th floor of the TD Centre Bank Tower at 66 Wellington Street. A good place to join the after-work crowd for a drink is the sophisticated **Bymark** in a low pavilion in the tower's courtyard.

Inuit art

Across the street on the ground floor and mezzanine of 79 Wellington is the impressive **Toronto Dominion Gallery of Inuit Art** ❸ (416-982 8473; www.tdretail.ca/ tourists; Mon to Fri 8am–6pm, Sat and Sun 10am–4pm; free; personalised tours available by appointment; subway: St Andrew) a collection of sculptures and other works of art by native people of Canada's Arctic region. This is one of the few galleries of its kind in the whole of North America.

Map on page 96

The TD Centre is the venue for a number of annual events, including the Canada Trust Jazz Festival and, in December, the Night of Dreams, a free concert and Christmas tree lighting ceremony that raises huge amounts for local charities.

BELOW: the art deco art from the old Stock Exchange trading floor lives on at the Design Exchange.

Maps are available to help visitors navigate the PATH, or you can print one from the city website: www.city. toronto.on.ca

BELOW: Old City Hall, a reflection of Toronto's past.

The Underground City

As you walk the streets of this busy area on an insufferably hot summer day or a freezing cold day in winter, you might just wonder where everyone is. The simple answer is that they have gone underground. Beneath the streets and buildings you'll find a labyrinth of hallways lined with shops, twisting and turning their way through the area, known as the **PATH**.

These passageways essentially link the separate shopping concourses found at the foot of every major skyscraper and hotel, and outside each subway entrance. In this way, the system forms one huge underground shopping complex. The PATH system took shape slowly over the years as buildings were constructed, but began as far back as 1929, when the Royal York Hotel built an underground hallway to connect it with Union Station.

Locals scurry along the corridors en route between offices, subway stations and business appointments, moving from building to building and running a few shopping errands along the way. It's not unusual on a sub-zero day in winter, to see office workers riding the subway in this area without a coat, and visitors can do the same, using the warm tunnels to travel between, say, their hotel room at the Fairmont Royal York and the Eaton Centre for shopping, then to Roy Thomson Hall to hear the symphony, or to the convention centre for an event or meeting.

Finding your way around

The system may sound easy, but you do need to know your way around to find your destination, and it can be quite a lengthy walk. City officials have tried to make some logic out of it all by naming it the PATH and posting comprehensive signs that tell you which building you're in or which street you're on, and the next building you will be entering. Colour-coded arrows on the signs indicate which direction each follows: blue for north, red for south, yellow for east, and orange for west. Sometimes arrows are on the ceiling, serving as a compass.

If you're the type of person who

gets lost easily, is low on patience, or who suffers from claustrophobia, it might be wiser to hail a cab.

Old City Hall

At the top of Bay Street, where it crosses Queen Street, is a familiar sight for Torontonians: the clock tower of the **Old City Hall** ❾ (130 Queen Street West; tel: 416-947 3300; www.city.toronto.on.ca/old cityhall; subway: Queen). This is actually Toronto's third City Hall, which replaced a temporary structure that was used after a fire in 1849 gutted the original 1845 city hall, located where the St Lawrence farmer's market stands today.

Built in the heavy-stone style of Romanesque Revival that was in vogue at the time, Old City Hall was the largest municipal building in North America when is was completed in 1899. It took nearly 10 years to build, dogged by scandal and corruption, political squabbles and public enquiries. It's said that the faces of each of the grotesques carved into the archways above the front doors are, in fact, caricatures

of city councillors at the time. The architect, Edward James Lennox, also slipped in his own portrait, which you can see on the western side of the centre arch (look for the gentleman with the moustache).

Of note inside the building is the massive stained glass window in the main hallway symbolising the union of industry and commerce, put in place at a time when Toronto was fully embracing the industrial revolution. When the building was opened in 1899, officials placed a time capsule in its cornerstone, filled with money, maps, city records, newspaper articles and other artefacts of the time. The building, now housing law courts, narrowly escaped being demolished in 1989. Instead, the structure was renovated, and a second time capsule was added during the building's centennial celebrations in 1999.

New City Hall

Across Bay Street next to Old City Hall stands today's **City Hall** ❿ (100 Queen Street West, at northwest corner of Queen and Bay; tel: 416-

The tables in front of City Hall are a good place to stop for a snack, a chat, and people watching.

BELOW: Viljo Revell's City Hall caused a stir when it was built.

The Henry Moore sculpture, Three-way Piece No. 2 *is also known as The Archer.*

338 0338; subway: Queen or Osgoode), one of Toronto's architectural gems and a defining element of the city's identity. Since it opened in 1965, the buildings have been pejoratively dubbed "UFO" or "flying saucer". Renowned architect Frank Lloyd Wright even derided it as "a head-marker for a grave… future generations will look to it and say, 'This marks the spot where Toronto fell'". But the building has proved to be a modern symbol of the city that's standing the test of time, and most Torontonians will tell you they like it.

The design was the winning project submitted during an international competition held in 1957 by the mayor, Nathan Phillips, following a 1950 vote in which Torontonians rejected a more classical design. The new City Hall contest attracted 520 submissions and was held five years after the completion of the United Nation's building in New York.

This could, to some extent, explain the choice of Finnish architect Viljo Revell's design, since it is similar in feel and form to the UN building. Revell was 48 when construction began in 1961, but died of a heart attack 10 months before its completion on 13 September, 1965. Revell based his design on the idea of the eye, which in Finland is a symbol for democracy. The two curved tower buildings form the eyelids, and the lower meeting hall in the centre, housing the city council chamber, the pupil.

Active public space

In front of the building is **Nathan Phillips Square** ⓫, perhaps the most active public space in the city. The site of art fairs and concerts, it throngs with tourists and workers in all weathers. Two giant concrete arches span a large pond with a fountain, around which people sit in summer. And in winter the pond is frozen for public skating and lit up at night.

To the right of the buildings near Bay Street is a sculpture by Henry Moore, a friend of Viljo Revell. The sculpture is officially named *Three-way Piece No. 2,* but is more commonly known as *The Archer.* There are no guided tours of City Hall, but a self-guided tour is available (visit: www.city.toronto.on.ca).

The Eaton Centre

Go south from City Hall, past Old City Hall and east on Queen Street and you'll reach Yonge Street, where you will find an architectural wonder, the **Elgin and Winter Garden Theatre** *(see page 138).*

Stretching north from here is a monument to our era of consumerism, the huge **Eaton Centre** ⓬ (subway: Queen or Dundas). It rises four storeys and fills an entire city block up to Dundas Street with 285 stores and three office towers. This is one of the most popular destinations in the city, with almost one million people visiting it every week, of which 25 percent are tourists. That volume is the equivalent of nearly one-fifth of the

BELOW: skating in Nathan Phillips Square.

population of the Greater Toronto Area and is equal to how many people visit the nearby Art Gallery of Ontario in a year. Although it was built in the late 1970s, the Eaton Centre doesn't look or feel its age, and is an attractive place to shop.

Inside the Queen Street entrance take a look up to the soaring glass-domed ceiling, patterned after the Milan Galleria by architect Vittorio Emanuelle. Hanging there is a beautiful mobile of flying Canada geese called *Flight Stop* by renowned Canadian artist Michael Snow.

In 1988, Snow took out a lawsuit against the Eaton Centre after the marketing department tied bright red velvet bows around the necks of the geese as Christmas decorations. The artist argued that the ribbons made his naturalistic work appear ridiculous and harmed his reputation as an artist. Judges found in his favour on the grounds of moral rights, and the case today stands one of the most important moral rights cases in Canadian law.

As you navigate your way around the centre, it helps to know the upmarket stores are on the upper two floors. At the northern end of the complex heading towards Dundas Street is what remains of the original Eaton's department store. The company went bankrupt in 1999 and its assets were acquired by the American department store chain, Sears, thus ending a family dynasty and a Canadian shopping tradition begun by Timothy Eaton in 1854.

On arrival from Northern Ireland, Eaton opened one of the most influential department store chains in Canadian history. The name is so emotive to Canadians that the title of the shopping centre has been retained.

Simpson's of Toronto

Across Queen Street is the original building of Timothy Eaton's main rival, Robert Simpson, creator of the defunct Simpson's department store chain. The 1895 building was the first in Canada with a load-bearing metal frame (a precursor to skyscraper technology).

Simpson's was taken over in the late 1970s by Canada's oldest corporation and currently its largest

On display at The Bay, the country's largest department store retailer.

BELOW: the Eaton Centre shopping mecca at twilight.

Map on page 96

department store retailer, the Hudson's Bay Company, now simply known as The Bay.

Trinity Square

Tucked in between the Eaton Centre and Old City Hall is **Trinity Square Park** ⓲, a quiet haven in a busy part of the city, perfect for a lunchtime sandwich. Or for spiritual calm, walk the **labyrinth** that's a copy of the 13th-century stone labyrinth at Chartres Cathedral in France (the labyrinth is closed when snow is on the ground).

Next to it stands the **Church of the Holy Trinity** ⓴ (10 Trinity Square, tel: 416-598 4521; www.holytrinitytoronto.org; subway: Dundas), a small church built in 1847 that's one of the most socially progressive in the city.

A monthly vigil is held here to mark deaths of the homeless; a few years ago, a group of 200 people attended the blessing of a same-sex union between two women. This sparked the landmark legal challenge in Ontario for same-sex marriages in 2001. The church is

The beautiful ceiling detail in the Great Library of Osgoode Hall. The library was built 1857–60.

BELOW: Osgoode Hall.

also home to Toronto's Early Music Centre, and concerts are performed here regularly at lunch time.

Osgoode Hall

If you go from City Hall south to Queen Street and head west, you'll reach an elegant building surrounded by immaculately manicured lawns and flower beds. **Osgoode Hall** ⓯ (130 Queen Street West; tel: 416-947 3300; www.osgoodehall.com or www.lsuc.on.ca; subway: Osgoode) was built between 1829 and 1832, and has had several major renovations and expansions.

This fine building is the headquarters of Canada's legal profession, the Law Society of Upper Canada, and several courtrooms here are used by the Ontario Court of Appeal. The imposing wrought iron fence may give the impression that ordinary folk can't penetrate this fortress of legal authority, but this is certainly not so.

Be sure to visit the Great Library, regarded by many as one of the most beautiful rooms in Canada. Also of note are the rotunda, the grand staircase and the fine collections of portraits and sculpture.

Across the street from Osgoode Hall is the **Four Seasons Centre for the Performing Arts** ⓰ (corner of Queen and University; www.four seasonscentre.ca; subway: Osgoode), the 2,000-seat home of the Canadian Opera Company and the National Ballet of Canada. The multimillion-dollar building, which opened in 2006, is Canada's first theatre to be built specifically for opera and ballet, and the best international experts in the business were called in to assist with the design and equipment. British theatre experts helped to create the state-of-the-art acoustics; technical advisors and some of the materials came from Germany, and the horseshoe-shaped auditorium is modelled on the best European opera houses. ❑

RESTAURANTS, BARS & CAFÉS

Restaurants

Biff's
4 Front Street East (at Yonge Street). Tel: 416-860 0086. Open: L & D Mon–Fri, D only Sat. **$$$**
Perfect for business lunches and pre- or post-theatre dinners. Top-notch bistro-inspired cuisine. Try the fried halibut with a potato "skin" or lunchtime fish cakes. Dinner is classic bistro with a few stretches. Options for sharing abound, including duck a l'orange. Fine cheese board and good desserts. Pleasant street patio.

Bymark
Toronto-Dominion Tower, 66 Wellington Street West (between York and Bay streets). Tel: 416-777 1144. Open: L & D Mon–Fri, D only Sat. **$$$$**
In the atrium of the TD Tower, this subterranean restaurant is one level below a busy bar. Power brokers go for lunch and evenings offer good people watching. The food is beautifully presented and easy on both the palate and the eye. Seared tuna is sushi grade and the speciality hamburger is huge, with porcini and shaved summer truffles. Dessert options don't disappoint; anything made with chocolate is especially fine.

Canoe
Toronto-Dominion Tower, 66 Wellington Street West (at Bay Street). Tel: 416-364 0054. Open: L & D Mon–Fri. **$$$$**
Specialising in the enigmatic "Canadian cuisine", this upmarket and high up (54th floor) spot creates beautiful and imaginative dishes using the freshest Canadian ingredients. Angus rib eye with northern woods mushrooms, Yukon confit and sherried truffles is classic Canadiana. Elegant minimalist decor.

Jump
18 Wellington Street West (between Bay and Yonge streets). Tel: 416-363 3400. Open: L & D Mon–Fri, D only Sat. **$$$**
Always fun and lively, Jump attracts a young business crowd. Choice menu items include a juicy hamburger with a short rib filling, roast chicken and excellent pastas. Look for new fusion, such as mussels in a green curry sauce, and jerk chicken with a not-too-spicy marinade. The wine list leans towards the New World.

Ki Modern Japanese
BCE Place, 181 Bay Street (at Wellington Street East). Tel: 416-308 5888. Open: L & D Mon–Fri, D only Sat. **$$$**
Sophisticated booths, high ceilings and an elegant sushi bar set the stage for small servings of beautifully prepared Japanese food. The patio is sublime and a plasma screen in the bar shows what the stock market is up to. Try chicken and leek skewers with kimchee glaze or crispy seafood tempura. Adventurous sushi rolls have top-notch ingredients and the torched fluke melts in your mouth. Well-chosen wine list and superb sakis, including a sparkler.

Reds
77 Adelaide Street West (between York and Bay streets). Tel: 416-862 7337. Open: L & D Mon–Fri. **$$$$**
This busy lunch spot is always bustling. Clever design makes the 300-seat restaurant cosier than you'd think. The café and bar offers tapas-size plates, while upstairs the fashionable bistro features food from wine countries of the world, paired with two wine choices. Named for its impressive red wine list, this is a deserving winner of a Wine Spectator Award.

Shopsy's Deli
33 Yonge Street. Tel: 416-365 3333. Open: L & D daily. **$**
A real city institution, founded in 1921, that attracts all levels of Toronto society, including visiting celebrities for its huge menu of deli favourites, from chicken pot pie or chicken parmigiana to corned beef and cabbage and their famous hot dogs, plus sandwiches, wraps, soups and salads. There are also branches of Shopsy's at 1535 Yonge Street and on King Street.

Bars & Cafés

Esplanade Bier Market
58 The Esplanade. Tel: 416-862 7575
A large selection of international beers is on offer here, as well as upmarket dining with a Belgian flavour.

Red's Bistro & Bar
1 First Canadian Place. Tel: 416-862 7337
Red's is a popular choice for a casual lunch or an evening gathering.

McVeigh's New Windsor Tavern
124 Church Street. Tel: 416-364 9698
McVeigh's is a real Irish pub with live music and home-style food. Definitely not the place for a quiet night out.

PRICE CATEGORIES
Prices for three-course dinner per person with a half-bottle of house wine:
$ = under $25
$$ = $25–50
$$$ = $50–70
$$$$ = more than $70

SERIOUS ABOUT SPORT

In Toronto enjoy everything from hockey to horse racing, and baseball to basketball

Torontonians are passionate about their sport and there are some spectacular venues across the city where fans can pay homage to the stars of hockey, lacrosse, basketball, baseball, Canadian football, soccer, horse racing, Formula One motor racing, and even cricket.

In Canada more young people are enrolled in soccer programmes than any other sport, including hockey. However, the game's popularity hasn't translated into a successful professional team for the city, but that might change with plans to build a soccer stadium at Exhibition Place. The 20,000-seat multimillion dollar complex is hosting matches during the FIFA World Youth Championship in 2007, and it will also be home to the Toronto Lynx soccer team.

Exhibition Place is the location of the Canadian Sports Hall of Fame (open Mon–Fri 10am–4.30pm; admission free), which pays tribute to athletes from all disciplines. Displays and touch-screen computers reveal the depth of Canada's sporting heritage. In town visitors shouldn't miss the Hockey Hall of Fame *(see page 97),* downtown at BCE Place, with interactive exhibits that will entertain all the family.

ABOVE: A bitter dispute between professional hockey players and team owners resulted in the cancellation of the 2004–05 season when players went on strike. Canada is one of the world's top hockey nations, a short list that includes the Czech Republic, Finland, the US, Russia and Slovakia.

BELOW: The Toronto Argonauts play their home games at Rogers Centre, which has a seating capacity of 53,000 and features a retractable roof high enough to accommodate a 31-storey building. Canadian football is similar to American football which is played across the border, with some rule differences. The Canadian game is generally considered to be faster with fewer stoppages. Since most clubs play outdoors the season is short, from August to the Grey Cup in November.

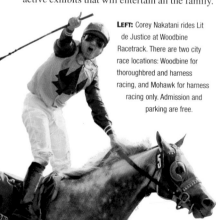

LEFT: Corey Nakatani rides Lit de Justice at Woodbine Racetrack. There are two city race locations: Woodbine for thoroughbred and harness racing, and Mohawk for harness racing only. Admission and parking are free.

HOCKEY ICON

Southern Ontario does not have winter like the rest of Canada. In regions where the ground is snow-covered and ponds are frozen for many months, it was natural that (ice) hockey would become the unofficial national sport. The fact that lacrosse holds this honour, being a traditional sport of First Nations, appears not to matter at all.

Before 1976, there were only six teams in the National Hockey League (NHL), with just two from Canada: the Toronto Maple Leafs and the Montreal Canadiens. Traditionally on Saturday nights the country tuned in to CBC (Canadian Broadcasting Company) radio or television for Hockey Night in Canada. During this time, the Maple Leafs were a winning team, and as a result attracted a devout following of loyal fans.

Today Torontonians are not so much hockey fans as Maple Leafs fans, creating heroes of Leaf captains such as Dave Keon, Wendel Clark, Darryl Sittler (above), Doug Gilmour and Mats Sundin. The club is the most financially successful in the modern expanded league, with almost every ticket sold out before the season begins. The Toronto Maple Leafs, the Toronto Raptors basketball team and the Toronto Rock lacrosse team all play at the Air Canada Centre.

RIGHT: Vince Carter, former Toronto Raptors and NBA (National Basketball Association) All-Star player made himself unpopular with sports fans, when he demanded to be traded in 2004. Carter played for the Raptors for seven years, but left the city and the team for the New Jersey Nets.

ABOVE: Professional baseball was introduced to Toronto in the early 1980s by the Toronto Blue Jays, a team in the American Baseball League. Local fans are notoriously fickle, withdrawing their support when the team isn't doing well. Following a decline in the game after back-to-back World Series Championships in 1993 and 1994, and the players' strike in 1995, the Blue Jays are finally enjoying a resurgence with more team wins, and better attendance at games.

RIGHT: Michael "Pinball" Clemons on the field in his last appearance as a player for the Toronto Argonauts. Clemons was much loved by Toronto players and fans alike. Under 1.7 metres (5 ft 6 inches) tall he was small for a football player, but he was fast and fearless running through defensive players earning himself the nickname, Pinball. He retired after 12 years with the Argonauts, but stayed on as the team's head coach leading them to league championship victory in the Grey Cup in 2004.

THE ENTERTAINMENT DISTRICT AND DOWNTOWN WEST

Toronto has a concentration of dynamic theatres and concert halls in its Entertainment District and a creative energy running through its downtown core

Practically stepping on the toes of the no-nonsense Financial District in the central downtown core is it's more vibrant, fun-loving neighbour, the Entertainment District. This is where people come to go to the theatre, concerts, restaurants, comedy clubs, boutique hotels and nightclubs; or to some of Toronto's principal tourist attractions such as the CN Tower, The Steam Whistle Brewery and the Rogers Centre, formerly known as the SkyDome, the city's excellent baseball and football stadium.

Spreading still further west is the creative Downtown West area, running along King, Queen, Dundas and College streets, out as far as Ossington Avenue. These long streets are some of the oldest in the city, over the years home to several of Toronto's most important ethnic enclaves such as Chinatown, Little Italy and the kaleidoscope of cultures found in Kensington Market.

On some stretches of these streets you'll find creative independent boutiques, shops, cafés and art galleries, particularly along Queen Street between Bathurst and Ossington. Also in this area is the highly respected and expanding Art Gallery of Ontario (AGO) at Dundas Street, lying between Beverley and McCaul streets.

For Torontonians, Downtown West is both a playground and a shopping haven, as well as an interesting place to live and work. And for visitors, this makes it a great place to discover some of the creative energy in the city.

Map on page 110

The Entertainment District

Toronto is proud of the fact that it's the third largest centre for the theatre in the English-speaking world, closely following New York and London. Many of the theatres

LEFT: the CN Tower is the city's most popular attraction.
BELOW: people watching downtown.

The Royal Alex in the heart of theatreland.

and concert halls are found in the **Entertainment District,** a section of downtown about eight blocks in size running from Lake Shore Boulevard in the south to Queen Street in the north, York Street to the east and Spadina Avenue to the west.

Just 20 years ago this area was a rather deserted part of town filled with run-down warehouses and wide, empty streets. Today the streets are busy, in part because of the new theatres and concert halls, and the restaurants that have opened in their wake, but also because of the hundreds of employees working at the headquarters of the Canadian Broadcasting Corporation (CBC) in the block between Front and Wellington streets, and at the flagship building for the CHUM television networks nearby at Queen and John streets.

Some of the city's new boutique hotels are here, as are many nightclubs, a cinema complex and a flurry of expensive condominiums is under construction. The action in the neighbourhood picks up after noon and lasts late into the night.

What started the transformation was the rescuing of the historic

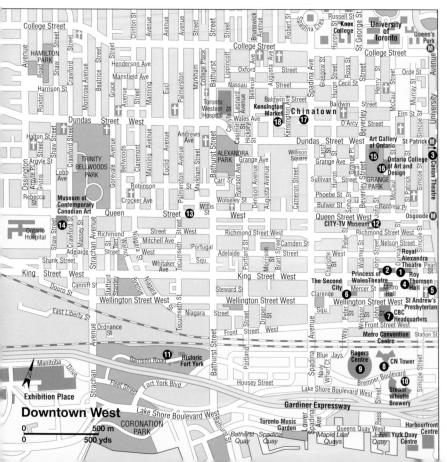

Downtown West

0 ___ 500 m
0 ___ 500 yds

Royal Alexandra Theatre ❶ (260 King Street West; subway: St Andrew) from the wrecking ball in 1963. It was restored to its original 1907 "Edwardian jewel-box" glory by the entrepreneurial Mirvish family, a colourful institution in the city.

Known by Torontonians as simply the "Royal Alex", the theatre was named after the wife of King Edward VII at a time when the neighbourhood was wealthy, with high-ranking government officials living on estates nearby.

The theatre is one of the city's first steel-framed structures, and one of its first air-conditioned buildings owing to a huge ice pit constructed beneath it that kept the air cool.

During the early 20th century, the theatre hosted such stars as Fred and Adele Astaire, Mae West and Edith Piaf, as well as visiting opera and ballet companies. More recently, Broadway and West End productions such as *Miss Saigon*, *Dame Edna* and *Mamma Mia* have been staged.

The connection to the London theatre scene is a strong one: the Mirvishes also restored and operated the prestigious Old Vic theatre in London in the 1980s and 1990s. The Royal Alex was declared a National Historic Monument in 1987. But strict building codes prevent the installation of a lift.

Theatre empire

The Mirvishes needed room to grow in the early 1990s and decided to take over the next block, building the **Princess of Wales Theatre ❷** (300 King Street West; subway: St Andrew) in 1993. The new theatre was named after Diana, Princess of Wales when she was still married to Prince Charles. The Mirvishes poured millions into the theatre, hiring respected contemporary artist Frank Stella to paint murals (one of his original models for the theatre now hangs in the National Gallery

in Ottawa). The design team Yabu-Puschelberg crafted the look of the lobbies and lounges.

The Mirvishes then took over the management of the former vaudeville palace, The Pantages, now the **Canon Theatre ❸** (244 Victoria Street; subway: St Andrew), which also hosts touring Broadway/West End productions.

Music venue

Opposite the Royal Alex sits another major cultural institution in the city, **Roy Thomson Hall ❹** (60 Simcoe Street; tel: 416-872 4255; www.roythomson.com; subway: St Andrew) with a sloping glass exterior and circular design. It's home to the Toronto Symphony Orchestra and its respected choir, the Toronto Mendelssohn Choir, and is a popular spot for performances by stars of the pop, jazz and opera world, as well as screenings during the Toronto International Film Festival.

Opened in 1982, the hall was designed by Arthur Erickson, a Canadian architect of Swedish

For theatre ticket information call Ticket King (416-872 1212; www.ticket king.com) or call Mirvish Productions for general theatre information (tel: 416-593 0351; www.mirvish.com).

BELOW: Peter Oundjian conducts the Toronto Symphony at Roy Thomson Hall.

Comedy Clubs

People aren't kidding when they say Canadians are funny – comedians such as Mike Myers, Jim Carrey, John Candy, Dan Aykroyd, Eugene Levy and Martin Short dominate the humour industry on both sides of the US-Canadian border. And many of them got their start doing stand-up and sketches in Toronto clubs such Second City or Yuk Yuk's.

Just why Canadians are so funny is often debated. Toronto-born Lorne Michaels, the legendary producer of the long-running hit comedy TV show *Saturday Night Live*, says he thinks his Canadian baby-boomer generation has a talent for comedy partly because it grew up on a diet of British humour, such as *Monty Python* and the *Carry On* films.

Eugene Levy and Martin Short agree there's more irony and humour in Canada than in the US, possibly because of the polite nature of Canadians and the country's clearly defined social rules – they create the perfect foil for comedy, which thrives on opposition and contrast. And being in the shadow of the all-powerful US of A for more than two centuries has finely honed the country's talent for self-deprecation.

Whatever the explanation, going to a comedy club in Toronto is a great – and inexpensive – way to spend an evening. Here are three of the best.

The Second City

Dan Aykroyd and Gilda Radner helped kick off the Toronto branch of this Chicago-based club in 1973. Since then it has spawned at least a dozen big-name comedians, and the hugely popular TV series *SCTV*, starring Eugene Levy, John Candy and Martin Short. The club has moved several times, but has kept its tradition of presenting fast-paced sketch comedy with top-notch talent. A cast of six present rapid-fire skits that skewer politicians, Canadian and American culture, relationships, even lizards, with some improv thrown in at the end of the evening. 51 Mercer Street; tel: 416-343 0011; www.secondcity.com; Tues–Sun; $20–28.

The Laugh Resort

For more than 20 years, The Laugh Resort has been showcasing rising stars in stand-up comedy from both the US and Canada (Ellen Degeneres, Adam Sandler and Ray Romano have performed here) in a warm and intimate atmosphere. The club presents edgy and intelligent humour that is "cleaner" than other clubs, but that doesn't make it boring. Standards here are high, with several comics appearing in one evening along with an MC. Concourse level of the Holiday Inn, 370 King Street West; tel: 416-364 5233; www.laughresort.com; Wed–Sat (Wed is new comic night); $7–15.

Yuk Yuk's

This brick-walled basement feels meaner and tougher than The Laugh Resort, and it is – comics and patrons here aren't afraid of taking a chance with risky humour. This is Toronto's oldest stand-up comedy club (now a national chain) and some of the biggest names in comedy have appeared here, including Jay Leno and Jim Carrey. Shows feature several comics and an MC. 224 Richmond Street West; tel: 416-967 6425; www.yukyuks.com; $2–17.   ❑

LEFT: Canadian kidders on *Saturday Night Live*.

descent, and named after Roy Thomson, the first Lord Thomson of Fleet, founder of a giant publishing empire, who donated nearly $5 million towards the total construction cost of $57 million. The concert hall recently underwent an extensive renovation of its acoustics at a cost of $20 million.

St Andrew's Church

Next door to Roy Thomson Hall on the corner of Simcoe and King streets is the historic **St Andrew's Presbyterian Church** ❺ (73 Simcoe Street, tel: 416-593 5603; www.standrewstoronto.org; subway: St Andrew) an example of how the city is still firmly rooted in its Anglo-Saxon past.

Built in 1876 in Scottish Romanesque style, the church was once the principal Presbyterian church in the city and today's congregation maintains ties to Scotland. It has strong links to the 48th Highlander Regiment, formed in 1891 by Scottish immigrants (its pipe band has played at the season opening for the Toronto Maple Leafs hockey team).

This is actually the second building constructed by the congregation, at a location that came to be known in the late 1800s as the "Four Corners" because of the buildings found at this intersection. The Four Corners were Salvation (the church); Legislation (the province's legislative building that stood at the time); Education (Upper Canada College was located here) and Damnation (a local tavern).

Today, the congregation is an active one, especially in its work with the poor. Toronto's well-known "Out of the Cold" programme helps feed the city's homeless and destitute.

The city's famous and successful are celebrated on the pavements outside the church and in front of Roy Thomson Hall and the Mirvish theatres. Brass and granite plaques have been embedded in the concrete as part of **Canada's Walk of Fame,** a sort of Canuck version of the well-known Walk of Fame in Hollywood. The stars in the pavement mark the achievements of well-known Canadian actors, singers, writers, ballerinas and even fashion models.

You'll find the names of Canadian comic greats including Dan Aykroyd, Mike Myers and Jim Carrey; actors such as Keifer and Donald Sutherland, and writers Margaret Atwood and Timothy Findlay. So far about 100 famous names have been laid in the pavement since the programme began in 1998.

Comedy theatre

Some of the big names in comedy in Canada's Walk of Fame got their start in the 1970s nearby at the Toronto comedy theatre **The Second City** ❻ (51 Mercer Street; tel: 416-343 0011; www.secondcity.com; nightly shows, improv and sketches on Mon; subway: St Andrew). Gilda Radner, Martin

Canada's Walk of Fame celebrates excellence in sport, the arts and entertainment. Visit www.canadaswalkof fame.com for a list of inductees.

BELOW: the beautiful interior of St Andrew's Church.

A sculpture of the Canadian pianist, Glenn Gould (1932–82), stands outside the CBC building, which also has a studio named for the renowned classical musician.

BELOW: on the glass floor of the CN Tower.

Short, Eugene Levy and Andrea Martin all performed here before moving on to join the casts of *Saturday Night Live* and *SCTV*. Originally located in just Chicago and Toronto, there are now three other branches of The Second City in the United States. The Second City in Toronto opened its doors to a 316-seat theatre on Mercer Street between John Street and Blue Jay Way, below King Street *(see page 112)*.

Restaurants and nightclubs

North of The Second City and about a block west on King Street, between John Street and Peter Street lies perhaps the highest concentration of restaurants in the city. Though you can't go wrong choosing any of these places, they mostly cater for tourists.

For a really good meal, head a couple of blocks further west to **Rodney's Oyster House** at 469 King Street West, or keep walking to No. 601, where you'll find upmarket **Susur**, an imaginative restaurant, with a less expensive spin-off, **Lee**, next door at No. 603.

Sports fans will enjoy the memorabilia at the restaurant of a hockey legend, **Wayne Gretzky's** (9 Blue Jays Way, south of King Street), has good food, and the decor pleasantly unlike the average sports bar.

This area comes alive at night, especially at weekends – it is a nexus of late-night dance clubs that draw in young crowds from all over town. Most come from outlying suburbs of the city, part of the great urban spread of Toronto that's officially called the Greater Toronto Area (GTA).

Some of the clubs are enormous, housed in former warehouses, and among the most popular are **Lot 332** at 332 Richmond Street; the club **West**, down a back alley at 510 King Street West; and **Fez Batik** at 129 Peter Street, which is also a restaurant. Be prepared for a stiff cover charge, expensive drinks and a wait outside at some of the clubs as doormen make their mandatory triage of who gets in first. So if you're skimpily dressed and it's winter, wrap up warm.

For those interested in broadcasting, it's worth a visit to the

Map on page 110

headquarters of the **Canadian Broadcasting Corporation** ❼ (CBC; tel: 416-205 8605 for tour information; www.cbc.ca; subway: St Andrew), located in the block east of John Street between Wellington and Front streets. Here you can go on behind-the-scenes tours of the newsrooms and control rooms and watch how shows are put together, or attend concerts in the Glenn Gould Studios.

The CN Tower

Down the street from the CBC, off of Front Street, is the pedestrian pathway leading to the **CN Tower** ❽ (301 Front Street West; tel: 416-868 6937; www.cntower.ca; subway: Union Station), also accessible from Bremner Boulevard to the south.

The tower *(see page 123)* is the number one tourist destination in the city, and the most recognisable edifice on the Toronto skyline. It's touted as the "world's tallest freestanding structure", taking into account the height of the tall spire that functions as a communication tower, which was the structure's original *raison d'etre*.

Now the building draws in crowds day and night. They zoom up the outside of the structure in glass-walled lifts in less than a minute. For those really wanting to test their bravery, the first observation deck has a glass floor giving you a view between your feet that drops 342 metres (1,122 ft).

Looking outward, you can see just how far this essentially lowlying city sprawls west, north and east. For an extra fee you can ride to a higher observation deck. You can enjoy a meal and the fabulous view at the **360 Restaurant**, the rotating restaurant, or a more casual snack at the Horizons Café or the Marketplace Café.

Rogers Centre

Nestled next to the CN tower is the **Rogers Centre** ❾ (1 Blue Jay's Way; tel: 416-341 3663; www.rogerscentre.com; subway: Union station), formerly known as the SkyDome, Canada's famous giant stadium with the world's first retractable roof. The stadium was renamed in early 2005 after the giant

The Audience *by Michael Snow, at Rogers Centre.*

LEFT:
the CN Tower, part of a distinctive skyline.
BELOW: the Blue Jays play baseball at Rogers Centre.

The Toronto Blue Jays play baseball in the American League East. Rogers Centre is the team's home ground.

communications company, Rogers – owner of the Toronto Blue Jays baseball team – purchased it for just $25 million. It was a tiny sum considering the $600 million it had cost to build by the time it opened in June 1989. The sale to Rogers had followed years of financial mismanagement by the owners (a combination of local and federal governments and a consortium of businesses) that led to bankruptcy and a highly controversial government bail out.

An impressive stadium

The 11-ton retractable roof can slide open or shut in less than 20 minutes, and when it is closed, the stadium is tall enough to hold a 31-storey building. Because the seats are easily removed, it can be reconfigured to suit both baseball and football set-ups.

It has room for up to 65,673, but it's usually more like 55,000 for most events, which have included not only sporting fixtures and concerts, but also readings by J.K. Rowling of her *Harry Potter* books and a speech by the Dalai Lama.

Each seat is cleaned after every event, which takes 14 staff members eight hours to complete. The seats are comfortable and well-spaced, but for sheer luxury and a good view of the action you can lounge in an armchair and gaze out from the privacy of your hotel room: 70 rooms in the Renaissance Hotel, built into the stadium structure, look directly out onto the field.

The Rogers Centre has its detractors among baseball fans. Some say it's simply too big for the sport, others claim that when the roof is open, the closed end acts as a wind scoop, creating a downdraft in the outfield that tends to prevent home runs.

Tours of the complex take visitors backstage to see the inside of dressing rooms and the private boxes known as "luxury suites", plus a walk out onto the field to get an idea of the player experience.

Just south of the Rogers Centre, beer fans can see how a microbrewery functions and taste its product at the **Steam Whistle Brewery** ❿ (255 Bremner Boulevard; tel: 416-362 2337; www.steamwhistle.ca; subway: Union Station), which is set up less than a decade ago in a former maintenance building for steam locomotives. Enthusiastic guides give tours of the historic building (officially known as the John Street Roundhouse) and demonstrate the brewing process for their award-winning premium Pilsner.

Fort York

Further along the lakeshore just past Bathurst Street stands **Historic Fort York** ⓫ (100 Garrison Road, tel: (416) 392-6907, www.fortyork.ca; subway: Bathurst, then streetcar 511). History buffs and military enthusiasts will enjoy visiting what is considered to be Canada's largest collection of War of 1812 period buildings, at what is the technical birthplace of the city. It was here in

1793 that a garrison was built for the then Lieutenant-Governor and representative of George III, John Graves Simcoe, at a time when Toronto was a small British trading post with less than 100 residents.

Fearing attack from America, Simcoe moved the capital here from the less-protected town of Niagara and planned to build a naval base to control Lake Ontario. In 1812, the Americans declared war on Canada, and they burned down the fort and town in April 1813.

The equipment at the rebuilt fort became obsolete by 1880, but the army continued to use it for training, barracks, offices and storage until 1930. It became a museum in 1934.

Military museum

Fort York houses a collection of military artefacts, and there are tours and demonstrations all year long, but it comes alive in the summer months when the Fort York Guard (many of whom are high school and university students interested in military history) give demonstrations of artillery firing, squad drills and battle tactics. There are fife and drum corps performers, tours every hour, and the firing of a cannon twice a day.

Unfortunately, Fort York is somewhat difficult to get to: it's a victim of poor urban planning, sitting on a small tract of land now hemmed in by railway tracks to the north and the busy Gardiner Expressway to the south. The best way to get to it is to take the 511 streetcar from Bathurst subway station and then cross a pedestrian walkway off the Bathurst/Front Street Bridge. Or you can drive there via a relatively new small road off Fleet Street to the south.

Queen Street West

Immediately to the west of the Entertainment District is a section of Toronto labelled the **Fashion District** by city officials. This was once the heart of the city's garment manufacturing industry; today most of the factory work is done elsewhere, but it remains the neighbourhood of choice for the offices, showrooms and work spaces of companies in the fashion industry.

Here, you can find great deals on fabric and notions (haberdashery) in dozens of small shops on the stretch of Queen Street between Spadina and Bathurst, or on furs in the cluster of fur shops on Spadina between Queen and Dundas. Further south at 400 King Street West, outdoor enthusiasts can stock up on clothes and equipment for all kinds of sports ranging from hiking to kayaking at the Mountain Co-op Equipment.

The most active street in the Downtown West area is without a doubt **Queen Street West**, lined with boutiques and small businesses, restaurants, cafés, art galleries and a major television network. It's a very long street and takes several hours to walk, so choose one section at a time to explore, or hop on the streetcars that run quite regularly along the

Map on page 110

A coat of arms over the entrance to Fort York.

BELOW:
troops re-enact a battle at Fort York.

The Rex Jazz & Blues Bar is a popular, casual venue on Queen Street West. Show times: Mon–Fri 6.30pm and 9.30pm; Sat–Sun noon, 3.30pm, 7pm and last show at 9.30pm

BELOW:
fashion in trendy Kensington Market.

street (make sure you have the exact change or a token).

This street has always been one of the principal roads in the city. It was originally called Lot Street because of the 40-hectare (100-acre) lots that once extended from the present-day Queen to Bloor Street, given to gentry at the time the city was settled in 1793. The street was renamed Queen in 1851 after Queen Victoria (King Street was named after George III, the reigning monarch during the early years of Toronto's inception).

Victorian architecture

Most of the architecture that lines the street dates back to Victorian times. In the late 1800s, the wealthy moved north to get away from the noise and the dirt from the nearby railway. Factories were built and houses constructed for the workers and their families who then flooded into the area. Most of the homes here date from this boom, between the late 1800s and the 1940s. These residential streets in the heart of the city, lined with trees and houses that have back and front gardens, are

part of what makes the city of Toronto so unique, and so "green".

Until recently, Queen Street and neighbouring Dundas and College streets linked one ethnic neighbourhood to another, reflecting waves of immigration in the city. There were major Portuguese, Ukranian, Hungarian and Italian sections. Most of these groups have moved on to other parts of the city and the suburbs, but some ethnic pockets remain. And it's the Hungarian bakeries, Italian and Korean restaurants and Portuguese food shops that give Queen and College Streets in particular their unique colour and flavour.

Queen Street between University and Spadina was a magnet for the counterculture and the creative beginning in the late 1970s. It still is lined with bookstores and record shops, secondhand clothes shops, funky boutiques, restaurants and a few of the best venues in the city for local and touring rock, blues, country and alternative bands.

These include the **Horseshoe Tavern** at No. 370), the **Cameron House** (No. 408) and the **Rivoli** (No. 334). But what's changed in recent years, is that the independent flavour of the neighbourhood has been compromised by the opening of mass-market outfits such as GAP and HMV, which have also contributed to an increase in traffic on the streets and sidewalks.

TV on the Street

The boom on Queen street solidified in 1988 when the Canadian television company **CITY-TV** moved its headquarters to 299 Queen Street West. The ornate Gothic-industrial facade of the building makes it one of the most noticeable in the city, and the CITY-TV news-truck embedded in the eastern side wall of the building, appearing to explode outwards with its wheels spinning, attracts attention too. The structure

Map on page 110

housed a Methodist bible factory in the early 1900s, then became the headquarters for the United Church of Canada until 1959. Today, the rapidly expanding CHUM corporation runs dozens of networks and programmes out of this building. It's become a dynamic part of the cultural life of Queen Street, too. TV programmes are shot on the ground floor, with windowed wall panels occasionally sliding open to the street, concerts are held in the parking area and there's a **television museum** ⑫ next door at No. 277.

And, for a dollar (which goes to charity), anyone can speak their mind into a permanently fixed camera on the corner of the CHUM-City building at John Street and Queen. Videotape from this "Speaker's Corner" is edited into a weekly programme or used for entertaining clips. For tour information or to watch a taping of a show call: 416-591 7400 or visit www.citytv.com.

West Queen West

Because of the commercialisation of the stretch of Queen between University and Spadina over the past 15 years or so, the more bohemian and creative energy that launched the street's cultural renaissance has now moved westward past Spadina to just beyond Ossington.

Known as **West Queen West** ⑬, this is a long stretch, but the flavour of the area is concentrated on the blocks between Bathurst and Ossington. Here you'll find the work of young up-and-coming Canadian fashion designers at stores such as **Willow Grant** (No. 960), vintage and cutting-edge furniture shops such as **Morba** (No. 665), or beautiful paper and origami workshops at the **Japanese Paper Place** (No. 887). There are handmade chocolates at **js bonbons** (No. 811) and trendy cafés and restaurants such as **Gypsy Co-op** (No. 817).

The people on the street are an interesting mix. The alternative set and students hang out at cafés, funky clothes stores and rundown bicycle repair shops; city professionals shop for designer goods that could be from the pages of glossy magazines, while down-and-outs break into fights outside cheap bars.

Art galleries

The borders of creative gentrification are spreading further west each year, but there's still a slight edginess to the area, especially beyond Trinity Bellwoods Park to just past Ossington, in the region of the city's mental health hospital.

This stretch is more deserted and quiet, but is lined with some of the most interesting contemporary art galleries in the city and a growing number of cafés and restaurants. Try a light meal at the vegetarian café/restaurant **Fresh** (No. 894). Some of the better galleries include the **Angell Gallery** (No. 890), which was the first in the area; the **Stephen Bulgar Gallery** and the **Edward Day Gallery** (No. 952).

The trendy Gypsy Co-op has coffee, tea, infusions and delicious cakes and pastries.

BELOW: a sunny smile from a vendor on Queen Street West.

*A visitor admires
an exhibit from
Ancient Egypt.*

BELOW:
young vegetable
vendors on Spadina.

The **Museum of Contemporary Canadian Art** ⓮ (www.mocca.toronto.on.ca) is at this address as well. **Camera Bar** (No. 1028; www.camerabar.ca) is a cinema-café, with a good wine, beer and cocktail list. It is partly owned by renowned Toronto-based filmmaker Atom Egoyan, and independent and foreign films are screened here five days a week.

Once a year, in September, you can tour the studios of artists in the neighbourhood as part of the week-long **Queen West Art Crawl** (www.torontoartscape.on.ca). Capping this stretch of creative activity on Queen is a hot spot, the **Drake Hotel** (www.thedrakehotel.ca), an avant-garde hotel-restaurant-art gallery-music venue that's become a creative focal point in the area. Nearby is the equally hip, but more genteel **Gladstone Hotel** (www.gladstonehotel.ca). Built in 1889, each guest room has been decorated by local artists, and the renovated hotel's public reception rooms and bars are popular venues for readings, screenings and exhibitions.

Art Gallery of Ontario

Less cutting-edge, but no less interesting, is an area north of Queen Street between University and Spadina avenues, stretching as far as the neighbourhood known as Grange Park, named after the grounds of an early 19th-century estate. The manor house, known as **The Grange**, stands behind the Art Gallery of Ontario at Dundas and Beverley streets. It's one of the oldest remaining private mansions of early Toronto, and was built in 1817 by D'Arcy Boulton, one of the city's wealthy estate owners at the time. Some other ornate homes still standing on Beverley (including one that now houses the Italian Consulate at No. 136) show the former grandeur of this neighbourhood.

The Grange now belongs to the the **Art Gallery of Ontario** ⓯ (AGO; 317 Dundas Street West; tel: 416-979 6648; www.ago.net; subway: St Patrick) which fills the block between Beverley and McCaul streets *(see also page 51)*. This is one of the city's most important art museums, housing treasured works of Canadian art, the largest collection of sculptures by British artist Henry Moore, and paintings by French impressionists.

The building is currently undergoing a $200 million expansion and renovation designed by the world-renowned architect Frank Gehry (the Guggenheim Museum in Bilbao, Spain and the Experience Music Project in Seattle, Washington) who spent many years of his childhood in the neighbourhood. Work on the gallery is expected to be completed by spring 2008, but it remains open (admission fees have been reduced) with selected works and exhibitions on show.

The renovation is part of a boom in important cultural projects in the city, along with the enlargement of the Royal Ontario Museum *(see*

page 153) by Daniel Libeskind and the construction of the opera and dance theatre, the Four Seasons Centre for the Performing Arts, at Queen and University *(see page 104)*.

Around the corner from the AGO is one of the more entertaining designs in recent years – the **Ontario College of Art and Design** ⓰ *(see page 50)* takes the form of a pencil box suspended in the air by 16 massive coloured pencils.

If you're hungry, head just north of the AGO above Dundas Street to unique Baldwin Street on the stretch between McCaul and Huron streets. This leafy block is like a neighbourhood in itself, running at its own casual tempo. It's lined with restaurants with outdoor patios, such as funky **Café La Gaffe** (No. 24), the classy French bistro **Bodega** (No. 30) and the Italian pizzeria **John's** (No. 27), plus several good ethnic eateries where you can eat in or take out.

Chinatown

Walk west along Baldwin to Spadina and you'll reach the heart of Toronto's central **Chinatown** ⓱

which runs west along Dundas Street and north on Spadina as far as College Street. There are several Chinatowns in the city, but this is the largest and best known, because of the number of stores and restaurants here that open until late at night, and its proximity to public transport. It sprouted up on these streets in the 1960s after the original Chinatown near Queen and Bay was razed to make way for the new City Hall. In recent years, the area has had an influx of other Southeast Asian nationalities, notably Thai and Vietnamese immigrants. There are concerns about the future of this area, however, because the population is aging as younger Chinese and recently arrived immigrants are choosing to live in the suburbs.

Kensington Market

Just west of Spadina between Dundas and College is one of the more colourful parts of the city – **Kensington Market** ⓲ – where several blocks of narrow streets are crowded with small stores opening onto the pavements. There are shops

Map on page 110

Enjoy the sweet aroma of freshly baked bread and pastries in My Market Bakery at 172 Baldwin Street.

BELOW: a streetcar passes through Chinatown.

Map on page 110

Little Italy has an infectious Mediterranean exuberance.

BELOW: vespas for sale in Little Italy.

selling fruit and vegetables, spices, grains and nuts as well as cheese stores; stands piled high with socks and boots; and Caribbean food storefronts crowd next to Eastern European butchers or organic ice-cream parlours.

The vibrant ethnic mix of the culture here reflects the waves of immigration into the city since the early 20th century, when Kensington Market was home to most of the city's Jewish population. By the early 1950s, most of them had moved to other areas, but the neighbourhood has retained it's character as an outdoor market, absorbing successive generations of immigrants from Asia, the Caribbean and Africa. It is also a hangout for students, the skateboard crowd and club kids.

Two of the city's best cheese shops are here – don't miss **Global Cheese** at 76 Kensington Avenue – along with one of Toronto's best butchers, **European Quality Meats** (176 Baldwin Street), making this a destination for well-heeled patrons shopping for dinner parties. Overall, Kensington Market feels not unlike

a hippy district, with a kind of 1960s/1970s Haight-Ashbury (San Francisco) atmosphere, particularly on Kensington Avenue, which is lined with vintage clothing stores and run-down Victorian townhouses painted in bright colours. You'll even find one of the few cannabis cafés in Canada at the **Hot Box** (191A Baldwin Street, corner of Augusta). Here people are free to light up, or munch on a "stonerwich", made with hemp seeds. (The sign outside their adjacent shop, Roach-O-Rama, reads, "Serving Potheads since… oh, I forget".)

College Street

North of Kensington Market along College between Bathurst and Ossington is the heart of the city's **Little Italy** *(see page 186)*, which still feels Italian even though many of the original Italian immigrants have moved to the suburbs. Some say the influx of Portuguese into the area is changing the emphasis, but remaining constant is the Mediterranean exuberance of this stretch of College, particularly in warm weather, when crowds fill the outdoor eating terraces. The vibrancy of the area has made it attractive to many of the city's media producers, writers and art directors, who live in apartments and houses on the side streets off College. They like to hang out at **Bar Italia** (No. 582) or at **Café Diplomatico** (No. 594), an institution for coffee lovers known simply as "The Dip" by locals. The café feels so authentically Italian it's been used in several films, and Sophia Loren once popped in.

Visiting big-name celebrities like to eat at the upscale and delicious **Trattoria Giancarlo** (41 Clinton Street at College). For those looking for a good selection of CDs to browse, try the eclectic music store **Soundscapes** (No. 572), considered one of the best in the city. ❏

The CN Tower

Torontonians may be a little blasé about the **CN Tower** (301 Front Street West; tel: 416-868 6937; daily 9am–11pm; admission charge; nearest subway: Union Station). They will tell you they went up it once, but probably wouldn't go again unless they were showing it to visiting friends or family. Nevertheless, it remains a powerful symbol of the city, and civic pride is never far from the psyche of citizens of Canada's largest city, however cool they may appear to be.

A trip to the top of the world's tallest building, gracefully rising 553.3 metres (1,815 ft 5 in) above the city, is pretty much a requirement of a visit to Toronto, regardless of the relatively high cost and crush of tourists standing in line to share the experience. From the adrenalin rush of the high-speed, glass-fronted lifts to the vertigo-inducing stand on the glass floor and the panoramic views from the Sky Pod, it really is a terrific thing to do. Choose a clear day, buy tickets in advance if you can, and either get there early in the day or arrive just before sunset to see the view then watch the city light up.

Attractions at the foot of the tower include a simulator ride, arcade games, a café and the inevitable retail opportunity, but most worthwhile is the "To the Top" movie about the tower and its construction. Otherwise get in line for one of the six lifts, with an info-screen to keep you interested while you wait.

The lift quickly exposes those who suffer from vertigo – they are the ones at the back with their eyes closed – while their fellow passengers are glued to the sight of the city disappearing below at a speed of 22 kph (15 mph). After 58 seconds, the lift deposits you at the **Look Out Level**, 346 metres (1,136 ft) above ground, with glass windows all around and the terrifying glass floor, where you can stand and look past your feet at the ground below.

Don't worry about safety; 14 large hippos could not break the glass. After this you can descend to an open-air observation deck, though the view is somewhat obscured by

the heavy, suicide/accident-proof mesh that encircles it.

Back inside, an internal lift whisks you up through the core of the tower to the **Sky Pod**, at 447 metres (1,151 ft) for the ultimate high-rise experience and incredible views. Be prepared for the encircling glass curving in at the bottom, which can be a little unnerving. Up here you can see for 120 km (75 miles) on a clear day, maybe even as far as the spray rising from Niagara Falls.

After the thrilling experience of going up the CN Tower, it is amazing to discover that it was built primarily not as a tourist attraction but to improve telecommunications in the city, after a spate of 1960s' skyscraper construction had disrupted radio and TV waves.

Torontonians had some of the worst TV reception in the whole of North America; now, not surprisingly, it has some of the best, with antennae serving all the major TV and radio stations and cellular phone networks. Started in 1973, the tower took 40 months to complete and cost $63 million. The highly regarded (and highly priced) **360 Restaurant** (tel: 416-362 5411 for reservations), which revolves once every 70 minutes or so, was added in 1995, and a further $40 million has been spent since then on improved security and visitor amenities. ❑

RIGHT: the CN Tower during construction.

RESTAURANTS & BARS

Restaurants

Amuse-bouche

96 Tecumseth Street (at King Street). Tel: 416-913 5830. Open: D Tues–Sun, L Thur–Fri. **$$$**

A small stylish restaurant serving beautifully prepared dishes. The co-chefs are from France and Barbados and both influences are seen on the menu; spicing is unusual and intricate. Try butter poached lobster served with braised pork belly and a star anise sabayon or the Bajan grilled shrimp with crispy wild salmon, wasabi gnocchi and yuzu drizzle. For dessert, try milk chocolate lemon tart with Szechuan pepper ice cream. Well chosen wine list.

Blowfish

668 King Street West (at Bathurst Street). Tel: 416-860 0606. Open: D only Mon–Sat. **$$$**

Located in a former bank building, with beautiful, minimalist interiors and warmer design accents. The fascinating menu fuses pan Asian, Japanese and French techniques in the secure hands of Chef G.Q. Pan. Interesting sushi options abound, but be sure to sample the other side of the menu. Salad with barbecued salmon skin and miso dressing is inventive and delicious. Other dishes include scallops wrapped in salmon topped with wasabi mayonnaise and beef tenderloin heaped with somen noodle fries.

Crush

455 King Street West (at Spadina Avenue). Tel: 416-977 1234. Open: L & D Mon–Fri, D only Sat. **$$$**

Bright, comfortable and airy, the layout provides tables far enough apart for either business or romance. High ceilings, sand-blasted natural brick walls and polished wood floors complete the picture. Within walking distance of the Entertainment District, this busy bistro features contemporary flavours, including superb tuna Nicoise salad, a popular choice at lunch, and has great takes on desserts. It's worth visiting in autumn for the pear tasting plate, featuring sticky pear and pecan brown sugar slice, poached pear with mascarpone mousse and pear fritters. Superb wine list.

The Fifth and Terrace at the Fifth

225 Richmond Street West (at Duncan Street). Tel: 416-979 3005. Open: D only Thur–Sat. **$$$$**

Essentially a private club with an open door policy, this fifth floor room located in a warehouse over a busy club is one of the loveliest in Toronto. The space is warm and inviting with top-notch, well-prepared food to match. The menu is short, but has some interesting choices. Excellent wine list and lots of help from servers when matching bottles with the French-inspired food. The Terrace, which overlooks downtown, offers grills and other casual options. Reservations essential.

Fred's Not Here

321 King Street (between Peter and John Streets). Tel: 416-971 9155. Open: L & D Mon–Fri, D only Sat–Sun. **$$**.

A bustling bistro at the centre of the Entertainment District. An eclectic menu with well-prepared standard and fusion dishes. Grills are a speciality. Service is quick and efficient to get you out on time for your show. A good choice of cocktails and wine by the glass.

Lalot

200 Bathurst Street (at Queen Street West). Tel: 416-703 8222. Open: D only Tues–Sun. **$$**

High style Vietnamese food is served here in a casual setting, and it's the vegetable dishes that steal the show. Caramelised catfish, served in a clay pot, is another highlight, and the fried squid stuffed with duck meat and shiitake is outstanding. Fresh flavours are spicy, herbal and very clean. There's a well-priced wine list.

Lee

603 King Street West (at Bathurst Street). Tel: 416-504 7867. Open: L & D Mon–Sat. **$$$$**

Foodies come to snack on superstar chef Susur Lee's "smaller" and cheaper dishes (see also Susur). Sharing from the global menu is a must and the recommendation of five plates per person adds up. The pink plexi-glass tables and giant budgies add to the funky vibe. The surprising combinations of flavours beg for bigger servings.

Monsoon

100 Simcoe Street. (at Adelaide Street). Tel: 419-979 7172. Open: L & D Mon–Fri, D only Sat. **$$$$**

This cool, award-winning restaurant is hip but very comfortable. The speciality is pan-Asian cuisine that's expertly cooked and beautifully presented. For an eclectic night out, make a meal of the appetizers. Try Kobe beef pan-stickers with a Thai dragon chilli sauce on daikon salad or the king crab cakes with cucumber namasa and coconut aioli. Entrées are delectable. Fish is always good. Wine suggestions are given with each dish.

Noce

875 Queen Street West (at Walnut Avenue). Tel: 416-504 3463. Open: D only Mon–Sat. $$$

Sophisticated Italian cuisine in an attractive room with large windows and a fabulous chandelier. Seafood includes outstanding shaved octopus on a slick of peppery olive oil. Main courses are standard, but are exceptionally well-prepared and attractive. Award-winning wine list.

Rodney's Oyster House

469 King Street West (at Spadina Avenue). Tel: 416-363 8105. Open: L & D Mon–Sat. $$$$

As Toronto's first oyster bar, Rodney's has maintained its high standards and sense of fun for more than 20 years. The oyster shuckers are all characters, led by Rodney himself. Choose from all kinds of oysters, including some harvested from Rodney's own oyster beds, the rest from all over the world. Fish and seafood dishes are cooked with flair. In the summer, check out the oyster garden patio with a barbecue. Great wine options.

Senses

SoHo Metropolitan Hotel, 328 Wellington Street West (at Blue Jays Way). Tel: 416-935 0400. Open: D only Wed–Sun. $$$$

A luxurious room sets the stage for the inventive food served up

by chef Claudio Aprile. There's a tasting menu as well as the à la carte selections, and a good example of the complex flavours in the dishes is the seared scallops with citrus fruit, galangal dressing, Thai herbs and coconut. Outstanding crab is accompanied by a luscious potato and goat's cheese panna cotta. Desserts are to die for, there's an excellent wine list, and service is smooth.

Susur

601 King Street West (at Bathurst Street). Tel: 416-603 2205. Open: D only Mon–Sat. $$$$

Susur Lee's eponymous restaurant is famous for his mind-blowing and highly original dishes. One of Canada's most famous chefs, Susur originally trained as a French chef in Hong Kong, but brings his Chinese roots to the table. The menu changes constantly, new dishes are always sensational and tasting menus show the breadth of Susur's experience. Excellent wine list, knowledgeable service *(see also Lee, page 126)*.

Tiger Lily's Noodle House

257 Queen Street West. Tel: 416-977 5499. Open: D only Mon–Sat. $

Create your own dishes, choosing from six types of noodle and various meats, vegetables,

wontons and broths. The menu also has satays, dim sum and other oriental delights, which you can enjoy in the mix of shoppers, office workers and TV people.

Ultra Supper Club

314 Queen Street West (at Peter Street). Tel: 416-263 0330. Open: D only Mon–Sat. $$$$

This ultra-glamorous Queen West rendezvous morphs into a nightclub after hours, but don't discount the cooking. Sit at one of the raised horseshoe banquettes and explore chef Chris Zielinski's contemporary cooking. Scallops get the full treatment, as a lychee-fragrant ceviche or fried as tempura, with shiso leaf and pan-seared with truffled butter. Desserts are deliciously inventive. The servers are serious about food and wine.

Bars & Cafes

Peel Pub

276 King Street West. Tel: 416-977 1881

A fun and lively pub with a good selection of beers and pub food.

Indian Motorcycle Café & Lounge

355 King Street West. Tel: 416-593 6996

A popular retro style café.

Queen Mother Cafe

208 Queen Street West. Tel: 416-598 4719

This cosy café is located in a historic building, it also has a garden patio.

PRICE CATEGORIES

Prices for three-course dinner per person with a half-bottle of house wine:
$ = under $25
$$ = $25–50
$$$ = $50–70
$$$$ = more than $70

RIGHT: a cosy cafe in a historic building.

TORONTO:
CITY OF FILM

From independent movies to big star productions, Toronto's film festivals show them all

Heralded as one of the most prestigious film events in North America, the Toronto International Film Festival (TIFF) was established in 1976 by film producers William Marshall, Henk van der Kolk and Dusty Cohl.

From small beginnings it has increased its influence, premiering the work of filmmakers, from art house movies to some of the most commercially successful films in history, which have gone on to win Academy Awards.

Spectacular red carpet gala screenings are attended by powerful movers and shakers in the industry, but the Toronto festival is also popular with local enthusiasts who are just as likely to sell out venues screening independent, foreign language films as a Hollywood blockbuster.

In September, during the 10-day event the city is awash with movie buffs eager to view hundreds of presentations from Canada, the US, Europe, Africa and Asia, which play venues such as Roy Thomson Hall, the Elgin Theatre, and Yorkville, the festival's original home. An offshoot of the TIFF is Sprockets, a children's event held in April. There are also several smaller festivals: the Hot Docs Canadian International Documentary Festival and the ReelWorld Film Festival in April; Inside Out Toronto Lesbian and Gay Film and Video Festival, and the Toronto Jewish Film Festival in May, and in June the Worldwide Short Film Festival.

International Festival passes are available from July. You can purchase them online, by phone or from the box office at the Manulife Centre, 55 Bloor Street West, tel: 416-968 3456.

ABOVE: Thandie Newton in *Crash*, a critically acclaimed movie set in racially charged, modern-day Los Angeles, which appeared at the Toronto festival in 2004. Canadian director, Paul Haggis, assembled a talented cast including Sandra Bullock, Don Cheadle and Matt Dillon for the feature that became one of the most successful independent films in America.

BELOW AND LEFT: *The Adjuster* caused a stir, and catapulted the director Atom Egoyan into the spotlight when it was released in 1991. The film, which explores the themes of sex and power, won the Best Canadian Feature category that same year.

THE DIRECTORS

In the 1980s the Toronto Film Festival Perspective Canada category took off. Originally introduced to showcase the work of Canadian filmmakers it promotes the independents, as well as Canadian-born directors such as Norman Jewison, Paul Haggis, David Cronenberg and Atom Egoyan, who have not only earned the respect of their peers, but have also forged lucrative careers across the border in the US.

Born and raised in Toronto, Norman Jewison has had a highly successful career as a director of films that reveal a social conscience. His body of cinematic work includes many award winning films stretching back to the 1960s, such as *Fiddler on the Roof*, *Moonstruck*, *The Hurricane*, and *Bread and Tulips*. Jewison was also instrumental in the setting up of the Canadian Film Centre.

Also making waves in Hollywood is Paul Haggis, director of the box office smash *Crash*, he also wrote the screenplay for Clint Eastwood's award winning film, *Million Dollar Baby*.

Independent filmmaker, Atom Egoyan's critically acclaimed films have film audiences flocking to see his powerful, often challenging dramas. Born in Egypt, he grew up in Victoria, British Columbia, but moved to Toronto to attend university at 18. His work includes *The Adjuster*, *Ararat*, about the genocide in Armenia, and award winning *Exotica* and *The Sweet Hereafter*.

RIGHT: *Mon Cousin Américain*, a coming of age drama about a young girl growing up on a ranch in rural Canada was written and directed by Sandy Wilson, and premiered at the festival in 1985. The film's success helped to elevate the Canadian category of the festival.

BELOW: Gabriel Arcand plays Mario in the French Canadian film, *Déclin de L'Empire Américain*, which won the festival's Audience Award in 1986, and was nominated for an Academy Award in the Best Foreign Language category the following year. Directed by Denys Arcand, who also wrote the script, the film which explores relationships was a box office smash, becoming one of the Canada's biggest selling films.

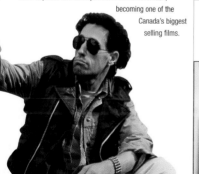

BELOW: Liam Neeson at the Toronto Film Festival, which showcased *Breakfast on Pluto* in 2005, an Irish/UK production directed by Neil Jordan. It is a rollicking tale of a transvestite cabaret artist, played by Cillian Murphy, searching for the mother who abandoned him at birth.

Cathedral Church
of
ST. JAMES
Anglican (Episcopal) Church of Canada
Sunday Services: 8:00 9:00 11:00 4:30
Weekday: 7:30 8:30 12:30 5:15
Saturday: 12:30
65 Church St.   416-364-7865
www.stjamescathedral.on.ca

OLD TOWN

The birthplace of Toronto has metamorphosed, finally, into one of the city's most lively quarters, with the revived Distillery District one of its biggest draws

A community of distinct yet connected neighbourhoods, Toronto's Old Town began as the Town of York, the capital of Britain's colony of Upper Canada, and then started to seriously grow with the commerce generated by the War of 1812. By the time the city was incorporated and renamed Toronto in 1834, it extended from Yonge Street to the Don River, and from Queen Street to magnificent Lake Ontario.

Over the past 200 years, Old Town has experienced highs and lows. From being the economic and political core of a young city, its fortunes plummeted when, at the beginning of the 20th century, Toronto's political, financial, judicial and industrial institutions headed north and west, leaving behind an increasingly decrepit collection of crumbling old factory buildings and cavernous warehouses, and in some cases less than inadequate housing.

Fortunately, in the 1970s, the city came to realise the urgency of saving and preserving the area's most historically important buildings and Old Town is once again a vibrant community, where people live, work and play. Sadly, none of the original wooden buildings have survived, but their worthy replacements include some fine 19th-century streetscapes.

Early buildings

In a small historic block, **Toronto's First Post Office** ❶ (260 Adelaide Street East; tel: 416-865 9414; daily; free; subway: King) was built in 1833 by postmaster James Scott Howard, who lived with his family above the post office until he was dismissed for allegedly sympathising with would-be reformers during the 1837 rebellion *(see page 21).*

Map on page 130

LEFT: the soaring St James Cathedral.
BELOW: modern sculpture in the Old Town.

Until its demise in 1866, the Bank of Upper Canada was one of North America's leading financial institutions.

Toronto's First Post Office is now a museum which houses a large collection of postal paraphernalia dating back to the 1830s and a full-service post office. Visitors are invited to try writing with a quill pen and sealing the letter with wax.

In the same block as the post office, at the corner of George and Adelaide Streets, the **Bank of Upper Canada** is an elegant stone building dating back to 1827. The first chartered bank in the province, it had a monopoly on government business until Upper and Lower Canada united as the Province of Canada in 1841. Facing competition for the first time, from the emergent Bank of Montreal, it succumbed in 1866, after granting too many loans on poor security.

Rising from the ashes

After most of its wooden buildings were destroyed in the Great Fire of 1849 *(see page 22)*, Toronto was rebuilt. Walking south on George Street visitors pass many of these solid brick replacements, mostly constructed in Second Empire (Italianate, with a mansard roof) or Georgian style.

In 1861, the city's first streetcars began operating from a grandiose, turreted castle-like building on Front Street. It housed the horses that pulled the streetcars, until the advent of electric power in 1891. After various incarnations the building was threatened with demolition, but, following a remarkable restoration in the 1970s, it is now home to the **Lorraine Kimsa Theatre for Young People** (165 Front Street East; subway: King).

Located two blocks east of St Lawrence Market the theatre stages critically acclaimed performances for and by children. Established in 1966, the drama school holds classes at its downtown base, in North York and Etobicoke.

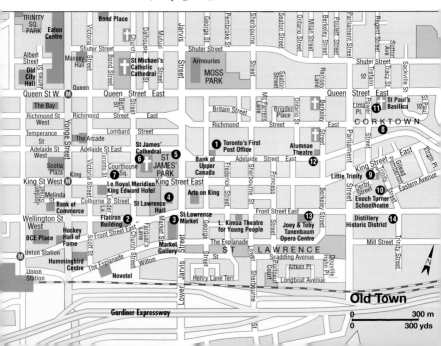

Old Town

West of here, one of Toronto's most photographed scenes comes into view. At the junction of Front and Wellington Streets, modern office towers frame the **Flatiron Building ❷**. Built in 1892, this wedge-shaped building – which predates New York's – was built for George Gooderham, a leading businessmen and son of the founder of Gooderham and Worts distillery *(see page 135)*. At its western end, an intriguing five-storey *trompe l'oeil* mural by Derek Besant gives the impression that there are many windows, although there is, in fact, only one.

St Lawrence Market

There has been a market at the intersection of Front and Jarvis streets since 1803, but the current **St Lawrence Market ❸** dates from 1844. It was once used as Toronto's second city hall, and enjoyed a prominent location on the bustling harbour. The wharf there was a secret stop on the Underground Railroad (the system set up to assist fugitive slaves from the United States escape to relative safety in Canada. *See page 200*). This changed with the advent of the railway in the 1850s, when the shoreline was deemed the perfect place for a rail corridor.

The Council Chamber and municipal offices occupied the upper floor of the building, while small shops, a market and a police station shared the ground floor. However, cells in the basement were frequently flooded and eventually the jail was moved. In 1899, the civic offices relocated too.

The market was restored in the early 1970s and its fresh produce and wise-cracking vendors continue to draw savvy local shoppers.

The only original part of the building that remains is the central portion. Upstairs, in the former Council Chamber, the **Market Gallery** (tel: 416-392 7604; Wed–Sun; free) houses a permanent exhibition on Toronto's history and offers a superb view through an old fanlight to the market below. On the opposite side of Front Street, the **North Market** has an equally long

Map on page 130

At the western end of the Flatiron Building is a five-storey trompe l'oeil *mural by Derek Besant.*

BELOW: service with a smile at North Market.
LEFT: the unmistakable Flatiron Building.

though less illustrious history, and hosts a lively farmers' market here every Saturday.

The **St Lawrence Hall** ❹ (157 King Street East) was built in 1850, and is Victorian neoclassical architecture at its best, with Corinthian columns, intricate stone carvings and a distinctive cupola. Political rallies, balls, lectures and concerts took place in the Great Hall, where distinguished guests included Canada's first prime minister, Sir John A. Macdonald and opera singer Jenny Nightingale. Now restored to its former splendour, it again hosts glittering social and cultural events.

On the north side of King Street, the Victorian-style gardens of **St James' Park** ❺ were once the cemetery for the city's early settlers, and are now a pretty and peaceful refuge for many harried office workers, who enjoy a picnic lunch here during the spring and summer.

At King and Church streets, **St James' Cathedral** ❻ (tel: 416-364 7865; tours Sun 12.30pm; subway: King), is the fourth church on the site, which was started after the

Great Fire of 1849 had destroyed its predecessor. Completed in the 1850s, it was possibly modelled on Salisbury Cathedral, and its Gothic Revival style was a Victorian revolt against the austerity of post-Reformation churches. The cathedral is magnificent, and its 96-metre (314-ft) spire is the tallest in Canada. The interior evokes equal drama with its elaborate hammer-beam ceiling, Queen Anne organ cases and a stained glass window by Tiffany & Co, New York (c.1900), in memory of William Jarvis, one of Toronto's founding fathers. Opposite the cathedral, the small **Toronto Sculpture Garden** really grabs the attention with its provocative experimental art.

Neoclassical architecture

Until 1826, hundreds of hangings took place at the corner of King Street and Leader Lane, site of the town of York's first jail, but since 1903 **Le Royal Meridien King Edward Hotel** (37 King Street East, tel: 416-863 3131; subway: King) has occupied the spot. It was

Little Trinity Church is the oldest place of worship in Toronto.

BELOW: St James' Park, an oasis in the middle of the city.
RIGHT: the dazzling stained glass windows of the cathedral.

Map on page 130

Toronto's first luxury hotel and continues to be among its most prestigious. Its architect, E.J. Lennox, was responsible for some of Toronto's most magnificent buildings, including Old City Hall, and it's neoclassical design oozes elegance, with soaring columns in the rotunda-like lobby. The hotel symbolises the standards and lifestyle of a period that has all but vanished.

The King Edward has played host to celebrities and colourful figures including Rudyard Kipling, Teddy Roosevelt and the Beatles. During the pop stars' stay 3,000 fans stormed the lobby of the hotel.

North of the hotel, almost every building on **Toronto Street** has a historical plaque and a story to tell. No. 10, built in the early 1850s as a post office, was designed by Frederic Cumberland and Thomas Ridout, the architects responsible for St James' Cathedral. Another neoclassical pile, with Ionic columns topped by a sculpted royal crest, it narrowly escaped demolition in the 1950s and later became the headquarters of Hollinger Inc., the holding company of tycoon Conrad Black, later Lord Black of Crossharbour, who faced fraud charges.

East of Toronto Street, a narrow passageway leads to **Courthouse Square** ❼, a real downtown gem. Tucked away between the buildings, the long-empty site has been delightfully transformed into a green oasis, awash with water courses, native trees, shrubs, vines, herbs, flowering perennials and grasses.

The square backs onto the 1851 **York County Court House** (57 Adelaide Street East), another striking example of Greek revival architecture by Cumberland and Ridout. In 1909, it became the home of the Arts and Letters Club of Toronto, an association for men only initially, who met regularly to promote their two great interests:

conversation and the arts. Cellist Pablo Casals and pianist Sergei Rachmaninov both performed here. Today, it houses an elegant restaurant where you can book one of the former cells for a cosy dinner.

Victorian Corktown

Extending southeast from Queen and Berkeley streets to the Don River, **Corktown** ❽ was settled in the mid-1800s by Irish immigrants who came to Canada during the Great Famine. The area had everything a community needed – gasworks, mills and distilleries for employment, schools, churches and taverns, and even the Don River for swimming.

Nestling in between were hundreds of workers' cottages, while larger, more gracious homes accommodated the business managers and their families. Now, the inevitable gentrification of these old homes is creating an increasingly desirable residential neighbourhood.

Close to Parliament Street, **Little Trinity Church** ❾ (417 King Street East), built in 1843, is the oldest church of any faith in the city.

Victorian houses in Corktown range from compact workers' cottages to villas.

BELOW:
a stack of books in
Courthouse Square.

Toronto's first free school was established in 1848 by Enoch Turner.

Wealthy philanthropists funded the neo-Gothic revival church, but their apparent generosity may well have simply been a means of retaining St James' Cathedral exclusively for their own use. Although a fire destroyed much of the church in 1961, the Communion table, the pulpit, the baptistery and the pews all date back to the 1840s.

Around the corner, on Trinity Street, cheerfully painted, 19th-century terraced houses are shaded by old trees. The 1848 **Enoch Turner Schoolhouse** ❿ (106 Trinity Street, tel: 416-863 0010; Mon–Fri; donation) was funded by local philanthropist Enoch Turner, to provide free schooling for the children of the parish. For 10 years, the modest one-room building was where two teachers instructed 100 pupils every day. Now restored to replicate the original mid-19th-century classroom, the schoolhouse offers today's youngsters a glimpse of Victorian education.

Three blocks north, Corktown's Roman Catholics attended **St Paul's Basilica** ⓫ (83 Power Street).

Founded in 1822, it was the first Roman Catholic parish in Upper Canada. Today's church was built in the 1880s and, in contrast to Toronto's many Gothic churches, is a magnificent Italian Renaissance-style building, with lovely rounded arches, glorious ceiling paintings and perfect acoustics. In 1999, Pope John Paul II designated the church a Minor Basilica.

Historic Berkeley Street

At the corner of Berkeley and Adelaide streets, the **Alumnae Theatre** ⓬ (70 Berkeley Street) occupies one of the city's first fire halls. The old Fire Hall No. 4 was constructed in 1859 and rebuilt in 1903. In 1919, the Alumnae Theatre was founded as a drama club by female graduates of the University of Toronto. In 1972, it was saved from demolition, and architect Ron Thom transformed it into an intimate space that is enjoyed equally by actors and audience, presenting a mixture of classic and contemporary plays.

Extending south from Queen to the Esplanade, Berkeley is a mix of

BELOW:
all the world's a stage on Berkeley Street.

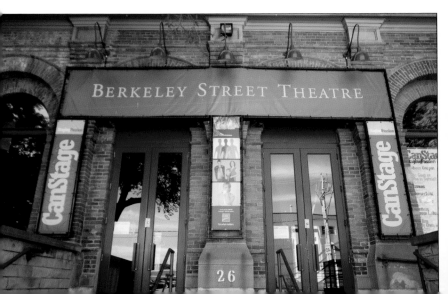

homes built in the 1870s that lie between Adelaide and King streets, and grander Georgian-style buildings at Berkeley and King streets – a reminder that King Street was Toronto's first commercial street.

The **Joey and Toby Tanenbaum Opera Centre** ⑬ (227 Front Street East) is part of a 19th-century factory and warehouse complex built by the Consumers' Gas Company between 1886 and 1892. The Imperial Oil Opera Theatre (originally 251 Front Street East) was the company's purifying house, and was designed like an early Christian basilica. Some suggest that the high Gothic roof was intended to lift off without destroying the building's walls, should an explosion occur.

The Canadian Opera Company purchased both buildings in 1985 and embarked on a massive restoration project to provide office, rehearsal and storage space.

Parliament Street is one of Toronto's most historic streets. Though there is scant evidence now, the first parliament buildings of Upper Canada were built in 1797 at the corner with Front Street.

During the War of 1812 American troops burned them down and, when the British eventually marched into Washington DC, they reciprocated, torching government buildings there, including the White House.

In the Neighbourhood

At the foot of Berkeley Street, The Esplanade is the main east–west thoroughfare of the **St Lawrence Neighbourhood**. Once again a tree-lined boulevard, it was conceived as a grand waterfront promenade, "where the people of Toronto would come to sport their Sunday best". This changed when the city turned the land over to the railways, which in turn attracted industry. St Lawrence became one of Toronto's most prominent industrial centres,

until the late 1940s, when industries began moving elsewhere.

Thankfully, in the early 1970s, it was decided to reclaim this badly neglected neighbourhood, and urban planners flock here to study one of the world's most successful revived residential areas, where significant landmarks sit alongside housing cooperatives, condominiums and artfully converted warehouses with trendy lofts, designer and film studios, boutiques and bistros.

The Distillery District

One of Old Toronto's most ambitious projects has been the transformation of the Gooderham and Worts Distillery into a cultural hotbed. The **Distillery Historic District** ⑭ (55 Mill Street; tel: 416-866 8687, www.thedistillerydistrict.com; subway: King) occupies what was once the largest distillery in the British Empire. Founded in 1832, the 44 buildings of this national historic site sprawl between Parliament and Cherry streets, the best-preserved collection of Victorian industrial architecture in North America.

Map on page 130

It's a dog's life at Mona's Dog Boutique (Trinity Street, tel: 416-361 9381) in the Distillery District.

BELOW: lights, camera, action in the Distillery District.

Map on page 130

TIP

Take an unusual tour around the Distillery District on a Segway, a type of motorised scooter. After a 30-minute training session small groups can explore the area with a guide. Contact Segway @ The Distillery, tel: 416-642 0008 or, 1-866-405 8687.

BELOW: exotic glass art at the Sandra Ainsley Gallery.

After more than 150 years in operation, the distillery closed in 1990 and, over the next decade, became Canada's number one film location – more than 800 productions have been filmed here, including Hollywood hits such as *Chicago* and *Cinderella Man*.

In 2001, a local company, experienced in historic restorations, purchased the complex and turned it into a burgeoning entertainment district. The maze of limestone and brick buildings, connected by cobbled walkways and courtyards, now house artists' and dance studios, art galleries, performance spaces, boutiques, restaurants and cafés as well as a microbrewery.

One of the first tenants in 2002 was the **Sandra Ainsley Gallery** (Cooperage Building; tel: 416-214 9490), showcasing breathtaking glass art. The gallery has on display the work of contemporary artists from Canada, the United States and all over the world, such as Dale Chihuly, Martin Blank and Ben Edols and Kathy Elliott.

Enthusiasts of fine art photogra-phy should head for the **Corkin Shopland Gallery** (Pure Spirits Building, tel: 416-979 1980), which represents some of Canada's best proponents of photographic art.

Adding to the buzz, Toronto's highly acclaimed **Soulpepper Theatre** (tel: 416-203 6264) is partnering a local college's theatre department to convert Tank Houses 9 and 10 into a shared permanent facility – the Young Centre for the Performing Arts (at the corner of Mill and Cherry streets), which includes five performing arts spaces, along with teaching and rehearsal studios.

Nearby Tank House 4, west of the main centre, will be the Baillie Centre, home to Soulpepper's education team, resident artists' offices, rehearsal halls, and set, paint and prop workshops.

A year-round calendar of events at the district includes the Distillery Jazz Festival, dance, comedy, music, antiques shows, vintage auto shows and fun outdoor exhibitions. It's a winning combination that keeps Torontonians coming back. ❏

RESTAURANTS, BARS & CAFES

Restaurants

George
111 Queen Street East, (at Jarvis Street). Tel: 416-863 6006. Open: D only Tues–Sat. $$$$
Situated in the Verity Club for Women, but open to the public, George takes small plate tapas to a new level. With a menu divided into three sections plus dessert, diners make up their own tasting menus. Dishes cover a lot of ground – a sheaf of red romaine lettuce with a crab mousse and hints of avocado drizzled with a miso dressing is as beautiful as it is exciting. Rabbit is perfectly cooked and succulent short ribs with a slab of foie gras are heavenly. Desserts are more mainstream. Magnificent outdoor dining in the summer; indoors, hardwood floors, exposed brick and beams give an inviting feel.

Hiro Sushi
171 King Street East (at Jarvis Street). Tel: 416-304 0550. Open: L & D Tues–Fri, D only Sat. $$$
This unpretentious sushi bar serves some of the freshest, most creative sushi in Toronto. Those in-the-know sit at the sushi bar and leave their choices up to Hiro. His inventive omakase dinners change weekly and always include flawless sushi. Smooth home-made soy sauce and pickled ginger are lovely compliments. Saki is available from a short list. Service is attentive but unobtrusive.

Jamie Kennedy Wine Bar
9 Church Street (at Front Street). Tel: 416-362 1957. Open: L & D daily. $$
Renowned chef Jamie Kennedy has been cooking exceptional food in Toronto for more than 20 years. His tapas-style wine bar churns out appetiser-sized portions of interesting dishes; his French fries and flat breads, with ever-changing dips, are famous. In the main restaurant, his creative approach to local ingredients shines; olive oil poached halibut and slow grilled rib eye are outstanding. Service is scattered but the food is worth it. No reservations in the wine bar.

Perigee
Distillery Historic District, Cannery Building, 55 Mill Street, Suite. 260 (at Parliament Street). Tel: 416-364 1397. Open: D only Tues–Sat. $$$$
Tucked away in the 19th-century Distillery Historic District, this unique room sets tables around an open kitchen where chef Pat Riley and his team create multi-course tasting menus suited to individual customers' tastes. They even take allergies into account. It's a foodie's dream, discussing ingredients and watching the dishes emerge – a mosaic of charcuterie or an avant-garde Caesar salad. Exciting options include veal cheek in caper sauce with sweetbreads or squab paired with figs and foie gras sauce. For dessert, how about whipped chocolate granité dressed in candied lime and salt crystals?

Romagna Mia Osteria Pizzeria
106 Front Street East (at Jarvis Street). Tel: 416-363 8370. Open: L & D Mon–Fri, D only Sat–Sun. $$$
From the checked table-cloths to the occasional table-hopping guitarist, this casual family style restaurant feels a lot like Old Italy. Featuring authentic fare from the Emilia Romagna region, the rich risottos are famous (and award winning) and fresh pastas are inventive and change frequently. The lasagna is the best in Toronto. Excellent wine list favouring Italian reds.

Starfish
100 Adelaide Street East (at Jarvis Street). Tel: 416-366 7827. Open: L & D Mon–Sat. $$$$
A jewel of a fish restaurant, where oysters are the speciality. Owner Patrick McMurray is the World Oyster Shucking champion and a fount of oyster and fish lore. The bar is perfect for savouring succulent bivalves with a glass of good white wine. Seafood dishes, such as roasted black cod, are creatively prepared and perfectly cooked. Those who don't like fish can choose between a rib-eye steak and a duck confit. Salads and desserts are superb.

Bars & Cafes

Balzac's Coffee Roastery
55 Mill Street. Tel: 416-207 1709
Fantastic coffee and excellent desserts make this one of the best coffee houses in Toronto.

b espresso bar
111 Queen Street East, Suite 102. Tel: 416-886 2111
A popular local coffee house.

C'est What
67 Front Street East. Tel: 416-867 9499
Pub with a live music section and a restaurant/café area; craft beers and good wines.

PRICE CATEGORIES

Prices for three-course dinner per person with a half-bottle of house wine:
$ = under $25
$$ = $25–50
$$$ = $50–70
$$$$ = more than $70

THE ELGIN AND WINTER GARDEN THEATRES

An architectural marvel and the world's last operating double-decker theatre

Intended as a flagship for Marcus Loew's chain of Canadian vaudeville theatres, Loew's Yonge Street Theatre opened to great fanfare in December 1913. Two months later, Toronto – indeed, Canada – had its first rooftop theatre, with the opening of Loew's Roof Garden Theatre. The entire complex, built at a cost of $500,000, featured one theatre stacked seven storeys above the other. Designed by noted architect, Thomas White Lamb, to support Loew's motto, "We sell tickets to theatres, not shows", the architecture and decor aimed to engage theatre-goers. Some of the world's greatest actors, singers and comedians have performed here.

Loew epitomised the American rags to riches success story. Born into a poor Jewish family in New York, in 1870, he worked hard to save his pennies. His first acquisitions, in the late 1800s, were penny arcades. Soon after, in partnership with others, he began to acquire nickelodeons (cinemas that charged a nickel admission fee), and in 1904 formed Loews Theatres.

Initially, the theatres offered performances of between eight and ten vaudeville acts, interspersed with newsreels and a silent movie, before focusing solely on cinematic shows. To secure a supply of movies, Loew purchased a failing film production company and then, together with Louis B. Mayer and Samuel Goldwyn, formed Metro-Goldwyn-Mayer (MGM) in 1924.

When Loew died in 1927, his was the largest cinema chain in the US, with 125, mostly opulent, theatres and another 24 under construction.

ABOVE: During the restoration, which began in 1987, concrete was removed from the orchestra pit, the plaster decorations on the opera boxes, the proscenium and balcony were recreated and regilted, and the original colour scheme was reinstated.

BELOW: The L-shaped complex occupies almost a city block, with a long narrow lobby extending back from Yonge Street more than 50 metres (165 ft), to the auditorium on Victoria Street. The stained glass doors were reproduced from photographs of the 1913 originals.

THE REBIRTH OF THE ELGIN

By the 1960s, the Elgin had become one of the city's foremost movie houses. The Canadian premieres of two of the most lauded MGM movies, *The Wizard of Oz* and *Gone With the Wind*, were held at the venue in 1939 and 1940 respectively.

New owners decided to convert the Elgin for Cinerama. The opera boxes, proscenium arch and cartouche were torn out, along with the front of the balcony, and the orchestra pit was filled with concrete. But, ironically, Cinerama's popularity waned by the time the work was complete, so the Elgin reverted to showing low-grade movies. When it finally closed, it was in a desperate state – so much had been removed or damaged, and up to 27 layers of paint covered the original colours.

Thankfully, in 1981, the Ontario Heritage Foundation came to the rescue, purchasing the entire building. This led to the commencement of the largest restoration project of its kind in Canada and the designation of the Elgin and Winter Garden theatres as a national historic site.

The lobby was the first area to be restored, and while money was being raised for the rest of the $29-million restoration, a Montreal production of *Cats* was brought to the Elgin in 1984. The producers had been looking for a venue that did not object to the entire theatre being painted black. This was the only theatre where another layer of paint was not going to make much difference. The four-month run extended for two years, and introduced more than 2 million people to the theatre. When *Cats* finally closed, the serious renovations began in 1987.

Using drawings and photographs found in the archives at New York's Central Library, the Elgin was faithfully renovated. More than 300,000 sheets of wafer-thin aluminium leaf were used in the seven-step process of regilding the plaster detail. And, as in 1913, all of the finishes were covered with a patina glazing that gave them an aged, mellow appearance.

Twice-weekly guided tours (tel: 416-314 2901; Thurs and Sat; admission fee) introduce visitors to the colourful history and remarkable restoration of the historic site.

RIGHT: The interior of the Elgin Theatre has been lovingly and faithfully restored to maintain the original grandeur of the performance space, which has gilded plaster details, faux marble finishes, red damask wall fabrics and a crimson carpet. Just outside the Corinthian columned lobby is an unusual exterior box office, still in use today.

RIGHT: Fittingly for a theatre, although for economic reasons, all was not as it appeared. The seemingly marbled fluted columns in the lobby, for example, were made of steel and covered by scagliola, an imitation marble made from plaster. The only real marble was – and is – at the base of the pillars, on the radiator caps, and on the treads of the sweeping Grand Staircase. The staircase connects the two theatres, spanning the equivalent of seven storeys.

ABOVE: The original Winter Garden Theatre auditorium seats were removed in the 1950s and when the restoration began substitutes needed to be found. Suitable replacements were located in the United States, in Chicago's renowned Biograph Theatre. The Biograph was notorious because it was where the gangster, John Dillinger was ambushed and shot by FBI agents in 1934. The shooting occurred just after he had seen a Clark Gable movie.

RIGHT: Seven storeys above the Elgin is the Winter Garden Theatre, with its whimsical decor, an excellent example of the Arts and Crafts movement. It had a rooftop garden in full bloom, with hand-painted garden scenes on its walls, columns were disguised as tree trunks, and the ceiling was a jungle of real beech leaves, cotton blossoms and pretty garden lanterns. The decorative leaves on the ceiling were rustled by carefully positioned small oscillating fans.

OPPOSITE PAGE TOP LEFT: Clarence Willard appeared as a novelty act during the vaudeville years.

OPPOSITE PAGE TOP RIGHT: During the restoration, an eight-storey backstage addition was built, with cascading lobbies, lounges, studios and rehearsal space. Since the grand opening in 1989, 76 years after the original opening of Loew's Yonge Street Theatre, Toronto audiences are once again flocking to the two beautiful Edwardian theatres.

OPPOSITE PAGE CENTRE: Husband and wife team, George Burns and Gracie Allen recreated parts of their vaudeville act for radio, and for a TV show in the 1950s.

OPPOSITE PAGE BOTTOM: Combining a desirable address with lower costs, Marcus Loew purchased the narrowest piece of land he could find on Yonge Street, in downtown Toronto, and a much wider – but less expensive – lot immediately behind, on Victoria Street.

ON STAGE

During vaudeville's heyday, both theatres accommodated the same productions. The continuous daylong show at the Elgin, with its cheap ticket prices, was geared to the masses, while the Winter Garden catered to Toronto's upper crust who purchased reserved seats for the evening's single performance.

Audiences flocked to see everything from the wackiest of acts to legendary performers, such as George Burns, Gracie Allen and Milton Berle.

In the 1920s, the movies took over – first silent, then talking. With the rapid decline in vaudeville's popularity, the Winter Garden closed in 1928 and remained boarded up, like a time capsule, for over 60 years.

After a successful reopening with a production of *Side by Side* by Sondheim, in 1989, most of the Winter Garden's productions have been Canadian, showcasing the work of some of the country's best artists, such as, Louise Pitre in *Piaf* and the comedic one-woman shows of writer/performer Sandra Shamus. Sarah McLachlan, Loreena McKennitt and Céline Dion, the New York City Ballet and the all-male Ballet Trocadero de Monte Carlo have also graced its stage.

THE WINTER GARDEN

The rediscovery of the 1,000-seat Winter Garden Theatre must have been like coming across a time capsule – albeit a filthy one, since years of dirt had been funnelled up the Grand Staircase. After carefully documenting everything, including every inch of wall surface, the branches and lanterns, the restorers decided that the best way to clean the hand-painted walls without removing the original paint was with bread dough. This labour-intensive process took four months, used up 680 kg (1,500 lbs) of dough, and restored 70 percent of the paintwork from 1914 .

Another challenge, which occupied 200 volunteers for years, was the harvesting, preserving, painting and fireproofing of 4,383 branches of beech leaves, before suspending them from the ceiling. Unfortunately an infestation of tent caterpillars and drought conditions, had destroyed many of the original leaves and branches, so a manufacturer in Hong Kong, which supplied the Royal Ontario Museum with its forest foliage, was contracted to supply the extra branches needed. And, since only 39 of the original 145 ceiling lanterns remained, volunteers were drafted in to recreate more, working with 40,000 glass beads.

The Winter Garden's renovations were further complicated by the absence of the elevators, which were being carefully overhauled elsewhere. Consequently, all supplies had to be either carried up the Grand Staircase or hoisted up the fire escape.

THE BEACHES

This laid-back neighbourhood really does have the best of both worlds, with peaceful streets and a lovely beachfront right on the doorstep of the city

One of the joys of Toronto is that you can escape the urban feel even within the city's boundaries – just drive east past Woodbine Avenue to the area known as The Beaches. This somewhat insulated neighbourhood includes 3 km (2 miles) of Lake Ontario beachfront, and there's an entirely different atmosphere and slower tempo here than in the rest of the city, with people strolling, cycling or rollerblading along the wooden boardwalk bordering the lake; there even seems to be more cafés per citizen than in any other part of the city.

The neighbourhood's roots as a resort area are evident in the nice old clapboard houses lining the narrow streets, and you could easily mistake the laid-back residents for relaxed vacationers. The short stretch of Queen Street East that dissects the area is lined with an intriguing mix of independent – sometimes quirky – boutiques, pubs and restaurants, and a local cinema shows quality films. All of this gives the neighbourhood its small-town feel – in fact, viewers of the public television network, TVOntario, voted this stretch of Queen the "Best Main Street" in the province.

But some complain that the area lacks the interesting ethnic mix of other parts of the city, and say it's too dominated by well-to-do Anglo-Saxons. There is some truth to this, despite the slightly dishevelled feel of the area, mostly because of soaring property prices and the appeal of living near the water. There are young professionals and families, who began moving here in the late 1970s, but there are also hippies, artists and students living in houses divided into apartments.

Some of the city's illustrious personalities grew up here, including

Map on pages 144–5

LEFT: relaxing on Woodbine Beach.
BELOW: little beachcombers.

pianist Glenn Gould and film director Norman Jewison – his father owned a dry goods store at 1925 Queen Street, and the family home was on nearby Lee Avenue. Comedian John Candy went to Neil McNeil high school on Victoria Park Avenue. Some people call the area simply "The Beach", but it's more generally referred to in the plural form because the lakefront is made up of three separately named beaches: Balmy Beach to the east, the central Kew Beach and Woodbine Beach to the west, given their titles in the late 1800s when the area really was three separate villages.

The main attraction here, of course, for both Torontonians and visitors to the city, has always been the beach and its wooden boardwalk. For more than two centuries, people have come here during the summer months to escape the city's oppressive heat and to enjoy the

The pretty clapboard cottages at the Beaches are among the city's most sought after real estate.

expansive views and breezes from the lake. It can be crowded during the summer with people walking their dogs and riding their bikes along the boardwalk, or sunbathing or playing volleyball on the beach.

There are lifeguards on duty, and the water quality of the lake is carefully monitored by city officials, who are are proud of earning a coveted Blue Flag several years in a row. However, E. coli levels occasionally rise above the acceptable mark and then swimming is prohibited. Most people choose not to swim anyway, aware that the beaches are located on the shoreline of a large industrial city.

Summer is the best time to visit or come in late spring or early autumn. At other times the cooling breezes from the lake become chilling, when only the very hardy will enjoy a beachfront or Queen Street East walk. The best way to get here

is on the 501 Queen streetcar, or you could take a bus from the Main Street subway station to Wineva Avenue and Queen Street East.

Kew Beach Gardens

The best starting point for a Beaches tour is **Kew Beach Gardens ❶**, between Waverley Road and Lee Avenue. This is the heart of the area, and a great place to enjoy outdoor concerts in the summer, toss a ball or a frisbee, or relax over a sandwich or an ice-cream cone. (For a good take-away burger or a milkshake try Lick's Homeburgers at 1960 Queen Street East.)

Kew Beach Gardens was created in 1879 by a wealthy property owner named Joseph Williams, who owned 8 hectares (20 acres) of land at this spot. He developed the park in honour of Kew Gardens in London, referring to it as "The Canadian Kew Gardens". You can tour the

home Williams built himself in the park in 1901 on Lee Avenue, which until 1995 was the house where the groundskeeper lived.

The Beaches area was first settled in 1793, but growth really didn't take place until the mid- to late 1800s when roads were developed, and stagecoaches, horse-drawn streetcars and the rail service reached the area. At this time, Kew Beach Gardens and Kew Beach were part of a small village that had schools, churches, a post office and a fire department.

Many Torontonians came to stay at residences built just for summer use, others pitched tents. The numbers of people coming during the summer months increased after the first electric streetcar lines began running in the early 1890s, and ferry boats brought in visitors from the centre of the city.

Developers took advantage of this influx of summer visitors, and in

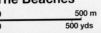

Map on pages below

Kew Gardens House, the groundskeeper's home at Kew Beach Gardens.

BELOW: the only way to travel at the Beaches.

The Beaches

| 0 | 500 m |
| 0 | 500 yds |

There are cycling and skating paths beside the boardwalk.

1907 constructed a huge amusement park on the lakefront between Kew Beach and Balmy Beach. Balmy Beach village had been settled by Adam Wilson, a wealthy landowner who owned a large waterfront lot, and in 1876 built small cottages and summer residences here. This area also had its own schools, churches and social clubs. When the amusement park was torn down in 1925, more streets and houses were built, linking the two communities.

One of the main entertainment draws here in the summer is the popular **Beaches International Jazz Festival**, held for a several-day stretch in mid- or late July every year. During the event, the streets are jammed with music fans and people who come for the festive atmosphere. Dozens of performers and bands play in back-to-back free concerts throughout the area, whether at the Main Stage in Kew Beach Gardens, along the boardwalk, on street corners and on rooftops along Queen Street. For more information and a schedule see www.beachesjazz.com.

Sporting passions

Some vestiges of the Beaches' British colonial roots and its era as separate villages can be found in the enthusiasm for lawn bowling around here. There are two clubs – one at the privately run Balmy Beach Canoe Club, which stands where the original club was built in 1905, and another at Kew Beach Gardens.

The Beaches has always been a popular spot for outdoor sports. Cycling enthusiasts can take advantage of the bike trail that runs parallel to the boardwalk. It follows along the shoreline of Lake Ontario across the city to the western edge, albeit with a few detours along busy roads. (There are no bike rental shops in the Beaches area.)

At the western edge of the Beaches alongside the boardwalk is the Olympic-size **Donald D. Summerville swimming pool** ❷ on the edge of Woodbine Beach Park and Ashbridge's Bay Park. If you're concerned about potential poor water quality in Lake Ontario, the outdoor Summerville swimming pool is a great place to cool off – and the pool is consistently voted one of the best outdoor pools in the city, thanks to its size, cleanliness and views of the lake and the city skyline. Popularity comes at a price, however – the pool can get very crowded on hot summer weekends, and some complain it's too much of a pick-up scene.

Further along the shoreline, beach volleyball tournaments often take place on the beaches of Ashbridge's Bay Park, where there are also three softball fields and a rugby pitch.

Along the boardwalk

The boardwalk continues on to **Woodbine Beach** ❸ and **Ashbridge's Bay Park** ❹, an often very crowded part of the beachfront, popular with families with children, and groups of friends, who come to splash in the water or play beach

games. A scenic lookout point gives great views across the lake and to the city in the west. For a snack or light meal, try the **Boardwalk BBQ Pub**, at the foot of Lakeshore Boulevard and Coxwell Avenue, and set back from the beachfront. Its menu is essentially fast food, and the plastic chairs on the outdoor terrace are uncomfortable, but there is a great view – and free parking.

These grounds and the beach are a prime location for viewing the sensational firework displays out on the water on Victoria Day (Monday preceding 25 May) or on Canada Day (1 July). Be prepared for a crush, though – there can be as many as 80,000 here to watch the show.

Loyalist origins

The name Ashbridge's comes from Sarah Ashbridge, the first settler in the area. She was a Quaker widow and United Empire Loyalist from Philadelphia who settled on a large estate here in 1793, the year the city of Toronto was formed. She joined a steady stream of Loyalists supporting the British in the American Revolution, who decided to desert their stakes in the US and migrate north to Canada.

At that time, Lieutenant-General John Simcoe was establishing Toronto as a city, dividing areas into large estates, and laying down central roadways such as the present-day Queen Street and Yonge Street. The Ashbridges were to remain here on the lakefront for years as prosperous farmers, surrounded by what was essentially a vast marshland. Sarah's sons defended Toronto as soldiers in the War of 1812, and a family home further west at Queen and Connaught streets still stands.

Urban development

As the years passed, the marshlands disappeared as city officials filled it in to create building land for indus-

trial purposes, but since the 1970s planners have protected this rough, man-made land as a public park.

These days, urban development is taking place north of Woodbine Beach, across Lake Shore Boulevard. The site of the Woodbine Racetrack, which was torn down several years ago, is now home to a burgeoning luxury townhouse development and a cinema complex, and by the end of the decade they will be joined by a huge $310 million retail and entertainment centre with a hotel, a performance hall, restaurants, bars and shops. There are also plans for a Canadian Music Hall of Fame.

It's not yet clear whether all the social and economic gyrations from this development will spill past Woodbine Avenue and into the Beaches proper, disrupting its valued tranquillity and its residential feel.

Places to eat

It is hoped that new development might bring one thing the area does need – a wider selection of good restaurants. Queen Street East is lined

Map on pages 144–5

Blue Flag awards are given by a Denmark-based environmental group and signify that a beach is clean – it must meet clean water standards at least 80 percent of the summer. Four Toronto beaches – Woodbine, Cherry, Ward's Island and Hanlan's Point – have met these standards. For information, or to find out the daily measurements of water quality, visit www.Toronto beaches.ca

BELOW: luxury townhouses.

Map
on pages
144–5

The cathedral-like building of the R.C. Harris Filtration Plant is surrounded by several acres of park.

BELOW: a couple stroll along the boardwalk.

with sushi restaurants, pubs, cafés, hamburger joints and their ilk, but this is not an area for those looking for a top-notch meal. However, for one of the best and richest ice-cream cones in the city, try **Ed's Real Scoop** (No. 2224); and a good place to enjoy a beer and do some people watching is on the outdoor patio of the **Lion Pub on the Beach** (No. 1958). You can nibble on some fusion tapas at one of the only trendy bar-restaurants in the area, the **Lounge Bar** (No. 2066). For a casual meal or take away visit the excellent **White Brothers Fish and Chips** (No. 2248) – be sure to try the homemade tartare sauce.

Solar and water power

Just a couple of doors down from here is one of the world's few solar-powered laundromats – the award-winning **Beach Solar Laundromat** at 2240 Queen Street East. It keeps its utility bills 30 percent lower by using rooftop panels to preheat water, and the air inside the building is kept cool by running municipal cold water through a network of coils in the ceiling.

The water comes from a building just a few blocks away, and it is one of the city's most admired pieces of architecture. The imposing **R.C. Harris Filtration Plant** ❺ can be found at the far eastern end of the Beaches, at Queen and Victoria Park Avenue. It's an art deco gem, built between 1937 and 1941, and is the city's largest water filtration and purification plant, providing Toronto with about 45 percent of the water it needs each day. The building was named after the city's director of public works at the time, Rowland Caldwell Harris. It's been nicknamed the "Palace of Purification" because of its dramatic design with vast art deco halls, marble floors and opulent attention to detail.

The place is a perfect blend of style and function: it works purifying water from the lake 24 hours a day. The water is treated and chlorinated inside the building before being pumped out to the city. Toronto is one of the first cities in the world to use chlorine to treat water and is considered a leader in the field today.

The building is described by author and poet Michael Ondaatje in his novel *In the Skin of a Lion*; and its exterior is used frequently as a setting for TV and film locations. Unfortunately, due to terrorism concerns and at the time of writing, public tours have been suspended.

The streets around the filtration plant, such as Fallingbrook Drive and Fallingbrook Crescent, are lined with the large homes of well-off residents. Five or six blocks west along Queen to Beech Street, then north brings you to Pine Crescent and Glen Manor Drive, a highly sough-after and peaceful residential neighbourhood of beautiful homes with **Glen Stewart Park** in the centre – a tranquil ravine filled with trees and shrubs with one of the city's few remaining natural streams running through it. ❑

RESTAURANTS, BARS & CAFES

Restaurants

Bonjour Brioche
812 Queen Street East (at Broadview Avenue). Tel: 416-406 1250. Open: B, Br & L Tues–Sun. **$**
This cheery French brunch spot entices with fresh baguettes, buttery brioche and the best croissants in the city – be quick, they're usually gone by mid-afternoon. Savoury tarts and quiches abound. Scrambled eggs with smoked salmon is divine, as is the cinnamon-laced baked French toast. You can eat on the adorable side-patio during the warmer months; inside the aroma of fresh pastries tempts all year-round.

Gio Rana's Really Really Nice Restaurant
1220 Queen Street East (at Leslie Street). Tel: 416-469 5225. Open: D only daily. **$$**
Discreetly located in a former bank building, the busy open kitchen is the star feature of this cosy Italian eatery.
Mis-matched chairs and cheap-chic chandeliers only add to the charm. The menu features robust flavours from the South of Italy and freshly made pastas.
There's an eclectic wine list and the service is friendly and unpretentious.

Il Fornello
1968 Queen Street East (at Waverly Road). Tel: 416-691 8377. Open: L & D daily. **$$**
Gourmet thin-crusted pizzas, baked in a traditional wood-burning oven, shine on a menu of familiar Italian favourites. The fun, casual atmosphere appeals to couples and families alike.
The weekend brunch buffets feature eggs benny, salads and pizzas. It's among the best of the Il Fornello chain. Many other locations around the Greater Toronto area. Affordable wines.

Sauvignon
1862 Queen Street East (at Woodbine Avenue). Tel: 416-686 1998. Open: D only daily. **$$**
This is the best of the Beaches bistros, a cosy, intimate place with a menu that features carefully prepared French fusion fare. The seared halibut and garlic-braised rapini on creamy herb polenta are highly recommended, and the roast rack of lamb with garlic mashed potatoes and sautéed vegetables is another popular choice. Fabulous home-made desserts include a decadent chocolate almond cake and a tarte citron in a crisp pastry shell. Wines are reasonably priced.

Tomi-Kro
1214 Queen Street East (at Leslie Street). Tel: 416-466 6677. Open: D only Tues–Sat. **$$$**
A Beaches favourite, this pleasant restaurant has exposed brick walls and gleaming hardwood floors complimented by retro lighting. An eclectic menu offers well prepared dishes with fun fusion accents. Juicy muscovy duck breast is positively divine, as are chocolate-rich desserts. The wine list is interesting and not over-priced and the service is friendly.

Verveine
1097 Queen Street East (at Winnifred Avenue). Tel: 416-405 9906. Open: Br Sat–Sun, D only Mon–Fri. **$$**
This relaxed neighbourhood eatery is one of the few places where you can expect fine dining in the Beaches. Popular for celebrations, the room features a big bar and a stunning reclaimed fireplace. The friendly owner is always on hand to give a warm welcome. Order succulent duck breasts pan-fried with crispy skin and served on top of couscous with beets. Seared scallops with a leek risotto is a signature dish. Brunch features a marvellous smoked salmon with truffles and scrambled eggs.

Bars & Cafes

Remarkable Bean Tea & Coffee Company
2242 Queen Street East. Tel: 416-690 2420
A highly rated Beaches coffee house. Vegetarian snacks.

Quigley's Pub and Bistro
2232 Queen Street East. Tel: 416-699-9998
A three-tier patio one block from the board-walk, a place to enjoy great food and live entertainment.

Miofrio
2169 Queen Street East. Tel: 416-693 7261
Recharge and relax with fresh blended juices, aromatic coffees and a selection of teas.

Castro's Lounge
2116 Queen Street East. Tel: 416-699 8272
Locals' favourite, with 97 brands of beer, none commercial. Great wings.

Murphy's Law
1702 Queen Street East. Tel: 416-690-5516
Three floors and a rooftop patio highlight this Irish pub. Great selection of single malts and Irish whiskeys.

PRICE CATEGORIES

Prices for three-course dinner per person with a half-bottle of house wine:
$ = under $25
$$ = $25–50
$$$ = $50–70
$$$$ = more than $70

UNIVERSITY AND THE ANNEX

Seat of the Ontario government and home to one of
Canada's premier seats of learning, this part of
the city has a somewhat rarefied atmosphere

Cutting a wide swathe north-
ward through the downtown
area, **University Avenue**
heads towards the legislative buildings like a processional route. South
of College Street it's lined by modern blocks, largely unremarkable
except for the fact that many of
them house hospitals – five of them
in a row on the west side alone. The
sound of ambulance sirens frequently cuts through the general city
noise and bustle down here. North
of College Street the atmosphere
changes as concrete and glass give
way to an area where dignified old
buildings set the scene on streets
that are full of academics, students
and government workers and where
traffic noise is less intrusive.

The Legislature

Here, the avenue becomes Queen's
Park Circle, taking the traffic out and
around the well-manicured lawns
and fine old trees of **Queen's Park**.
This is the location of the **Ontario
Legislature ❶** (tel: 416-325 7500;
www.ontla.on.ca; open Mon–Fri
8.30am–6.30pm, also Sat & Sun
9am–4.30pm from Victoria Day to
Labour Day; guided tours; free; subway: Queen's Park), seat of the government of the province since 1893.

The Romanesque Revival building, designed by Richard Waite in

pink-tinged stone, is sturdy and
impressive – certainly a place to
inspire confidence, whoever its
incumbents happen to be – its central block with monumental arches
and towers, flanked by two equally
stately wings.

Guided tours take visitors
through the lobby and up the grand
carved-oak staircase to the richly
decorated Chamber, where parliament sits; when it's in session during spring and autumn visitors can
watch the debates from the public

Map
on page
152

LEFT: University of
Toronto building.
BELOW: the police
memorial in front of
the Whitney Block.

The statues in front of the Legislature include one of Sir John A. MacDonald (1815–91), who emigrated to Ontario from Glasgow, Scotland. In 1820 he was elected to the Legislature and became the first Prime Minister of Canada after playing a leading role in the country's Confederation in 1867.

galleries. The two wings, with their lofty corridors, are quite different from each other due to a fire in 1909 which destroyed the west wing. Rather than restore its original decor, it was fitted out entirely with pale Italian marble, while the east wing retains its original style, with pale walls picked out by dark wood pillars, floor and beams. The tour includes exhibits that follow the history of Ontario and give an insight into its culture. Portraits of former premiers and speakers of the house line the grand staircase and the walls of the east wing.

University of Toronto

Clustering around the Legislature are further government buildings, embassies and consulates, but dominating the surrounding streets, particularly on the west side, are the buildings of the St George campus of the **University of Toronto** ❷. The university, founded in 1827 as King's College and achieving university status in 1849, is the largest and one of the most prominent seats of learning in Canada, with 14 faculties including the arts, medicine, science, architecture, music, IT, engineering, education and theology. It comprises four colleges (University, New, Innis and Woodsworth), plus three federated universities and four federated colleges, and is loosely based on the college systems of Oxford and Cambridge in England, though colleges here have less autonomy.

The university also encompasses the Institute for Aerospace Studies in the northwest part of the city, the Dunlap Observatory at Richmond Hill and the Koffler Scientific Reserve at Jokers Hill.

An impressive list of achievements includes groundbreaking work in the medical field, including the discovery of insulin and the first electronic heart pacemaker, the

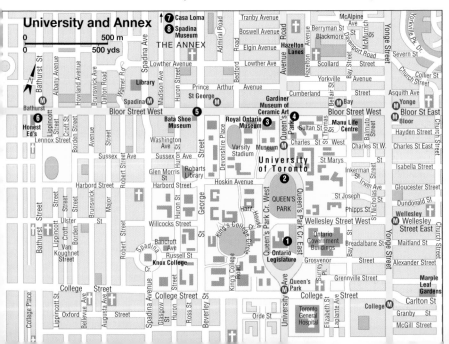

development of chemical lasers, contributions to aerospace technology, the establishment of the Royal Ontario Museum, the Canadian Opera Company, the Toronto Symphony and the Royal Conservatory of Music. This impressive record makes Toronto University very attractive to prospective students, many of whom come from abroad, and the university is currently in the throes of a huge expansion programme which will add 93,000 sq. metres (1 million sq. ft) of tuition and research space and additional student residences.

Front Campus

Although it's relatively young by European standards, the university area makes for a pleasant stroll, with a number of distinguished old buildings, particularly around the central lawn of the Front Campus. Here, stately University College and the classical-style Convocation Hall face each other on the north and south sides. Bounding the western edge of the lawn is the medieval-style Knox College building, where the **Nona Macdonald Visitors Centre** is geared mostly to the needs of students, tourists can also pick up a leaflet detailing some general information about the university.

There are more fine old buildings on Queen's Park, including ivy-clad Emmanuel College and the Faculty of Law. Of the notable modern buildings, the Robarts Library, west off Queen's Park along Hoskin Avenue, is an interesting composition in pale brick that witty Torontonians have likened to a giant turkey.

Further buildings extend the downtown campus west as far as Spadina Avenue, north to Bloor Street (where a Varsity sports ground is located) and south to College Street, and its most picturesque areas are much loved by film companies for location shooting. There are additional, more modern, campuses at Mississauga, 30 km (18 miles) west of Toronto and at Scarborough, about the same distance east of the downtown campus.

The Royal Ontario Museum

Queen's Park north of the Legislature is a delightful little park, where on warm days students relax in the shade of the trees, and black squirrels wait expectantly around people enjoying lunch at the picnic tables.

Walk north a little further and on the west side you'll see the huge building that is home to the **Royal Ontario Museum** ❸ (100 Queen's Park; tel: 416-586 5549; www.rom. on.ca; Mon–Thur 10am–6pm, to 9.30pm Fri; admission charge; subway: Museum).

The ROM, as it is popularly known, is in a state of flux at the time of writing due to a massive expansion project, aptly named **Renaissance ROM**, which is due to be completed towards the end of 2006. Already Canada's foremost international museum, with more than six million objects, the ROM

Map on page 152

Free walking tours of the St George campus are available, departing from the Nona Macdonald Visitors Centre on weekdays at 11am and 2pm and on weekends at 11am only (no tours on holiday weekends). There's no need to book unless you are in a group of more than 10 people, in which case you should call 416-978 5000.

BELOW: happy graduates from the University of Toronto.

will be expanded to house a total of 43 galleries and 19,880 sq. metres (214,000 sq. ft) of exhibition space.

A prominent feature will be the new Michael Lee-Chin Crystal, named in recognition of a $30 million gift from Michael Lee-Chin, which will contain six new galleries. Designed by the renowned architect Daniel Libeskind, the glittering aluminium and glass structure will send a starburst of prismatic points out from the north side of the building in a manner that has raised many Torontonian eyebrows.

Further gifts of $30 million from the government of Ontario and another $30 million from the federal government are enabling additional expansion, together with the renovation of the existing historic buildings. There are also plans to demolish the now unused planetarium that stands alongside the museum and sell the land to a developer for a block of condominiums, a controversial scheme that is defended by the museum as a means of raising even more funds for its improvement.

Inevitably, during the extensive rebuilding and renovation some galleries will be closed, so check before you visit. If you have children with you, for instance, make sure the excellent **Dinosaur Gallery** will be available. Canada's "Badlands", in Alberta, have proved to be of the best source of Cretaceous dinosaur skeletons in the world, and a large number of them have found their way into the ROM, where they are displayed in imaginative settings among Jurassic skeletons from Utah in the US.

The dioramas exhibit complete skeletons in realistic situations amid authentic landscapes. You will see meat-eating dinosaurs squaring up to each other for a fight or see how the plesiosaur and mosasaur would have swum through the shallow sea that once covered much of North America. With video stations to provide explanations along the way, this is the highlight of the Life Sciences and Palaeontology department.

Another exhibit that's popular with children is the **Bat Cave**, based on the St Clair cave in Jamaica, complete with a bat nursery in its

TIP

Admission to the ROM is free on Friday after 4.30pm, and discounts are available for special ticketed events and exhibitions. These include live music, lectures and film screenings.

BELOW: exhibits at the Dinosaur Gallery.

crevices and a reproduction of the twilight exodus of thousands of bats, off in search of food.

There are also excellent dioramas in the **Mammal Gallery**, while the **Evolution Gallery** groups examples of various types of animals together and explains how the ground beneath our feet can reveal the history of the planet and its life forms. There's a fascinating display of fossils from the Burgess Shale of British Columbia, which spawned the first animal life more than 545 million years ago.

The ROM has a first class range of oriental exhibits, including artefacts, textiles and costumes. The **Bishop White Gallery of Chinese Temple Art** is outstanding, and there are further areas containing Chinese and Korean art, gold and gemstones, and a Ming Tomb. European cultures are represented with exhibits from ancient Egypt, Greece and the Roman Empire, a reproduction of an Islamic town, the **Weinberg Judaica Collection**, a large collection of armour and weapons and displays of decorative and applied arts.

One area that should not be missed contains the galleries that cover the history of Canada, including the **Indigenous Peoples Gallery**, the **Sigmund Samuel Canadiana Galleries** and the **Ontario Archaeology Gallery**.

When Renaissance ROM is complete, there will be a good range of places to eat or just get a reviving beverage within the museum. Other visitor facilities include free use of wheelchairs, inexpensive pushchair (stroller) rental and a coat check where all visitors must check in extraneous baggage, such as shopping bags, backpacks and umbrellas, before entering the museum.

Ceramics treasurehouse

Across from the ROM is a modern building, and the decorated pottery motif above its entrance announces it as the home of the **Gardiner Museum of Ceramic Art ❹** (111 Queen's Park; tel: 416-586 8080; www.gardinermuseum.on.ca; Mon, Wed and Fri 10am–6pm, Tues and Thur am Sat–Sun 10am–5pm; admission charge; subway: Museum).

Map on page 152

Among the many distinguished graduates of the University of Toronto are several prime ministers of Canada, six nobel laureates, authors, scientists, the president of Latvia, and Daniel Libeskind, architect of the Renaissance ROM project.

BELOW:
decorative ceiling detail at the ROM.

Throwing pots in a museum is usually frowned upon, but aspiring potters inspired by the collections at the Gardiner Museum might like to call and enquire about the Clay Pit programme, in which professional potters run a variety of classes and workshops.

BELOW AND RIGHT:
books and blooms
for sale.

Established around 20 years ago, the basis of the museum is the priceless collection of financier and businessman George Gardiner and his wife Helen. Now a widow, Helen Gardiner is still the Honorary Chair of the museum.

Other pieces have been added and other collections have been donated – most recently the Robert Murray Bell and Ann Walker Bell Collection of Chinese blue and white porcelain, the Hans Syz Collection of European porcelain and the Aaron Milrad Collection of American, British and Canadian contemporary ceramics. Together, they provide a superb timeline of important developments in world ceramic art from ancient times up to the present and form the only museum of its kind in North America.

The ancient American pieces are particularly interesting, the Meissen services are exquisite, and there are fine examples of delftware, Italian maiolica, English slipware and earthenware, and translucent porcelain.

Modern pieces include Karen Dahl's wonderful *Cabbages and Kings* (1998), featuring incredibly realistic cabbages set on a brown paper-wrapped parcel, all made of clay, and the stunning piece by Roseline Delisle, in rich royal blue, that combines geometric shapes and a fluid imagery inspired by a ballet dancer. At the time of writing, the museum was closed for expansion and renovation and is set to re-open during 2006. A number of remarkable works of innovative ceramic art have been specially commissioned for the re-opening, including some modern works by First Nations potters, which will add to the already superlative permanent collection. If you are here around lunchtime, the **À la Carte at the Gardiner** restaurant is a good place for lunch, but it's quite small, so reservations are recommended.

If you walk north and east from here across Bloor Street, you enter the **Bloor–Yorkville** area, which borders the exclusive residential area of Rosedale *(see page 186)* and is renowned as one of Toronto's most upmarket shopping areas. Here you'll find some of the most

exclusive clothing and interior design boutiques in the city and the chic **Hazleton Lanes** mall. Mingle with visiting celebrities, or sit among the city's "ladies who lunch" at a pavement café in one of the leafy streets to watch the well-heeled passers-by, soak up the atmosphere and sniff the sweet smell of affluence wafting on the breeze. Bloor West is also a great place for restaurants and bars (*see page 163*), as long as you like them trendy and crowded.

The Annex

Beyond the ROM's north side – where its new entrance will be – on Bloor Street West you enter **The Annex**, one of Toronto's oldest suburbs. Until 1835, this was outside the city boundary – it ended at Bloor Street in those days – and is full of historic homes, the earliest of which can be identified by their red sandstone walls and fanciful Romanesque decorations.

In spite of its history and because of its proximity to the university the Annex has a youthful atmosphere

and is a great area to shop for art and crafts, secondhand books, used CDs and vintage fashions – **Divine Decadence**, upstairs at 136 Cumberland Street (tel: 416-324 9759; Mon–Sat 11am–6pm), has clothed such celebrities as Renée Zellweger, Celine Dion and Diana Krall.

Walk west along Bloor Street West to the St George intersection and you'll spot an unusual building that, apart from its triangular glass entrance, is reminiscent of a giant shoe box. This was a deliberate move on the part of architect Raymond Moriyama because his remit was to design a suitable home for the **Bata Shoe Museum** ❺ (327 Bloor Street West; tel: 416-979 7799; www.batashoemuseum.ca; Tues–Wed and Fri–Sat 10am–5pm, Thur 10am–8pm, Sun noon–5pm, also June–Aug Mon 10am–5pm; admission charge; subway: St George). Within you will find a truly fascinating journey (on foot, of course) through the history of footwear, starting with replicas of shoes from 6,000 years ago and covering shoes from just about every

Fancy footwear on display at the Bata Shoe Museum.

BELOW: the triangular glass entrance of the Bata Shoe Museum.

Tourism Toronto provides an excellent service to visitors who want a more in-depth view of the city than any sightseeing tour could provide. They have volunteer "greeters" who have first-hand knowledge of a particular area, and they walk you around their favourite spots. Tours are available for individuals, couples or groups of less than eight people. Call 416-338-2786 for information, or visit www.toronto.ca/tapto.

BELOW: out for a stroll on Bloor Street West.
RIGHT: driving through The Annex.

age, up to modern times. You'll see what kept ancient Egyptians, Greeks and Romans from getting their feet dirty, and be shocked by the astonishingly tiny size of the Chinese shoes from the time when the women's feet were bound to make them appear more dainty. Beautiful bejewelled footwear worn by Indian royalty is on show, alongside medieval European shoes with turned-up toes, foot sections from suits of armour with incredibly long points, and ornate Renaissance, baroque and rococo shoes. There are shoes with religious relevance, occupational footwear, such as spiked contraptions for tree-climbing, delicate dance shoes, clogs with wheels and skates, and a display relating to shoes in fairytales, including glass slippers, of course.

Displays change year by year, but some have included exploration of the Alaskan Coastal Cultures, including exhibits on loan from the Peter the Great Museum in St Petersburg, Russia, and the Star Turns exhibition.

Star Turns includes shoes that belonged to such stars as Jimi Hendrix, Gene Kelly, Phil Collins, Elizabeth Taylor, Madonna and Britney Spears, a pair of pink shoes that belonged to Diana, Princess of Wales (spares in case anything happened to the originals), Ronald McDonald's size 29s and a pair of size 20 basketball shoes that belonged to sportsman Shaquille O'Neal.

Celebrity footprints

Perhaps more interesting than the shoes themselves is discovering how small some celebrity feet are (or were). The footprints of stars, projected onto the floor, show a similar discrepancy between size of foot and celebrity status. These include David Bowie, Indira Gandhi, Kate Bush and the poignant single footprint of Terry Fox, the courageous Canadian who lost a leg to cancer and yet, in April 1980, inspired the world with his attempt to run across Canada from coast to coast to raise money for cancer research. Tragically, the disease prevented him from completing his run, but he ran from St John's, Newfoundland to Thunder Bay, Ontario (where he

died), at an astonishing rate of 42 km (26 miles) per day.

Terry Fox features in yet another display, which also contains shoes that once belonged to Elvis Presley, Picasso, Tiger Woods, Marilyn Monroe, Rudolf Nureyev and Sir Winston Churchill.

Further along Bloor, at the Bathurst Street intersection, is **Honest Ed's ❻** (581 Bloor Street, tel: 416-537 1574), one of the most famous stores in Toronto. The vast 14,864 sq. metre (160,000 sq. ft) emporium of bargain goods, heralded from the outside by hundreds of coloured lights and giant slogans ("Don't Just Stand There – Buy Something!"), is tacky with a sense of humour, full of cheap goods and some unusual items.

It was opened in 1948 by Ed Mirvish, whose empire now includes a number of Toronto's best theatres (*see pages 41 and 111*), and there's much theatrical memorabilia inside the store, including autographed photographs of many Hollywood stars. The area around Honest Ed's is now known as **Mirvish Village** and is home to an interesting range of shops, including antiques, art galleries, bookstores and restaurants. West from here is Koreatown (*see page 185*).

The northern Annex

The Annex stretches north from Bloor, and if you take Spadina Avenue north, you will pass the **Toronto Archives** (255 Spadina Avenue; tel: 416-397 5000; open Mon–Fri 9am–4.30pm, Sat 10am–4.30pm except July and Aug; free; subway: Dupont), repository of millions of documents, maps and photographs which chronicle the city's past. Special exhibitions are frequently staged here to highlight particular aspects of Toronto.

Every so often on your route to this point you will catch a glimpse of a particular hilltop building that excites a tremendous sense of curiosity. The towers and turrets of **Casa Loma ❼** (1 Austin Terrace, tel: 416-923 1171; www.casaloma.org; open: May–Oct daily 9.30am–4pm; admission charge; subway: Dupont) loom over the northern Annex like a

The Kiwanis Club is a global organisation that was founded in Detroit in 1915 and now has its HQ in Indianapolis. With 600,000 community-minded members worldwide, it does much work to benefit children, and a 2004 statement declared that they are "dedicated to changing the world one child and one community at a time".

BELOW: the towers and turrets of Casa Loma.

During World War II, when its manufacturing plant in England was bombed, the ASDIC device (a predecessor of the modern-day sonar) was produced in the basement of Casa Loma's stable block.

grandiose enchanted castle, a fairy-tale mansion set on a hilltop with a story of enormous success (and excess) and equally monumental bad fortune.

It was the dream home of Sir Henry Pellat, born in Ontario in 1859, a well-rounded and well-travelled individual who was ambitious in business, enthusiastically athletic, a passionate devotee of the arts, a philanthropist and a military man (his distinguished service earned him his knighthood).

In his twenties, Sir Henry founded the Toronto Electric Light Company and by the time he was in his thirties he was chairman of more than 20 companies, with interests encompassing insurance, mining, property, the Canadian Pacific Railway and a Niagara Falls power plant.

The vast fortune that resulted from these ventures enabled him, in 1911, to embark on the building of what was to become North America's finest private home. Canadian architect E.J. Lennox was hired to bring Pellatt's imaginative ideas to life, and in 1911 work began.

BELOW: the marble-floored Conservatory in Casa Loma.
RIGHT: the Great Hall.

Three years later a task force of 300 workmen had finished Casa Loma (the "house on the hill") at a total cost of $3.5million. Fanciful in the extreme, it features medieval-style battlements and turrets above walls of pale stone. The interior is a sumptuous array of wood panelling, intricate carvings and decorations, marble and fine furnishings, secret passages and every comfort that the early 20th century had to offer.

Dream turned sour

The idyllic lifestyle was not to last. One by one, Sir Henry's financial interests turned sour as electricity moved into public ownership and World War I had a far-reaching effect on how people invested their money. After occupying his dream home for just 10 years, Sir Henry was up to his medieval turrets in debt and the bank eventually fore-closed, forcing him to move into a small apartment. He tried to sell Casa Loma for a tiny fraction of its building cost, but its quirkiness had little appeal to any prospective purchaser and there were no takers.

Sir Henry could not even afford the annual taxes on the property, and it was eventually seized by the government, standing empty for years while an unresolved debate continued about how it should be used. There was even talk of tearing the whole thing down.

Fortunately, in 1937, the charitable organisation, the Kiwanis Club came up with the idea of restoring the building and opening it to the public. They have done a tremendous job here – a display on the third floor explains their work – and Casa Loma is now one of the city's major attractions. Had the tourist industry begun a few decades sooner, no doubt the tenacious Sir Henry Pellat would have been one of its early beneficiaries, and found a way to hang on to his grand lifestyle.

Casa Loma tour

Through the entrance you go first into the imposing, balconied **Great Hall** which has a sweeping staircase, fine fireplace and a few nice pieces of furniture – including a somewhat incongruous Wurlitzer organ. You can pick up handsets for the self-guided tour here. You proceed into the library and dining room, originally separate, but now one huge oak-floored area lined with bookshelves.

Leading off from here, and in complete contrast, is the lovely **Conservatory**, with Italian marble floor and Canadian marble lining the planters around the wall. It opens out into the beautiful gardens, restored by the Garden Club of Toronto.

Each of the three floors has a long central corridor – an idea Sir Henry borrowed from Windsor Castle. Off the one on the ground floor, called Peacock Alley, you can step into Sir Henry's Study, the nerve centre of his financial empire, with secret passageways leading from either side of the fireplace. The one on the left leads upstairs, or you can return to the Great Hall and use the main staircase (there's a lift for those who can't manage stairs; ask a member of staff).

On the first floor are the suites once occupied by Sir Henry and Lady Pellat, each reflecting the particular interests of the couple. **Sir Henry's Suite** features dark heavy furniture and decor, with a small canon by the foot of the bed, while his wife's suite is in a lighter, prettier style with a sitting area and balcony overlooking the gardens and a display relating to her involvement in the Girl Guides movement. Both have sumptuous bathrooms, reflecting Sir Henry's penchant for gadgets and the latest technology.

Upstairs again are a number of rooms devoted to a **Queens Own Rifles Museum**, with uniforms and other items recalling the volunteer regiment to which Sir Henry devoted both time and money. Along the corridor you can gain access to two of the towers, via wooden stairs then spiral staircases, for superb views across the city.

Map on page 152

One thing you should remember: unlike the pronunciation of the city's Spadina Avenue, Spadina Street and Spadina subway station (Spadie-na), the name of Spadina House is pronounced Spa-dee-na, which comes from an Ojibwe word meaning hill.

BELOW: perennial displays at Casa Loma.

Map on page 152

Getting around Toronto, especially the University and Annex area, is simple by bike.

BELOW: sidewalk art.

If you look northwards you will see another ornate building, which is, in fact, Casa Loma's stable block, connected via a long tunnel that leads from the lower level of the main house beneath the road outside. The horses evidently enjoyed a superior lifestyle too. The tunnel also gives access to the garage where Sir Henry kept his motor vehicles, including Toronto's first electric car.

Returning along the tunnel to the main house, if you wonder why the wall alongside the café is lined by movie posters, these are all the feature films that include scenes shot at Casa Loma.

Spadina Museum

After visiting Casa Loma you can leave your car in the Casa Loma car park and walk, turning right outside the gates, to the end of Austin Terrace to visit the **Spadina Museum: Historic House and Garden ❽** (285 Spadina Road; tel: 416-392 0382; Apr–Labour Day Tues–Sun noon–5pm; Sept–Jan Tues–Fri noon–4pm, Sat–Sun noon–5pm; admission charge; subway: Dupont). If you expect this more modest home to be overshadowed by its flashy neighbour, think again. It may be on a different scale, but the visit is equally – perhaps even more – enjoyable because it provides an intimate portrayal of the family who lived here.

The house, which predates Casa Loma, belonged to the Austin family, who came from Ireland and made good in their adopted country, building their fine home around the shell of the former Baldwin home. As they prospered they made additions and updated the decor, but the 50-room mansion still seems far more "livable" than the ostentatious place next door.

The tour begins with a video in which the house itself speaks (in a soft Irish accent) about its own history, its occupants and the social occasions that took place there. A knowledgeable guide leads you from room to room, showing family photographs and portraits, explaining the changing lifestyles and etiquette of successive generations of the family, and inserting fascinating family stories along the way.

In addition to the fine furniture in the house, there are some interesting artworks, including silk wall coverings and a superb art-deco style freize in the billiard room.

The house has delightful gardens and grounds, which were much more extensive before the Austins sold part of their land to Sir Henry Pellat for his Casa Loma, and once included a private golf course and country club where the family did their entertaining.

From here you can turn left out of the entrance gates and either retrieve your car from the Casa Loma car park or walk due south on a path between tree-shaded lawns, down some steps and on down the road to Dupont subway station. ❏

RESTAURANTS, BARS & CAFES

Restaurants

Joso's
202 Davenport Road (at Avenue Road). Tel: 416-925 1903. Open: L & D Mon–Fri, D only Sat. **$$$$**
The speciality here is pristine, fresh fish and seafood. Grilled fish with herbs and olive oil is always superb. Risotto nero and crispy calamari (great for sharing as a first course) are house specialities. Kitschy wall decorations add character to this small room, as do controversial nude female sculptures. Outdoor dining in summer. Excellent service.

Lai Wah Heen
Metropolitan Hotel, 108 Chestnut Street (at Dundas Street West). Tel: 416-977 9899. Open: L & D daily. **$$$**
High-end juicy dim sum in classic, serene surroundings, carry unusual ingredients like shark's fin or foie gras. More familiar offerings are plump and juicy with a lighter touch than most. At dinner, the room is a more formal Cantonese restaurant, and dishes include an outstanding lacquered crisp Peking duck. Good wine list.

Mistura
265 Davenport Road (at Avenue Road). Tel: 416-515 0009. Open: D only Mon–Sat. **$$$$**
Attractive, upmarket Italian food in a warm, relaxing environment. Chef Massimo Capra's geniality shows in the restaurant and on the plate. The menu changes seasonally, and fresh pastas are always interesting. Try the red beet risotto and innovative takes on duck, veal and fish. The wine list is heavy on Italians. Staff are attentive without being intrusive.

Opus
37 Prince Arthur Avenue (at Avenue Road). Tel: 416-921 3105. Open: D daily. **$$$$**
Wine lovers flock to this chic spot to dip into the Amaro brothers' staggering list of French and American reds. The elegant room is a perfect frame for a *grand cru*, and Jason Cox's seasonal cooking is harmonious. Lobster wontons garnish gorgeously moist East-coast halibut.

Pangaea
1221 Bay Street (at Bloor Street). Tel: 416-920 2323. Open: L & D Mon–Sat. **$$$$**
A corporate haven at lunchtime, this midtown spot is serene and luxurious at dinner, with a focus on Canadian ingredients and an innovative approach to vivid seasonal flavours. Banana coconut cream tart is sublime. Knowledgeable servers.

Sassafraz
100 Cumberland Street (at Bellair Street). Tel: 416-964 2222. Open: L & D daily. **$$$**
Yorkville yuppies come to see and be seen at the popular outside patio. Great for people watching, visiting celebs are often spotted grabbing a bite in this trendy, high-ceilinged room. French and Italian-inspired mains are supplemented by signature dishes such as their trio of lamb, which includes braised shank, seared chop and grilled tenderloin. Service is hushed and discreet. Excellent wine list.

Splendido
88 Harbord Street (at Spadina Avenue). Tel: 416-929 7788. Open: D only Tues–Sun. **$$$$**
Surroundings are elegant with romantic lighting and modern art on the walls. Chef David Lee's dishes are nuanced and delicious. Try rack of lamb with lamb osso buco and fingerling potatoes with a touch of garlic foam. Desserts include outstanding lemon tart. The wine list – over 700 bottles – is pricey, but there are some well-priced unusual bottles.

Truffles
Four Seasons Hotel, 21 Avenue Road (at Yorkville Avenue). Tel: 416-928 7331. Open: D only Mon–Sat. **$$$$**
A landmark of meticulous old-school service and elegance, the hushed room is benefiting from a fresh, youthful attitude in the kitchen and a creative approach to wine pairing. There's a fine sense of balance in such ingredients as crayfish and caviar to garnish salmon ballotine or chanterelles for superb venison.

Bars & Cafes

Panorama
55 Bloor Street West. Tel: 416-967 0000
Romantic place with great views from city's highest outdoor patio.

Ein Stein Café & Pub
229 College Street. Tel: 416-597 8346
Friendly cellar bar full of welcoming regulars.

Victory Café
581 Markham Street. Tel: 416-516 5787
Wraparound summer patio, and eclectic theatre, music and literary events upstairs.

Tik Talk Café
96 Harbord Street. Tel: 416-964 6414
Menu features vegetarian soups and sandwiches.

PRICE CATEGORIES

Prices for three-course dinner per person with a half-bottle of house wine:
$ = under $25
$$ = $25–50
$$$ = $50–70
$$$$ = more than $70

THE WEST END

Leafy streets and eastern European neighbourhoods
cluster around a vast and verdant park that
brings the countryside right into the city

N ow an integral part of Toronto, the West End was once a bucolic area of rolling hills and meadows, woodland, streams and small villages – a place where city dwellers came to escape the hurly burly of city living. Easy to reach by TTC, High Park is at the area's heart, with a sizeable chunk of natural wilderness, while the "villages" around it – Roncesvalles to the east, Bloor West and Swansea to the north and west – capture the best of town and country living, just minutes from the centre.

High Park

One of Toronto's oldest and largest parks, **High Park** ❶ stretches south from Bloor Street West almost to Lake Ontario. It began as a 67-hectare (166-acre) donation to the city in 1873 and has grown to 161 hectares (399 acres) of lovely parkland. Bordered by residential neighbourhoods, it is regarded by those who live nearby as their own. That said, they share it with many others who come from all corners of the city – especially at weekends – to picnic, jog, fish, swim, play tennis, practise tai chi, walk their dogs or play with their kids.

The original lot, then in the town of York, was purchased in 1836 by John Howard, the surveyor and city

engineer of the newly incorporated city of Toronto, and his wife Jemima. It was just an hour to the west – on horseback – from Toronto, and they named it High Park, because of its lofty view of Lake Ontario.

A year later, the Howards built a small three-room cottage facing the lake. It was called **Colborne Lodge** ❷ (Colborne Lodge Drive; tel: 416-392 6916; Jan–Apr and Sept weekends; May–Aug Tues–Sun; admission charge; subway: High Park), after John's patron, Sir John

Map on page 168

LEFT: leafy High Park and Grenadier Pond.
BELOW: a cannon on the lawn of Colborne Lodge.

The Humber River pedestrian bridge, at the mouth of the river, is an eye-catching addition to Toronto's Waterfront. Its soaring tubular arches and intricate cross-bracing motif incorporating design elements – from snakes and turtles to thunderbirds – reflect the spirituality of the First Nations, who used the Humber River as a trading route between Lake Simcoe and Lake Ontario.

BELOW: you can learn about the flora and fauna on a walking tour of the park .

Colborne, Lieutenant-Governor of Upper Canada until 1836. Additions were subsequently made, and it is one of the few remaining examples of Regency-style picturesque architecture in North America. One of the first houses in York to enjoy indoor plumbing, Colborne Lodge's parlour has expansive bay windows opening onto a wide verandah facing the lake (which, pre-landfill, was much closer), some of the original furnishings, and lovely watercolours of early Toronto painted by John Howard, who was also an accomplished artist.

The Howards deeded their property to the citizens of Toronto in 1873. Three of many provisos were that people should be able to visit the park free of charge in perpetuity, that it must retain the name High Park, and that no "drinking booths or intoxicating liquor" be allowed on the grounds. While the park's only restaurant is not licensed, picnickers are largely unaware of this latter prohibition! Since then, the city has acquired neighbouring land, to bring the park to its current size.

A naturalist's delight

High Park is one of Toronto's most ecologically significant areas, and efforts continue to restore its vegetation to pre-settlement conditions. More than a third of the park is in a natural state, with an oak savannah ecosystem (the fourth largest in the world) that shelters rare plants such as shrubby St John's Wort and the wild blue lupine, a boreal forest and a tallgrass prairie, full of wild flowers, similar to that which once covered much of southern Ontario.

Some 200 bird species live here or pass through; and each autumn enthusiasts from across North America come to **hawk hill**, to participate in the annual hawk migration watch. Walking tours (www.highpark.org) led by knowledgeable volunteers are an excellent way to learn about the flora and fauna, but if you prefer to explore on your own, the **Spring Creek** and **West Ravine** nature trails offer the best views of the natural forest.

Just below Colborne Lodge is **Grenadier Pond ➌**, named after the British Grenadiers who were

Map on page 168

once stationed at nearby Fort York. Almost as long as the park, it is popular with skaters in the winter, and with anglers from the moment the ice melts. Much of the area surrounding Grenadier Pond, particularly at its upper and lower limits, has been restored to natural vegetation. Most of the time you don't need binoculars – though many regulars always carry them – to spot herons, egrets and even turtles among the reeds.

In the central ravine of the park, on Deer Pen Road, the **animal paddocks** date back to the 1890s, and today's enclosures hold yak, bison, Highland cattle, llamas, mountain sheep and peacocks, as well as deer. North of the zoo, the **Grenadier Teahouse and Café**, with indoor and outdoor seating, is very popular.

A cherished part of Toronto summers is **Dream in the Park**, featuring productions of Shakespeare in a small outdoor amphitheatre, backdropped by trees. Produced by **CanStage** (tel: 416-368 3110), they attract good crowds, who come with

picnics, blankets and cushions (if you're planning to picnic, arrive well ahead of the performance). As dusk turns to black, and the lights strung through the trees begin to twinkle, the setting is absolutely magical, whether or not the production is to your taste.

Roncesvalles Village

To the east of High Park, Roncesvalles Avenue (affectionately referred to as "Roncey") separates the larger Edwardian and Victorian homes along Parkside Drive, Indian Road and the connecting network of streets, from the smaller homes of Parkdale. The name originates from one of the early settlers to the area, an Irish colonel, Walter O'Hara, who had fought against Napoleon at the Battle of Roncesvalles in northern Spain.

After World War II ended, **Roncesvalles ❹** was transformed from a community that was mostly English, Scottish and Irish by the arrival of many European newcomers, including a large number of Poles. In no time, they had established their own shops and their own

An organic food market takes place in a corner of the parking area in High Park on summer Sundays.

LEFT a view over Grenadier Pond.
BELOW: strolling through Roncesvalles.

church. Another influx of Polish immigrants, fleeing marshal law in communist Poland, arrived in the 1980s, and now their presence is the predominant one, celebrated at the annual Roncesvalles Polish Festival in mid September.

Although the face of Roncesvalles is changing, it still has an Old World feel. Tantalising aromas of fresh-baked goods and traditional smokehouses waft from Polish bakeries, delis and butchers' shops that advertise their wares in English and Polish, while window displays advertise Polish events.

Granowska's (No. 175) is a bakery and café with a reputation that goes far beyond the Polish community, although it can't have hurt when the late Pope John Paul ll declared the Napoleons here to be his favourite pastry.

St Casimir's ❺ (No. 156) was Toronto's third Polish Roman Catholic church, built in the late 1940s. Poles who have moved out to the suburbs still come back on Sunday, remaining loyal to both the religious and social aspect of their Polish heritage. Beside the strikingly modern **St Stanislaus-St Casimir's Polish Parishes Credit Union** (No. 220), elderly Poles enjoy the calm of a small corner garden, where a monument and a statue commemorate the visits of Pope John Paul ll, in 1984 and again in 2002.

A lively scene

The liveliest stretch of the village encompasses a 10-block stretch from Galley Avenue to Howard Park Avenue in the north. Corner grocery stores, fruit and vegetable markets and hardware shops share the pavement with cheerful pubs and well-reviewed restaurants. At the north end of Roncesvalles, **Hugh's Room** (6621 Dundas Street West; tel: 416-531 6604) is an intimate cabaret-style club frequented

Praline-pear, lemon meringue, pecan and chocolate ganache are just a few of the delicious tarts for sale at this fine bakery at 283 Roncesvalles Avenue.

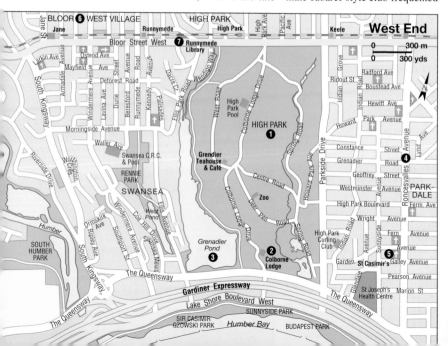

by some of the top names in Canadian and international roots music. South of Howard Park, live jazz and blues is offered most nights at **Gate 403** (403 Roncesvalles; tel: 416-588 2930) in a jazz lounge reminiscent of New York in the 1950s. Over the road, the **Revue** (400 Roncesvalles; tel: 416-531 9959) is for serious movie buffs. One of the oldest continually running theatres in Toronto, it offers an eclectic repertory of foreign, arthouse and classic films.

Touted as the next hot neighbourhood, Roncesvalles is good for browsing or serious shopping, with something for everyone – from antiques to boutiques to children's clothing, organic pet food and wine bars. A sure indicator of neighbourhood interests are establishments such as the **Kennel Café** (No. 295) for dogs, cats and their owners, **Alternative Grounds** (No. 333), a throwback to the 1960s, peddling organic and fairtrade coffees and teas, and **She Said Boom** (No. 393), a local secret that has a superb collection of used books along with new and used vinyl and CDs for music hounds. In **Butler's Pantry** (371 Roncesvalles), a popular café that serves international comfort food, the noticeboard promotes Buddhist retreats, yoga classes and local artists' showings.

For those with a serious interest in antiques, walk to the **Sunnyside Antique District**, with its 20 or more antiques shops on Queen Street West, just east of Roncesvalles.

Bloor West Village

Boundaries blur, when it comes to **Bloor West Village ⑥**. Officially, it extends from Glendonwynne Road in the east to South Kingsway in the west, and the streets north of Bloor. However, when Torontonians talk about Bloor West Village, they are generally including the older village of **Swansea**, which is bordered by the Humber River, Bloor Street, High Park and Lake Ontario.

Swansea's exposure to Europeans goes back to 1615, when the explorer Etienne Brulée set foot on the east bank of the Humber River. Close to two centuries later, Jean Baptiste Rousseau became the first permanent European settler in the area, running a small trading post on the shores of the Humber in the early 1790s.

Fast forward to the early 1900s, when Swansea became incorporated as a village in 1926, and its inhabitants were mostly of British extraction. Swansea's hilly and wooded terrain apparently reminded the early settlers of their Welsh roots.

Bloor West Village became an official neighbourhood in 1970, and its East European influence is as strongly felt today as it was then. The annual **Ukrainian Festival** (www.ukrainianfestival.com) that takes place at the end of August attracts more than 300,000 people from North America and Europe.

While Bloor West Village is mostly known for its shops and restaurants, it has a few other dis-

Map on page 168

The architect, John Lyle, used native Canadian motifs on the Runnymede Library building (see page 170).

BELOW: fresh flowers at the market.

Map on page 168

*There's a dog-
friendly welcome at
Chapters bookstore.*

BELOW:
Runnymede Library.

tinctions as well. The building of the
Runnymede Library ❼ (2178
Bloor Street West, at the corner of
Glendonwynne Road) in 1930 caused
considerable uproar. Irish-born John
Lyle was the first architect to use
native Canadian motifs such as totem
poles and animals in his work; this
was considered far too avant-garde by
the conservative denizens of
Swansea. In a recent expansion, the
unconventional theme has been continued in a modern vein, with a large
curved and punctured copper wall
and huge 5-metre (16-ft) windows
overlooking a neighbouring park.

Two short blocks west, at the corner of Runnymede and Bloor, the
bookstore **Chapters** (2225 Bloor) is
housed in the former, and historic,
Runnymede Theatre. Built as a
vaudeville house in 1927, with
courtyard-like murals, it was later
converted into a movie theatre.
When the cinema closed in the late
1990s, Chapters acquired the building and restored it beautifully, inte-
grating the proscenium stage and the
balcony into the store's layout. The
(rare) dog-friendly store offers a

wide-ranging book selection and a
programme of author readings.

There was a time when Bloor West
Village was a 10-block stretch of
bakeries, delicatessens, greengrocers
and butchers, many run by immigrants from Ukraine, Poland and the
former Czechoslovakia. Despite a
few chain stores moving into the
neighbourhood, independent store
owners are still holding their ground,
joined by more recent newcomers –
from Korea, Japan, and Thailand –
who are opening trendy restaurants,
flower shops and elegant boutiques.

Books and refreshments

Book City (No. 2350) deservedly
retains a loyal following, despite
Chapters a couple of blocks east. For
unusual presents, consider **Say Tea**
(No. 2362), experts in all things tea,
Durie Lane (No. 2140) for gifts, fun
accessories at **eriAle** (256A Willard
Avenue) or more global offerings
from **Quipus Crafts** (No. 2414).

If you've worked up a thirst or an
appetite try the **Coffee Tree Roast-
ery** (No. 2412), where a traditional
coffee roaster churns out fresh
roasted beans, **Max's Market** (No.
2299), with gourmet foods that are
perfect for a High Park picnic, or
Vineyard Estate Wines (No. 2273),
with Niagara-area wines. There are
at least four British-style pubs, each
with an outdoor or rooftop patio, and
a raft of cafés and bistros.

For literary connections, head
down **Riverside Drive**, south from
Bloor above the Humber, west of
South Kingway. Most of the houses
are larger and more elegant than
Swansea's modest brick homes.
Lucy Maud Montgomery, author of
Anne of Green Gables, spent the lat-
ter part of her life at No. 210, while
Morley Callaghan lived at No. 316
upon his return from Paris in 1929 –
after some creative years, fraternising
with Ernest Hemingway, F. Scott
Fitzgerald and James Joyce. ❑

RESTAURANTS, BARS & CAFES

Restaurants

Bloom
2315 Bloor Street West (at Jane Street). Tel: 416-767 1315. Open: D only Tues–Sat. **$$$**
This is a sleek restaurant with a menu to match. Chef Sam Gassiara's creative flair takes the simplest ingredients and gives them interesting twists. Try the pheasant leg stuffed with duck sausage or the fillet of sole folded around a medley of crab meat, squid and shrimp. Desserts are a high point, beautifully presented with out-of-the-ordinary flavours, such as the inventive stilton cannoli with peppered cherries. The wine list is small, eclectic and reasonably priced.

Merlot
2994 Bloor Street West (at Royal York Road). Tel: 416-236 0081. Open: L & D Mon–Sat, D only Sun. **$$$**
This traditional French bistro has a lively atmosphere and serves generous helpings of classic bistro food. The cooking is accomplished, and includes the ever-popular mussels steamed with white wine, shallots and garlic. Juicy duck breasts are served with potato

gratin, while veal comes with fresh tomatoes in a white wine sauce; both are served with pasta and are typical of the traditional French dishes on the menu. Service is attentive.

Sushi Kaji
860 The Queensway (at Islington Avenue). Tel: 416-252 2166. Open: D only Wed–Sun. **$$$$**
This is a gem of a restaurant that serves authentic omakase dinners. Fresh fish is prepared using both classic and innovative techniques and chef Mitsuhiro Kaji's masterful touch (he trained with a number of Japanese master chefs) results in intensely flavoured dishes with interesting textures. The menu changes daily. Many patrons come for the sushi bar, full of tempting, expertly prepared morsels. There is a small list of imported sakis.

Via Allegro
1750 The Queensway (at Highway 427). Tel: 416-622 6677. Open: L & D daily. **$$$$**
Holding its fair share of Wine Spectator Awards, the Via Allegro has a magnificent wine cellar with a team of sommeliers to ensure that everyone has the perfect wine to accom-

pany their meal. The innovative Italian fare never strikes a wrong note, and for dedicated meat-eaters, the steaks and veal chops are outstanding. The decor is flamboyant Italian – the food is anything but. Do not be put off by the mall location – it is well worth the drive.

Bars & Cafes

Loons
416 Roncesvalles Avenue. Tel: 416-535 8561
This friendly locals' bar has the advantage of a heated outside patio.

Whelan's Gate Irish Pub
1663 Bloor Street West. Tel: 416-531 1311
A neighbourhood bar with great chicken wings and much more.

Alternative Grounds Coffee House
333 Roncesvalles Avenue Tel: 416-534 5543
This coffee house serves its very own brand of fairtrade organic coffee, and has a menu of vegetarian and vegan food.

The Dark Horse
2401 Bloor Street West. Tel: 416-769 4696
English style pub in the heart of Bloor West Village.

RIGHT: decorative cabbage.

SCARBOROUGH BLUFFS

A magnificent geological record of the
last ice age, Scarborough Bluffs are unique
in North America, their earliest origins
dating back some 70,000 years

Rising dramatically up to 106
metres (350 ft) high along a
14-km (9-mile) stretch of
Lake Ontario coast, **Scarborough
Bluffs ❶** have attracted worldwide
scientific attention. You can probably best appreciate what makes
them so distinct by looking up from
the shore, rather than looking down.
Starting around the watermark, the
first 46 metres (150 ft) of sediment
contain plant and animal fossils
deposited during the first advance of
the Wisconsin glacier, some 70,000
years ago.

Over the next 58,000 years, these
were gradually covered by 61 metres
(200 ft) of boulder clay and sand left
by four subsequent advances and
retreats of the ice. Each time the
glacier retreated, deep valleys were
created,which can still be traced in
cross-sections through the Bluffs.

After the final withdrawal of the
ice took place, Lake Iroquois – the
larger predecessor of Lake Ontario
– was created, and lasted for 1,000
years or so. It was this lake's waves
that undercut and eroded 70,000-
years worth of sediment to create
the spectacular geological formation
that is marvelled at today.

Aboriginal peoples lived here
from around 8000 BC, until European colonisers arrived in more
recent times. Scarborough Bluffs

acquired their current name when
Lady Elizabeth Simcoe – wife of
John Graves Simcoe, the first
Lieutenant Governor of Upper
Canada – spotted them, as she sailed
in a small boat to the town of York.
They reminded her of the English
cliffs, in Yorkshire, and she wrote in
her diary, on 4 August, 1793, "after
rowing a mile we came within sight
of what is named in the map the
highlands of Toronto. The shore is
extremely bold, and has the appearance of chalk cliffs but I believe

Map
on page
180

LEFT: the towering
cliffs of Scarborough
Bluffs.
BELOW: the perfect
place to picnic.

View Lake Ontario from the cliffs atop Scarborough Bluffs.

BELOW: walking the dog on the beach at Bluffers Park, near Cathedral Bluffs.

they are only white sand… they appeared so well that we talked of building a summer residence there and calling it Scarborough."

Although the Simcoes ultimately built their summer residence further west at Castle Frank, overlooking the Don River, many others were drawn to this area, particularly after World War II, when a mix of residential communities – some noticeably more affluent than others – gradually settled along the top of the Bluffs.

Since the sandstone is vulnerable to erosion, much-used trails leading down from the numerous cliff-top parks have gradually been cordoned off by concerned municipal authorities. At the foot of the Bluffs, despite the never-ending pounding by the waves, erosion is being slowed down to some extent by various forms of artificial protection – such as landfill – that have been introduced to stabilise the cliffs.

Scarborough, a part of Toronto since amalgamation in 1998, extends east along Lake Ontario, from Kingston Road and Victoria Park Avenue to the Rouge River. If

you're coming from the centre of Toronto, Scarborough Bluffs are about 8 km (5 miles) east of The Beaches, continuing along Kingston Road. The journey is a slice through the best and worst of suburban development, with communities of older homes, trendy stores and cool cafés close to soul-destroying shopping arcades and dreary motels.

Keep a look out for the dozen or so eye-catching murals that bring some of Scarborough's history cheerfully to life – from *Remembering Spiritual Ancestry* (2378 Kingston Road), which honours the aboriginal people who first lived in the area, to *The Bluffs as viewed by Elizabeth Simcoe* (2384 Kingston Road).

Cliff-top treasures

With the disappearance of some paths, and a new multi-purpose waterfront trail from Port Union to Bluffers Park not opening until 2008, exploring Scarborough Bluffs is not as easy as you might think. Ask many a Torontonian about how to reach them, and you're likely to get a rather vague reply. That said,

Map on page 180

there are numerous places to appreciate their magic and majesty, high above the lake or at water level.

The entrance to the **Rosetta McClain Garden** is at Kingston Road and Glen Everest Road. At the turn of the 19th century, it was a farm, but it was later donated to the city by Robert McClain in memory of his wife Rosetta, whose family – the Wests – had owned the land since 1905.

A mix of formal and more natural gardens, the 9-hectare (23-acre) park offers a wonderful bluff-top view. It is one of the city's more tranquil parks, with sweeping lawns, a large limestone rockery, a rose garden, and an unusual fountain made from huge granite boulders. A pet cemetery dates back to the days when the land still belonged to the West family. Signage in Braille, along with a herb and scented garden full of plants with distinctive fragrances, make the garden especially enjoyable for the blind.

Two adjoining parks along the cliff top, **Scarborough Heights Park** and **Scarborough Bluffs Park**, are accessed from Fishleigh Drive and Undercliff Drive respectively. Mainly mown grass with thick vegetation at the edge of the cliffs, they offer a few paths and some excellent views, but no official route down to water level.

On the other side of Midland Avenue, however, take Scarborough Crescent down to Scarborough Bluffs Park. From here, footpaths wind through old fields and provide a cliff-top walk with breathtaking views all the way, eventually, to Brimley Road.

If you're approaching by car, continue east along Kingston Road. On the south, just before you reach Brimley Road, is **St Augustine's Seminary**. Superbly located on the bluffs, it was built in 1913 and its imposing dome continues to be a convenient landmark for sailors on Lake Ontario.

Once a year, during Doors Open Toronto *(see Events, page 228),* hordes of visitors come to admire the broad rotunda, the chapel with its Italian-style frescoes and the glorious lake views.

TIP

There are parking restrictions on Ravine Drive, particularly from Monday to Friday, so you might have more luck finding somewhere to park on Windy Ridge Drive.

BELOW: Scarborough Bluffs Park has designated trails.

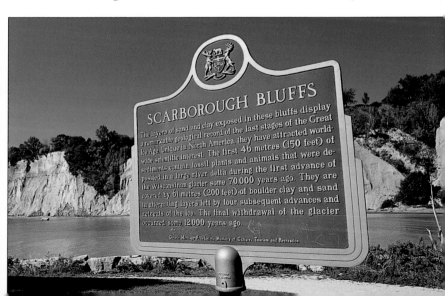

TIP

If you're looking for refreshment the Dogfish Pub at Bluffers Park Marina (7 Brimley Road South, tel: 416-264 2337) is worth a stop, otherwise the area immediately around Scarborough Bluffs has limited pubs or cafés of note. Given the proximity of The Beaches, travellers would do well to make their way there.

Down to the lake shore

Turning right on Brimley, the road down to **Bluffers Park** is steep and winding, built in one of the few locations where a descent to Lake Ontario was possible (if you're coming by TTC, it's about a 10-minute walk from Kingston Road). Whether you're driving or walking, you will have an excellent close-up view of the various levels of sand and gravel that comprise what is known as the Dutch Church formation. This is one of the best spots to fully appreciate the Bluffs' odd-shaped pinnacles and buttresses.

Bluffers Park seems far removed from the rest of the city, its bay cosily protected from the "outside" world by the towering cliffs. Four yacht clubs and a small community of year-round houseboats call the park home. At **Bluffers Restaurant** and **Dogfish Bar**, surrounded by sparkling water, you can enjoy what is unquestionably one of Toronto's most glorious lakeside views.

At the park's eastern end, a long broad stretch of sandy beach – that you can walk along as far as water levels allow – is popular for picnicking and swimming. Behind the beach, a gravel footpath meanders peacefully along the foot of the cliffs, through bulrushes, sweet-smelling wild flowers and wetland trees.

East of Bluffers Park, turn south off Kingston Road onto Cathedral Bluffs Drive, which leads to **Cathedral Bluffs Park**. Here, the 90-metre (300-ft) cliffs mark the highest point on Scarborough's shoreline and you'll find some of the most spectacular views of the Bluffs' pleistocene deposits. It's also popular with bird-watchers, who come to see the harrier hawks heading south in the autumn.

Art and nature

One of the loveliest walks down the Bluffs is along the **Doris McCarthy Trail**, at the western end of Sylvan Park. To access the nature trail, turn south from Kingston Road onto Ravine Drive, and the entrance is right in front of you. The trail winds steeply down beside a babbling stream that runs through the forested gully, known as Bellamy Ravine.

In 2001, the nature trail was officially named the Doris McCarthy Trail after one of Canada's more cherished artists whose property, **Fool's Paradise**, borders the ravine's western edge.

The beauty of Scarborough Bluffs has drawn countless artists and art lovers over the years, and nowhere is this more in evidence than in **Guildwood Park** (191 Guildwood Parkway). It is part of what was the 35-hectare (88-acre) Ranelagh Park estate, which surrounded a white stucco Arts and Crafts-style mansion built in 1914 for Harold Bickford, a retired American soldier with a penchant for polo ponies and cars. It was acquired in 1932 by Rosa Breithaput Hewetson, shortly before her marriage to Spencer Clark. After visiting

Doris McCarthy

Landscape artist Doris McCarthy is a legend in her own time. Born in Calgary in 1910, she moved with her family to Toronto in 1913. After winning a full-time scholarship to the Ontario College of Art, she studied under Arthur Lismer – one of the Group of Seven – and graduated with honours in 1930. A teacher for 40 years, she retired to paint full time, and her love of travel to all corners of the world, and particularly to Canada's Arctic, shines through the vast body of her work.

McCarthy's connection with the Scarborough Bluffs began in 1939, when she purchased a remote cliff-top property. Reflecting both her humour and her feistiness, she called it Fool's Paradise, since her mother had referred to "that fool's paradise of yours". The name stuck, and it has been home and inspiration to McCarthy ever since. Seeing how many artist friends visited to renew their creative energies, McCarthy generously decided to donate her home to the Ontario Heritage Foundation. Once she no longer lives there, it will become a retreat for individual artists of all disciplines. During Doors Open Toronto, however, anyone may experience its tranquillity.

Roycroft, an artist colony in East Aurora, New York, the socially conscious couple decided to found a similar colony at their new home.

The property was requisitioned by the Canadian government during World War II, but the Clarks returned to it in 1947. By this time, since interest in The Guild had disappeared and property taxes had risen, the Clarks sold off much of their land to developers – who built the residential community of Guildwood Village – and devoted the next 35 years to being patrons of the arts and preservationists.

Architectural antiques

During the 1950s, 1960s and much of the 1970s, many of Toronto's historic buildings were being torn down, often to make way for some rather ugly replacements. The Clarks made it their mission to amass a collection of as many architectural fragments and sculptures from the old buildings as they possibly could. In 1978, Spencer Clark sold the property to the Government of Ontario, and it is now maintained by the city of Toronto as a public park and historic site.

The more than 70 architectural fragments and sculptures could not have a more lovely setting, within the 36 hectares (90 acres) of forest, gardens, lawns and woodland trails atop the Scarborough Bluffs. Each has its own small plaque stating where it came from, the architects who designed it, when it was built… and when it was demolished.

Ironically for a site dedicated to the preservation of fine architecture, Guildwood Park's own building is an unmitigated eyesore. Just beyond the entrance, the boarded-up hulk that is the former Guild Inn is impossible to miss. Although many local families fondly remember occasions celebrated in such stunning surroundings, the inn was never financially successful and has been boarded up for some years, though plans are proposed for another hotel complex.

Happily, the building quickly fades into insignificance once you come to the **Guild Sculpture Gardens** on the far side. Scattered among the lawns are treasures salvaged from Toronto's past – such as the art deco panels from the former *Toronto Star* building, decorative terracotta elements from the Royal Conservatory of Music, marble Ionic columns from the Bank of Nova Scotia's 1903 headquarters on King Street West, and the hefty stone mantelpiece from the home of Sir Frederick Banting, the man who discovered the existence of insulin. The centrepiece of the gardens is the soaring Greek amphitheatre of columns and archways from the 1912 head office of the Bank of Toronto.

Beyond the manicured lawns, handsome iron gates lead to the top of the Scarborough Bluffs, from where trails heading east and west offer more glorious views. ❑

Decorative sculpture in the gardens.

BELOW: footpaths snake through the clifftop landscape.

TORONTO'S NEIGHBOURHOODS AND VILLAGES

Multicultural Toronto is at its very best in those enclaves that preserve the culture and atmosphere of the "old country" – wherever that might be

Map on page 180

LEFT: a striking church building in Little Italy. **BELOW:** a welcoming smile at the farmer's market, Front Street.

To the First Nations peoples of Canada, Toronto was a meeting place and this has never changed. It is one of the most ethnically diverse cities in the world – more than half the population was born outside Canada – and just about every city street contains a culturally mixed crowd of citizens going about their daily business.

The level of integration here is a monument to the widespread Canadian ethic of friendship and tolerance (some say that political correctness was born in Toronto), and this makes for a particularly pleasant downtown atmosphere.

However, there is nowhere better to explore the city's diversity than in its neighbourhoods or "villages", many of which are clustered around the downtown area. Most colourfully, these include areas that are home to a concentration of people whose origins go back to a particular nation, but others are distinguished by historic architecture, as in Cabbagetown, or social standing (Rosedale).

Three Chinatowns

Many Western cities have cultural enclaves such as this, but Toronto is particularly well endowed with them. It has no less than three major Chinatowns: the main downtown one is covered in the Downtown West

chapter *(see page 121)* and there's another at Markham, on the northern fringes. Several of the ethnic neighbourhoods are in close proximity, a few even overlap, and this not only makes them easy to explore, it also helps to highlight the differences. The changing shopfronts and restaurants stamp a new identity on otherwise similar streetscapes and the local populations provide an unmistakable "old country" character and atmosphere.

What distinguishes Toronto from so many other Western cities, in

*Heritage Toronto
runs free guided
walking tours
exploring the city
neighbourhoods,
July–September.
Pick up a leaflet from
the tourist office,
visit www.heritage
toronto.org or call
416-338 1338 for
information.*

terms of cultural identities, is the fact that it is a city that has grown as a result of large-scale immigration. It began with the first French and British settlers to Canada, then during the American Revolution it became home to a wave of Loyalists, heading north across the border so that they could maintain their ties with Britain.

Those early citizens were followed by a large number of incomers from all parts of Europe – migrant workers, people escaping persecution or hardships in their own countries, and families who were simply coming in search of a better standard of living in a new and exciting country.

During the second half of the 19th century, the population surged from 30,000 in 1850 to more than 180,000 by 1900. There was another substantial wave of immigration from Europe and Asia after World War II, when many of the city's neighbourhoods were established, and there are now around three million people living in the Greater Toronto Area.

The city, now the largest in Canada, is still the first choice for many new immigrants, though efforts are being made to encourage many of them to settle elsewhere and boost less populous areas of the country.

Cabbagetown

Toronto's neighbourhoods and villages that are not ethnically themed are based principally on the unified style of historic homes that are clustered together there. These areas offer a stylish kind of living that has attracted Toronto's well-off citizens, who preserve not only the architecture but also the sedate atmosphere and lack of commercial activity.

One of the oldest such areas is **Cabbagetown ❷** (subway: Sherbourne or Castle Frank), noted for its fine Victorian houses, lovely parks and Toronto's oldest cemetery,

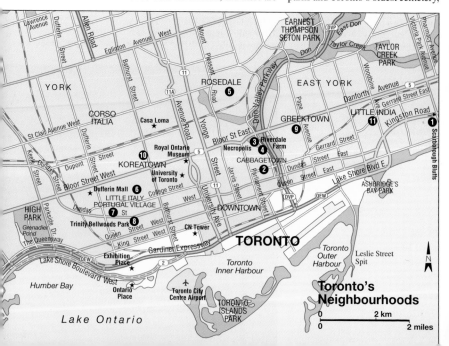

**Toronto's
Neighbourhoods**

the Necropolis. The district covers an area bounded by Parliament Street, Wellesley Street East, Gerrard Street East and the Don River, and gets its curious name from the simple fact that its early residents, Irish settlers who came to escape the Great Famine at home, grew vegetables in their front gardens. It was a working-class area back then, but it later transformed into a desirable neighbourhood, with a number of notable residents – you'll see blue plaques in some of the well-tended front gardens (no cabbages in sight these days): two on Sackville Street mark the homes of the poet Al Purdy (1918–2000) and Nobel physics laureate Dr Arthur Schawlow (1921–99).

Flags bearing the cabbage symbol denote buildings of particular architectural interest.

Notable resting place

If you make your way along Winchester Street you will come to the **Toronto Necropolis ❸** (200 Winchester Street; tel: 416-923 7911; daily from 8am, closing time varies

seasonally; free), one of the oldest cemeteries in the city. Established in 1850, it is the resting place of many notable citizens, including Toronto's first mayor, William Lyon Mackenzie, and world champion rower Ned Hanlan *(see page 92)*. There is also a monument commemorating Samuel Lount and Peter Matthews, who were hanged in 1838 for taking part in the Mackenzie Rebellion. The area designated "The Resting Place of Pioneers" is where the remains of 984 early settlers were re-interred between 1851 and 1881.

Elsewhere pathways wind their way among splendid Gothic monuments, shaded by wonderful old trees, and down into a grassy vale which contains a "scattering area" for cremated remains. The main entrance gate on Winchester Street is flanked by twin buildings, one housing a nice little chapel, the other containing the cemetery offices.

Cross the road here and enter the park on the south side of Winchester Street. On the left is the gate into **Riverdale Farm ❹** (201 Winchester Street; tel: 416-392 6794; daily

Map on page 180

During the week-long Cabbagetown Festival in early September, visitors can actually go inside some of the historic homes on a tour. The festival also offers concerts, films, a dog show and other events.

LEFT: Cabbagetown doorway detail.
BELOW: Riverdale farm hand.

Rosedale Park was the venue for the first ever Grey Cup (Canadian football) championship in 1909. Canadian football is similar to American football, and consequently incomprehensible to most European visitors.

BELOW:
upscale shopping.

9am–5pm). If you are travelling with small children, this is one of the nicest places in the city to take them, and is actually the original site of Toronto Zoo *(see page 193)*. Covering nearly 4 hectares (7½ acres) in the heart of the city, it is set up as a farm from the turn of the 20th century and has a full complement of domestic animals to see, plus woodland, ponds and gardens to wander around. There's also a programme of storytelling and musical events for little ones.

Rosedale

North of Cabbagetown across Bloor Street is **Rosedale ❺** (subway: Rosedale), where some of Toronto's most desirable properties are to be found, a place that some of Canada's most prominent people have called home, including politicians and media celebrities. Developed between 1884 and the outbreak of World War I, it is full of beautiful Queen Anne-style mansions, well spaced out along quiet, tree-lined streets, with little to disturb the peace.

Cutting a swathe through the area is **Rosedale Valley**, a 40-hectare (100-acre) ravine with a network of pathways through parks and woodland that provide a home for wildlife right in the city and is a great place for walking, jogging, cycling and rollerblading. The most secluded part of the valley is **Severn Creek Park**, at the top of Aylmer Avenue. Other parks include **Rosedale Park**, in the heart of the neighbourhood, and **Chorley Park**, on Douglas Drive, another popular place to walk along nature trails among the plentiful trees; there's a wonderful view of the Don Valley from the eastern end.

Good shops abound mostly in the luxury category because of their proximity to all those multi-million dollar homes. **All The Best Fine Foods** (1099 Yonge Street; tel: 416-928 3330) is a good place for top-quality delicatessen foods and gift baskets, **Harvest Wagon** (1103 Yonge Street; tel: 416-923 7542) has excellent fruit and vegetables, and antiques hunters will not be disappointed by the selection of shops and galleries on the stretch of Yonge Street between Rosedale and Summerhill subway stations.

Nightlife in Rosedale also centres on the area of Yonge Street just north of Bloor, where there are plenty of restaurants, bars and cafés – arty **Rosedale Perk** is a favourite.

Little Italy

Some of Toronto's neighbourhoods have changed over the years as the original nationalities moved on to new areas and were replaced by new groups. The area that is now **Little Italy ❻** (subway: Ossington then walk south, or Queen's Park then streetcar 506 west), home to Toronto's Italian population since the mid-20th century, was originally the home of the city's Jewish community, who moved north many years ago. Its character is beginning to shift again as Portuguese citizens are replacing some of the Italian residents. You might not realise this, though, as you stroll the stretch of College Street between Euclid Avenue and Shaw Street, particularly during the Italian Street Festival, which takes place here in late August every year.

There has been an Italian population in Toronto since at least the early 20th century, but it really blossomed after World War II when Little Italy was established around these streets, and the city now has more than half a million citizens of Italian descent.

Among the shops here is a real Italian icon – a little place selling Vespa scooters. The nightlife is vibrant, and as the sun goes down the volume goes up in the restaurants and cafés, many of which spill out onto the pavements on summer evenings. Coloured lights illuminate the trees, and streetcars trundle up and down. This is a great place for an evening stroll, dropping in, perhaps, at the renowned **Café Diplomatico**

at the corner of Clinton Street for a cup of their excellent coffee.

It would be a dreadful waste, though, to come to Little Italy and not dine out on truly authentic regional Italian cuisine. You can try good, wood oven-baked pizzas (and other fare) at the **Standard Club Pizza and Pasta Bar** (667 College Street; tel: 416-588 8170), and there are plenty more to choose from.

Portugal Village

Walk down College Street as far as its junction with Crawford Street (aka Praça Luis de Camões) and you'll see the Portuguese influence creeping in, with a bust of the famous Portuguese poet, Luis Vaz de Camões (1524–80), whose epic poem *Os Lusiadias (The Portuguese)* extols the achievements of his countrymen around the world, and whose death is commemorated with a national holiday in Portugal. **Portugal Village** ❼ (subway: Ossington then walk south), though, is primarily in evidence along Dundas Street, where the section from Ossington to Bathurst is lined

Map on page 180

As you stroll through Little Italy, look for a corner restaurant called Eat More Amato, then look up at it's fun paint job, which gives the impression that it needs a paint job – peeling paint and exposed bricks have been cleverly re-created by the talented decorator.

LEFT: brightly painted homes in Portugal Village. **BELOW:** coffee-break at Café Diplomatico in Little Italy.

A statue of Alexander the Great in Greektown, where the Greek community of Toronto celebrate their homeland's cuisine in early August each year, with the Taste of the Danforth Festival.

BELOW:
relaxing in Greektown on the Danforth.

with bakeries, bars and restaurants with a Portuguese flavour – **Caffé Brasiliano, Portuguese Café Bar** and **Musa**, at 677 Dundas Street, which goes a step further than others with an attractive painted facade that has a decidedly Iberian flavour. Churches along the street, include **Santa Ines** (St Agnes) and **San Juan** Batista, both Roman Catholic.

At the west end of the village, stretching down as far as Queen Street, **Trinity Bellwoods Park ❽** was the original location of Trinity College, of which only the gates, at the southern end of the park, remain. Today, the spacious park has picnic tables, a children's playground and tennis courts. The side streets here are all strictly residential, but the Portuguese are known to be keen gardeners so it's worth taking a stroll to see what they have made of their little front gardens.

Corso Italia

Since the 1960s, many of the Italians who moved out of Little Italy made their way to a new enclave in the West End, known as **Corso Italia** (subway: Lansdowne then bus 47 north), which stretches along St Clair Avenue West, from Lansdowne to Westmount. Here, they have gone decidedly upmarket, with a number of designer fashion boutiques and classy shoe shops. There are chic restaurants too, and some wonderful places to shop for Italian provisions. The **Tre Marie Bakery** (1311 St Clair Avenue) has been making and selling delicious European-style bread and other Italian foods here for more than 40 years, and the friendly **Diana Grocery**, just up the avenue, has terrific delicatessen goods, meat, fresh fruit and vegetables and a range of imported and Canadian groceries.

Greektown

One of the most vibrant of all the neighbourhoods is **Greektown on the Danforth ❾**, home of Toronto's Greek population for more than 50 years. Extending along Danforth Avenue, it is concentrated between Chester and Jones Streets, where there's a truly Mediterranean atmosphere, bursting with exuberance.

You will know when you've arrived, because the street signs are in English and Greek, and banners hanging from lamp posts proclaim "Greektown". Then you'll notice the Greek food shops, including bakeries tempting passers-by with pastries dipped in distilled honey and other similar goodies; travel agents offering trips to Greece; shops selling traditional Greek music CDs and a Greek pharmacy. In the middle of all this, Starbucks, Tim Horton's and Canadian burger joints, commonplace elsewhere, look strangely incongruous.

On summer evenings, as dusk falls, the best thing to do is to join the procession of people strolling past restaurants that spill out onto the pavement and listen for cries of "*Opa!*" (the Greek equivalent of

"Hurrah!") as waiters astonish their patrons with a flambée dish from an authentic menu. Better still, stop and sample the cuisine, which includes all the best-known favourites – souvlaki, moussaka, calamari, tsatsiki – and less famous dishes from the old country. Some of the restaurants will have traditional Greek music or even a belly-dancer gyrating around the tables, and the standard of cooking is very high.

At the corner of Danforth and Logan, there's a pleasant little square with a fountain, which is a popular meeting place for local families on summer evenings, with children playing happily and old men sitting on benches conversing in Greek. You could be in a quiet corner of Athens.

Asian communities

Communities that have made a substantial impact on Toronto are those who have come from the Far East and re-created their colourful lifestyle. Even outside the China-towns, you'll find plenty of Chinese restaurants, Japanese sushi restaurants are everywhere, and Thai cuisine is among the most popular.

Less well known – even some Torontonians are unaware that it's here – is **Koreatown** , which extends along Bloor Street West between Bathurst and Christie. The Bathurst end is dominated by Honest Ed's *(see page 161)* and Mirvish Village, but the Korean influence becomes more apparent the closer to Christie you get. Here, both sides of the street are lined by brightly coloured shops with Korean lettering, selling a range of goods that includes low-cost clothing and Oriental remedies, or places offering acupuncture. There are also plenty of restaurants, some purely Korean and others offering fusion cuisine. It's a fairly small neighbourhood, but worth a look if you are in the vicinity.

Over in the eastern part of the city you'll find Toronto's **Little India** , sometimes called Indian Bazaar, stretching along a colourful section of Gerrard Street East. Streetcar 506 goes to it, or take the subway to Greenwood or Coxwell and walk south. Though its official boundaries are Greenwood and Main, once you have negotiated the dog-leg junction at Coxwell Street, it's mostly residential, with not much to interest visitors.

However, the main part of the neighbourhood has a fascinating mix of grocery shops, selling exotic foodstuffs and Halal meats, cookware shops with stacks of massive curry cauldrons and utensils, clothing shops hung with colourful saris. There are restaurants serving Indian cuisine, such as the **Lahore Biriani House and BBQ** and one that's simply called **Famous Indian Cuisine**.

Come and visit after dark when the street is really bustling, with strollers wandering along beneath garlands of coloured lights, and an inviting aroma of Indian spices pervades the air. ❑

Map on page 180

TIP

The Corso Italia Toronto Fiesta in July celebrates all things Italian in a free three-day community event. Visitors can enjoy musical performers and sample authentic Italian food from street vendors and local restaurants. Visit: www.torontofiesta.com for more information.

BELOW: Buddha statues in Chinatown.

RESTAURANTS, CAFES & BARS

Restaurants

Greektown on the Danforth

Allen's Restaurant Bar
143 Danforth Avenue (at Broadview Avenue). Tel: 416-463 3086. Open: Br Sat–Sun, L & D daily. **$**
A well-loved pub on the souvlaki-dominated Danforth, Allen's has the lively atmosphere of a neighbourhood watering-hole but the food of a more serious restaurant. A traditional oak bar dominates the front of the room, and behind it an incredible array of whiskeys, beers and what may be the best Caesars in town (on the plate and in the glass). Irish food dominates, but global influences creep in. Authentic hamburger, while not on the menu, is available for those in the know.

Avli
401 Danforth Avenue (at Chester Avenue). Tel: 416-461 9577. Open: L & D daily. **$$**
An air of authenticity sets Avli apart from its more generic neighbours in Greektown. The garlicky dips are addictive and a meal can be had from the many hot and cold appetisers. Succulent lamb shank sits on bed of tasty orzo; the chicken and rosemary pie tastes as if it

came straight from mama's kitchen. The wine list offers high-quality Greek vintages, rarely seen. The casual taverna is always lively with friendly servers that make diners feel like part of the family.

Café Brussels
124 Danforth Avenue (at Broadview Avenue). Tel: 416-465 7363. Open: D only Tues–Sat. **$$$**
This traditional, art deco-inspired Belgian brasserie offers more than 30 ways of preparing mussels, served with Belgian fries and mayonnaise. Sensational lamb shanks shine on a typical brasserie menu. Try the unusual Belgian speciality, waterzooie chicken, which features poached chicken in a strong chicken sauce. Confit of garlic with goat's cheese makes an interesting first course. Wine Spectator Award list.

Embrujo Flamenco Tapas Bar
97 Danforth Avenue (at Broadview). Tel: 416-778 0007. Open: L & D Thur–Sat, D only Mon–Wed. **$$$**
Full of charm and very romantic, this authentic Spanish tapas bar features live flamenco performances and gentle guitar. Tapas are outstanding. Quintessential tortilla presents thick

wedges of perfectly cooked egg and potato with a subtle whisky-butter sauce. Cod croquettes are crispy outside and delightfully creamy inside. Aromatic paella features saffron-infused rice with choice of seafood, chicken or veggies. Choose from Spanish wines or fruity sangria.

Eglington West Village

Zucca Trattoria
2150 Yonge Street (at Eglinton Avenue). Tel: 416-488 5774. Open: D only daily. **$$**
Co-owner, chef Andrew Milne Allen brings downtown sophistication to this midtown favourite. From the complimentary chick pea pancake to creative salads and outstanding fresh grilled whole fish, Zucca never disappoints. Pastas are house-made and change with the seasons. Expertly chosen wine list.

Little Italy

Tempo
596 College Street (at Clinton Street). Tel: 416-531 2822. Open: D only daily. **$$$**
Tom Thai is an incredibly talented chef and loves to play with flavours, creating small Asian fusion plates, as well as inspired sushi. This small, hip restaurant is sophisticated and busy

with a jazz beat in the background. The patio is cool. Sea bream ceviche with yuzu, shiso and crisp shallot is delicious; lobster maki with white truffle oil shows the breadth of his brilliance. Desserts include superb organic ice cream in fusion flavours. Lots of fun cocktails to choose from.

Trattoria Giancarlo
41 Clinton Street (at College Street). Tel: 416-533 9619. Open: D only Mon–Sat. **$$$**
A classy intimate Italian restaurant in the heart of Little Italy. Inventive pastas and seafood. Great grills, especially the veal chop. Desserts are fabulous; in the summer, go for the chocolate cake with salt-water taffy sauce. Good wines, though they are on the expensive side.

Koreatown

Buk Chang Dong Soon Tofu
691 Bloor Street West (at Clinton Street). Tel: 416-537 0972. Open: L & D daily. **$**
Specialising in fiery soon tofu, this popular Korean eatery offers six varieties of the silken tofu stew, including seafood, veggie, dumpling, and, of course, kimchee. Stews arrive in bubbling stone hot pots and are seriously spicy (you can request mild or medium

hot). Non-stew options include the more familiar dolsot bi bim bap and bulgogi. Prices are cheap and service is cheery and extremely helpful.

Portugal Village

Cataplana
938 College Street (at Dovercourt Road). Tel: 416-538 1562. Open: L & D daily. **$$**
Traditional Portuguese cuisine with lots of flavour. Several dishes, including pork and clams, are cooked and served in a *cataplana* (a copper cooking vessel that goes on the grill) – hence the name. Simply served grilled Mediterranean fish always fresh that day. Grilled sardines are a speciality.

Chiado
864 College Street (at Concord Avenue). Tel: 416-538 1910. Open: D only daily. **$$$$**
Chiado is a sophisticated, urban Portuguese restaurant with modern Portuguese food. Grilled squid and crisply grilled sardines for appetisers start off your trip through Portugal. Specialities include the freshest fish, grilled whole, and grilled Portuguese salt cod. There are meat and game dishes, too. Roast pheasant flavoured with a crackling crust of sage, lemon thyme and marjoram. Traditional desserts. The setting is formal, with service to

match. Excellent wine list with Portuguese options with plenty by the glass.

Rosedale

Scaramouche
1 Benvenuto Place (at Avenue Road). Tel: 416-961 8011. Open: D only Mon–Sat. **$$$$**
A sophisticated dining room with a lovely view of the city and romantic atmosphere for a special night out. Discreet service and top-notch seasonal food that is perfectly balanced. Simple dishes with complex flavours star on the menu. Ontario veal with porcini mushrooms and halibut with foie gras are both superb. The Pasta Bar and Grill next door offers a simpler, less expensive menu with the same attention to detail. Excellent wine list.

Cabbagetown

Provence Delices
12 Amelia Street (at Parliament Street). Tel: 416-924 9901. Open: D only daily. **$$$$**
A recent renovation has transformed this bistro into one of the most delightful restaurants in Toronto. There's a beautiful covered patio to dally on and a casual menu. Duck confit is wonderfully crispy and served with skinny French fries. Liver is a speciality, heaped with sautéed onions. Fish changes daily. Good wines and service.

Rashnaa
307 Wellesley Street. Tel: 416-929 2099. Open: D daily. **$$**
Spicy Sri Lankan cuisine with flavoursome appetisers. Try the clove-fragrant lentil dumplings with piquant tomato sauce – accompanied with superb chutneys.

The Town Grill
243 Carlton Street (at Parliament Street). Tel: 416-963 9433. Open: D only Mon–Sat. **$$**
This busy restaurant is a favourite with couples and quiet parties looking for American Continental food and friendly service. Owners are always on hand to ensure that this place continues to be one of the top neighbourhood bistros in the city. Beef tenderloin with a horseradish crust is the tried and true favourite.

Cafes & Bars

Greektown on the Danforth

Café Frappe
519 Danforth Avenue. Tel: 416-462 0693
A European-style café in the heart of Greektown.

Little Italy

Kalendar Koffee House
546 College Street. Tel: 416-923 4138
Come here for a coffee and read in the daytime, or cosy up with a cocktail in the evening.

Corso Italia

La Paloma Gelateria & Café
1357 St Clair Avenue West.

Tel: 416-656-2340
Tuck into delicious homemade ice cream in a comfortable café setting.

Koreatown

Clinton's Tavern
693 Bloor Street West. Tel: 416-535 9451
Popular and lively karaoke bar, which doubles as an improv comedy location.

Portugal Village

Caffe Brasiliano
850 Dundas Street West. Tel: 416-603 6607
This is a traditional Portuguese bar and coffee house.

Rosedale

Rosedale Diner
1164 Yonge Street. Tel: 416-923 3122
Mediterranean and Middle Eastern menu. Great wine menu and selection of single malts, which can be enjoyed on the large heated garden patio.

Cabbagetown

The Brass Taps
221 Carlton Street. Tel: 416-966 9440
The food is good here, and there are pool tables and a nice patio.

PRICE CATEGORIES

Prices for three-course dinner per person with a half-bottle of house wine:
$ = under $25
$$ = $25–50
$$$ = $50–70
$$$$ = more than $70

AROUND TORONTO

Clustering around the suburbs are several worthwhile attractions, and within easy reach of the city you can discover the many delights of rural Ontario, two theatre festival towns and the most famous waterfall in the world

There is much in Toronto to keep visitors absorbed for far longer than they can usually stay, but radiating out from the city are some very special places that it would be a shame to miss. How could you not go and see Niagara Falls, for instance, a world-class attraction just a couple of hours away by road.

In the following pages we explore not only this unmissable sight, but also a number of less well-known but fascinating parts of Ontario. Many are accessible by bus or train, but travelling by car will give you infinitely more flexibility. Each destination, with the exception of Prince Edward County, is an easy day trip, but if you decide to take in a theatre performance at Stratford or Niagara-on-the-Lake, then you'd probably want to stay overnight.

Driving out of Toronto is not difficult as long as you avoid rush hours – Friday afternoons in summer are particularly bad, with highways getting very congested from around 2pm as Torontonians set out for a weekend in cottage country (and, of course, they all come back again on Sunday afternoons). It's probably best not to set out before 9.30am either, because traffic is heavy in all directions with people heading to work in the city or suburbs.

The Northern GTA

Dotted around the northern reaches of the Greater Toronto Area are a number of attractions that are quick and easy to reach from the city via a combination of subway and buses or, in the case of Unionville, on the GO Train.

Out in the northwest, there's a living, breathing reminder of the early settlers of this part of Ontario. The **Black Creek Pioneer Village ❶** (1000 Murray Ross Parkway, near Steeles Avenue and Jane Street; tel:

Map on page 194

PRECEDING PAGES: Niagara Falls.
LEFT: a statue of George Bernard Shaw on Queen Street, Niagara-on-the-Lake.
BELOW: Ontario is wine country.

*Crafts and artefacts
are on display at
Black Creek Pioneer
Village.*

BELOW: a visit to
Toronto Zoo is a fun
day out for the family.
RIGHT: step back in
time at Black Creek
Pioneer Village.

416-736 1733; www.blackcreek.ca;
May–Dec weekdays 9.30am–4pm;
July–Labour Day 10am–5pm; weekends and holidays 11am–5pm, until
4.30pm after Labour Day; subway:
Finch then bus 60 west, or Jane then
bus 35 north) is on the site of an old
farm, with 40 historic buildings
faithfully restored and laid out as a
working 19th-century village.

The whole place is populated
by costumed guides and artisans,
who demonstrate the type of
crafts that were the life blood of a
self-sufficient village and talk to visitors with both enthusiasm and
knowledge about pioneer life.

The buildings are furnished and
equipped as they would have been
more than 100 years ago, with some
50,000 artefacts bringing the whole
thing to life, including furnishings,
textiles, glass, ceramics, tools,
books, domestic articles, toys and
period clothing.

Theme-gardens grow medicinal
herbs, kitchen crops and heritage
flowers, and the farm produces grains
that are ground at the watermill.
There are also rare breeds of animals,

and the whole site can be explored on
foot or via a carriage ride.

Over in the Don Valley, northeast
of the downtown area, the **Ontario
Science Centre** ❷ (Don Mills Road;
tel: 416-696 1000; www.ontario
sciencecentre.com; daily 10am–5pm;
admission charge; subway: Eglinton
then bus 34 east, or Pape then bus 25
north) couldn't be more of a contrast
– bang up to date, with around 800
interactive displays to grab the
attention of visitors of all ages.

From the basics of physics or
biology to the latest technological
advances, there's a fascinating array
of things to see and do – you can
wander through a rainforest, generate pedal power, have fun with
optical illusions, test your reflexes
and heart rate, see lasers at work,
land a spaceship on the moon and
much more. Demonstrations – often
with audience participation – are a
real highlight of this hands-on
funfair of science and technology,
always a favourite with children.
There's also an IMAX theatre here.

Out in the lovely Rouge Valley in
Scarborough is one of the city's

biggest attractions, the wonderful **Toronto Zoo ❸** (Meadowvale Road, tel: 416-392 5929; www.toronto zoo.ca; daily, mid-Mar to mid-Oct from 9am, winter from 9.30am, closing time depends on season; admission charge; GO Train: Agincourt, then bus 85 east). One of the world's largest zoos, it has 10 km (6 miles) of walking trails, or you can hop on and off the open-air tram or ride the Zoomobile.

The 50,000 animals represent more than 460 species and are housed in six zoogeographic areas. Within these areas are naturalistic environments, including the award-winning African Savannah and the Gorilla Rainforest, and tropical pavilions. Children, of course, love the whole place, but they also have some special areas, including the Kids' Zoo, the interactive children's wildlife experience, Splash Island (a huge water-play area) and the Waterside Theatre, where the *Amazing Animal Show* is staged. There are also camel and pony rides and themed Safari Simulator rides.

Unionville

Further north, historic **Unionville ❹** (north from Highway 7 between Warden and Kennedy; GO Train: Unionville) is a lovely old community known for its abundance of festivals and fun events throughout the year (www.unionvilleinfo.com/events.htm) and its delightful Main Street. Stroll down here on a summer's day and your first impression is of the abundance of flowers. Then you'll discover its historic houses, shops, mills and churches, and the pedestrian-friendly shopping. Over 60 speciality shops and galleries sell fashions, jewellery, crafts, antiques and much more. Entertainment includes a series of free concerts at the Millennium Bandstand (July–mid-Sept, Thur and Fri 7–9pm, Sun 4–6pm, holidays 1–3pm), and

there's the Unionville Festival and parade (first weekend in June), the Unionville Celtic Festival in July, the Simcoe Day Festival (first weekend Aug), the Markham Jazz Festival (mid-Aug), the Labour Day Festival (first Mon Sept), Oktoberfest (second weekend Oct) and the Olde Tyme Christmas and Candlelight Parade (first weekend Dec).

Kleinburg

Heading north from Toronto, a 40-minute drive will get you to **Kleinburg ❺** (www.kleinburg village.com), established in 1848 and now a showcase of early Canadian architecture and traditions. Its appeal lies not just in its picturesque location and historic buildings, but in its country village atmosphere right on the edge of the city.

Shopping is good, too, with boutiques and galleries offering fine art, books, clothing, furniture, crafts and one-of-a-kind gifts.

At the weekend after Labour Day, the town comes alive with the annual Binder Twine Festival, an event which began in the late 1800s

Map on page 194

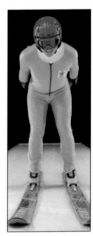

On display at the Science Centre.

BELOW: climbing the wall at the Ontario Science Centre.

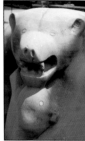

The statue (above), is the work of Inuit sculptor, Pauta Saila, at the McMichael Canadian Art Collection, which also shows the work of other artists including Group of Seven member, Tom Thomson (see page 46).

when farmers came to town to purchase binder twine for tying sheaves of harvested grain crops. Today, there's not so much call for the twine, and the event has turned into a festival of crafts, food, activities and entertainment, but there's still a definite agricultural theme. The Binder Twine Queen won't win her crown on looks alone, but has to succeed in a contest involving hog-calling, flipping a pancake, hammering nails and milking a cow.

On the outskirts of Kleinburg, the **McMichael Canadian Art Collection** (tel: 905-893 1121 or 1-888-213 1121; daily; admission charge) is a wonderful gallery that's best known as the spiritual home of the Group of Seven *(see page 46)*. The original collection was amassed by Robert and Signe McMichael, whose focus of attention was on Tom Thomson and the Group of Seven. In the 1950s, they opened their pioneer-style log home to the public and, as the collection and number of visitors increased, several more galleries were added.

In 1964, the McMichaels gave their home, property and collection of 194 paintings to the province of Ontario and, since then, the collection has grown to more than 5,000 pieces, including works by First Nations and Inuit artists. The sprawling complex, built from fieldstone and hand-hewn logs, is surrounded by 40 hectares (100 acres) of woodland, a sublime setting and a fitting reminder of the importance of Canada's landscape to the Group of Seven.

A five-minute drive away, between Rutherford Road and Major MacKenzie Drive, the **Kortright Centre for Conservation** (9550 Pine Valley Drive; tel: 905-832 2289; Mon–Fri 9am–4pm, Sat–Sun 10am–4pm; admission charge) presides over 320 hectares (790 acres) of woods, meadows and marshland in the Humber River valley. Educating visitors on the environment, including renewable energy, is the Centre's main goal, and it's heavily used by school groups and summer camps. Weekends are quieter and guided

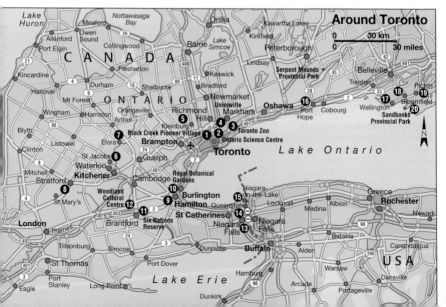

walks are available then too, but you can also explore the 6 km (10 miles) of nature trails on your own, with the aid of a trail map and the informative plaques along the way.

For a different spin, follow the Power Trip Trail to learn about solar, wood and wind energy. Various events during the year add to the attractions here, including the Maple Syrup Festival from early March to early April, with demonstrations in a traditional "sugar shack", the Fall Colour Festival in the second week of October, and the "frightful" Hallowe'en fun during the last two weeks of October, suitable for children aged six and up (advance registration required). The Visitor Centre has a range of interesting exhibits, in addition to a theatre, café and gift shop stocking maple syrup products, nature-themed books and educational gifts.

Mennonite country

Drive for about 1½ hours west from Toronto, and just beyond Waterloo you'll reach the once sleepy Mennonite village of **St Jacobs ❻**, settled in the 1840s by German Mennonites. Owing to its huge farmers' market, an outlet mall and a main street chock-full of craft, antiques and gift shops with historic storefronts, St Jacobs is now renowned for its shopping.

Many heritage buildings along Front Street have been converted for imaginative settings for artisan studios and attractive stores. In the Country Mill, at the corner of Front and King Streets, The **Quilt Gallery** (tel: 519-664 2728; daily) is dedicated to preserving and promoting the art of quilting. Exquisite examples adorn the walls, and advice is willingly dispensed to would-be quilters.

Among the shoppers, you will usually see some of the local Mennonites, solemnly dressed in black, the women in bonnets and the men sporting black, broad-brimmed hats. They come here to sell their farm produce and hand-made quilts, and can be seen speeding along the country roads in their horse-drawn buggies.

To learn more about this community, visit the **Mennonite Story** (tel: 519-664 3518; daily; donation) in the Visitor Centre on Front Street, which explains the history, culture and religion of the Mennonite people. Founded in 1525 in Switzerland during the Reformation, they established the first "free church" and introduced the now widely accepted principle of separation of church from state. Considered revolutionaries, they were severely persecuted for several generations, before migrating first to Pennsylvania and then, after the American Revolution, to this corner of southern Ontario.

The St Jacobs Country Market District is a few minutes' drive west of the village. Go with an appetite to **St Jacobs Farmers' Market** (tel: 519-747 1830; June–Sept Tues, Thur and Sat; Oct–May Thur and Sat). Besides stalls overflowing with fresh Ontario produce, you'll find all

Map on page 194

Fresh fruit and vegetables on sale in St Jacobs.

BELOW: a young Mennonite girl at the farmers market.

things maple – syrup, butter, fudge, even lollipops – and old country specialities such as homemade perogies, butter tarts, German apple cake or raspberry apple cobbler. Somewhat incongruously, the St Jacobs Outlet Mall across the street offers a 21st-century shopping experience, with more than 30 stores selling discounted top name brands.

Elora

Northeast of St Jacobs, just off Highway 6, the village of **Elora** ❼ nestles between the Grand and Irvine rivers, on the edge of a spectacular gorge. Its sheer limestone cliffs rising 22 metres (70 ft) from the Grand River, where, in the midst of the roaring falls, a remarkable rock formation known as the Tooth of Time withstands the powerful waters.

Many of Elora's solid limestone homes and buildings date back to the early 1800s, when the area was settled mainly by Scottish pioneers. With the rivers powering an assortment of mills by the 1870s, the town prospered as an agricultural and market centre.

Elora has also been home to countless artists, writers and photographers over the years, including Group of Seven artist A.J. Casson. More recently, craftspeople and artists have been transforming its old buildings into shops and galleries, and a historic school has been converted into the **Elora Centre for the Arts** (75 Melville Street, tel: 519-846 9698; Mon–Sat), which hosts a variety of events and shows by local artists.

Propelled by so much creativity, Elora hosts some remarkable arts events for such a small community (population around 4,500), from the Elora Writers' Festival in June to Jazz on the Grand and the Elora Festival (tel: 1-800-265 8977) – a long-established July celebration of song that attracts international performers of the classics, gospel, jazz and blues. In the autumn, there's the Elora-Fergus Studio Tour.

Besides the many galleries and craft stores offering one-of-a-kind items in Elora, you will find speciality kitchen and food shops and riverside cafés.

It's standing room only at the Royal George Theatre during the Shaw Festival, held every summer in Niagara-on-the-Lake.

BELOW: the Elora Mill Inn. **RIGHT:** climbing the walls at Elora Gorge.

This is also a great place for walking, with trails in the village, beside the Elora Gorge and along the Elora Cataract Trailway – also good for cycling – a 47-km (29-mile) trail that links the Grand River and Credit River watersheds, following the old Canadian Pacific railway bed.

In the countryside outside Elora, the imposing **Wellington County Museum & Archives** (tel: 519-846 0916; daily; small admission charge) overlooks the Grand River. Now a national historic site, it was built from locally quarried limestone in 1877, and provided shelter for the "deserving poor", the aged and the homeless for almost a century. With exhibitions depicting 19th-century life in southwestern Ontario, magnificent gardens and contemporary art by talented local artists, it pays tribute to the area's agricultural roots.

Stratford

A two-hour drive from Toronto, **Stratford ❽** not only shares its name with the English birthplace of Shakespeare, it embraces that connection with an outstanding theatrical heritage of its own. Today, the city's engines are fired by theatre and tourism and, specifically, by the **Stratford Festival** (tel: 1-800-567 1600; www.stratford-festival.on.ca; mid-Apr–early Nov). It is North America's largest classical repertory theatre, which was founded in 1952.

Tom Patterson, a Stratford-born journalist and a then unknown visionary, managed to persuade theatre giant Tyrone Guthrie to come to Canada as the festival's first artistic director, and actors Alec Guinness and Irene Worth were also enticed to join the company for its first season. Performances took place in a huge tent in Upper Queen's Park.

More than half a century later, the festival mounts up to 15 productions a year in four theatres, and continues to attract top-notch actors and directors such as Christopher Plummer, William Shatner, William Hutt and John Neville.

The Festival Theatre was the event's first bricks-and-mortar home, surrounded by parkland overlooking the river, its crennellated roof reflecting the theatre's early beginnings under canvas. If you are a serious theatre buff, check out the Festival Fringe programme, which offers entertaining lectures by performers and writers, backstage and costume warehouse tours and post-performance discussions.

The site that Stratford now occupies was part of the 405,000-hectare (1 million-acre) Huron Tract, given to the Canada Company to settle in 1824. A community began to grow around the river, which was originally known as the Little Thames but, in another nod to it's English counterpart, was re-christened the Avon. By the 1880s, the settlement was a major furniture manufacturing centre and railway stop.

Map on page 194

TIP

If you are attending a performance at Festival Theatre, parking is free on the circular Queen's Park Drive, and you can almost always find a good spot.

BELOW: sailing in swans on Victoria Lake, Queen's Park.

Shakespeare Gardens has fragrant flower beds and water features.

BELOW: sculptures in the grounds of the Festival Theatre.

In addition to its theatre tradition, Stratford has also become a foodie paradise, thanks largely to the presence of the Stratford Chefs School. Many of its graduates have stayed on, creating a hot restaurant scene, and the choice of places to eat is astonishing for a small (pop. 30,000) country town. Many regular festival-goers, however, opt for a pre- or post-theatre picnic beside the tranquil Avon, and places like **York Street Kitchen** (41 York Street; tel: 519-273 7041) or **Pass da Pasta** (127 Albert Street; tel: 519-272 1956) offer picnics to go.

Near Perth County Court House, you can visit the **Shakespeare Gardens** (tel: 1-800-561 7926; guided tours July–Aug Mon and Thur; free), a riverside treasure, built on the site of an old woollen mill. There are flower-wreathed arbours, banks of thyme, rosemary and woodbine, elaborate fountains, even a birdhouse for purple martins, and many of the plants are mentioned in Shakespeare's plays. The **Arthur Meighen Gardens and the Elizabethan Gardens** (tours June–Sept

Tues–Fri 10am) also reflect the festival's ties with Shakespeare.

Stratford has a number of other attractions. **Gallery Stratford** (54 Romeo Street North; tel: 519-271 5271; closed Mon, seasonal hours) has a constantly changing schedule of exhibitions, and the **Stratford-Perth Museum** (270 Water Street; tel: 1-519-271 5311; Sept–Apr Tues–Sat; May–Aug daily; donation) takes a look at the area's military role up to World War ll, at pioneer life and the craft of quilting.

Gallery 96 (tel: 519-271 4660; Wed–Sun) is an artists' cooperative that shows everything from flat-to-the-wall paintings and prints to 3-D sculptures and installations. More arts and crafts are featured in **Art in the Park** (Lakeside Drive and Front Street; June–Sept; Wed, Sat and Sun, weather permitting), a 30-year tradition of regional artists gathering to present their work – sculpture, leather, glass, clay, wood, jewellery and photography.

Being in the heart of Perth County's richest farmland, the **Stratford Farmers' Market** (Stratford Agricultural Fairgrounds; every Sat) has been a fixture since 1855, and is the place to come to sample such local delicacies as organic maple syrup, sublime sourdough rye or creamy concoctions by artisanal cheese-makers.

Hamilton

A 45-minute drive from Toronto, **Hamilton** ❾ sits in a natural bay formed by the Niagara Escarpment – a forested ridge that extends 725 km (450 miles) from Queenston, near Niagara Falls, to Tobermory, at the tip of the Bruce Peninsula. Long known as Steel City, because of its steel industry, it's a place that few people, especially Torontonians, would have considered as a great a day out. Today, however, this gritty steel town is transforming into a

cultural centre and the environmental clean-up of its harbour and waterfront is creating a much-loved outdoor playground.

On Pier 8, the **Canada Marine Discovery Centre** (57 Guide Street East, tel: 905-526 0911; mid-May to mid-Oct daily 10am–6pm; mid-Oct to mid May Tues–Sun 10am–5pm; admission charge) will introduce you to Canada's national marine conservation areas, which encompass 243,000 km (151,000 miles) of coastline and another 9,500 km (5,900 miles) along the Great Lakes. A special section is devoted to Hamilton Harbour, and through riveting interactive displays – such as tests on navigating the Great Lakes – and lively guides, visitors can absorb the importance of conserving Canada's marine heritage.

War and art

Nearby, on Pier 9, HMCS *Haida* (tel: 905-526 0911; mid-May–Labour Day daily; Labour Day–mid-Oct Thur–Sun) is the world's last remaining Tribal Class destroyer. Now a national historic site, it served in many theatres of operation from World War ll to the Cold War and offers a realistic glimpse of life and work on board. Make sure you wear sensible shoes to safely negotiate the sometimes slippery decks and steep ladders.

Downtown, the **Art Gallery of Hamilton** (123 King Street West, tel: 1-905-527 6610; Tues–Sun; admission charge) is Ontario's second largest art gallery. Recently expanded and transformed with a striking gold-and-glass exterior, it has an exceptional collection of Canadian art – historical, modernist and contemporary – and frequently has thought-provoking exhibitions. One of the more intriguing permanent installations is *Bruegel-Bosch Bus*, by Kim Adams, in which a 1960 Volkswagen is enveloped by a profusion of disconnected discombobulating objects, apparently representing a post-industrial universe.

Prominently located overlooking Hamilton Harbour, **Dundurn Castle** (610 York Boulevard; tel: 905-546 2872; Victoria Day–Labour Day daily; Labour Day–Victoria Day Tues-Sun; admission charge) was built in 1835 for Sir Allan Napier MacNab, one of Upper Canada's first premiers. The lavishly decorated house featured the latest in technology, including an Ablutions Room that was equipped with running water and gas lighting. Restored to how it was in 1855, the great house has costumed guides who provide vivid descriptions of the family and its servants during tours of the 40 rooms.

Out on the periphery of Hamilton International Airport, the **Canada Warplane Heritage Museum** (9280 Airport Road, tel: 905-679 4183; daily; admission charge) captures the magic of flight with displays on Canada's aviation history, and you don't have to be an aviation enthusiast to enjoy a visit.

The lush interior of Dundurn Castle, which had all the mod cons of the day including gas-powered lights.

BELOW: rural Ontario.

A full programme of events at the Six Nations Reserve includes the Grand River Powwow in July, showcasing traditional performance arts, crafts and food. Visit www.grpowwow.com for information.

Covering the period from the 1930s to the present, it contains many of the world's greatest aircraft, including those that played a vital role in World War II. One of its biggest attractions is the only operational Lancaster bomber in North America, and one of only two in the world. You can even book a ride in it – or in the open-cockpit Stearman or a Harvard trainer.

On the borders of Hamilton and Burlington, the **Royal Botanical Gardens** ❿ (680 Plains Road West, tel: 905-527 1158; daily; admission charge) has five remarkable gardens and four nature sanctuaries. The 0.8 hectare (2-acre) rose garden is outstanding, and Cootes Paradise, a sprawling forest and wetland preserve, has oak trees almost 400 years old. The gardens are home to more than 250 species of breeding and migratory birds.

Six Nations Reserve

Long before Europeans arrived in North America, six nations – the Mohawk, Oneida, Cayuga, Seneca, Onondaga and Tuscarora – came together to form the Six Nations Iroquois Confederacy. During the American Revolution many of the Iroquois Confederacy, led by their Mohawk leader, Captain Joseph Brant, fought with the British. For their loyalty, the Six Nations were relocated in 1784 from their homeland in the Finger Lakes region of New York State, to settle within the "Haldimand Grant", an extensive area of Upper Canada, on either side of the Grand River, which was within their traditional beaver hunting grounds.

Eventually, much of the original land was surrendered to the Crown or otherwise taken; by the mid-19th century, a much smaller **Six Nations Reserve** ⓫ of 18,820 hectares (46,500 acres) remained within the original Grant on the river's south bank, southeast of Brantford. Nevertheless, it is the largest First Nations community in Canada, and it lies just 1½ hours drive, from Toronto. Allow plenty of time for absorbing the reserve's history and culture, and if you would like to experience a traditional pow wow, check dates on www.sntourism.com.

Culture and heritage

On the outskirts of Brantford, the **Woodland Cultural Centre** ⓬ (184 Mohawk Street; tel: 519-759 2650; daily; admission charge) preserves and promotes the culture and heritage of the First Nations of the Eastern Woodlands. The Centre's starkly modern museum presents a compelling overview of their history, via a journey that begins in a Neutral village, some 600 years ago. It continues through the first contact between First Nations and Europeans, when the Algonkian and Iroquoian Nations neither feared nor were intimidated by the first Europeans, the gradual colonising and growth in paternal attitudes, to the loss of land and so much more.

Ontario's Freedom Trail

In the 18th and 19th centuries enslaved Africans fleeing bondage were assisted by anti-slavery abolitionists who formed a complex network of safe houses and hiding places throughout America and Upper Canada, known as the Underground Railroad.

Fort Erie in Niagara, was an important "station" on the railroad, because of its location directly across the Niagara River from Buffalo, New York. It is here that fugitives made their final crossing to relative freedom, some settling in a town known as Little Africa. The town has gone, but a plaque on the riverbank commemorates the crossing spot.

Many escaped slaves ended their journey in St Catharines, Ontario and one of the best known railroad "conductors" lived here. Harriet Tubman, an escaped slave lived for years near the Salem Chapel on Geneva Street in St Catharines. A plaque in the chapel honours her achievements. Tubman led hundreds to freedom, including her parents, and she never lost a charge. An exhibit at St Catharines Museum reveals the local characters who worked on the local freedom trail. For a guided tour of the region, or of Underground Railroad sites, contact Niagara Bound Tours (Tel: 905-984 5375).

The museum's journey ends in the present day, with the active pursuit of land rights, language rights, cultural rights and rights to self-government. First Nations' contemporary art is exhibited in an adjoining gallery, and the museum shop offers an impressive selection of art and jewellery.

Church for the Mohawks

Nearby, overlooking the Grand River, **Her Majesty's Royal Chapel of the Mohawks** (301 Mohawk Street, Brantford; tel: 519-756 0240; Victoria Day–June Wed–Sun; July–Labour Day daily; Labour Day to Thanksgiving, weekends only) was built in 1785, on behalf of King George III for the Mohawks who had supported the British. It was the first Protestant church in Upper Canada, and continues to be the only Royal Chapel to belong to native people. Among its treasures are communion silver and a bible presented by Queen Anne to the Mohawks who visited her court in 1712. A guide is always on hand to explain the Six Nations story, told through the chapel's decorative stained glass windows.

From here, it is a 15-minute drive to the **Chiefswood National Historic Site** (Highway 54 at Chiefswood Road, Ohsweken; tel: 519-752 5005; May–Oct, Tues–Sun; Nov–Apr, by appointment only; admission charge). Chiefswood was built in 1856 by Mohawk Chief George Johnson, for his English bride, Emily, and is where their youngest daughter, E. Pauline Johnson, was born in 1861.

Pauline became an internationally acclaimed poet and performer, also known by her Mohawk name, Tekahionwake. The Six Nations and European cultures and traditions merged in the Johnson family, and Pauline's writings reflect this shared heritage. A tour of Chiefswood offers an intriguing glimpse into the life and times of a respected Six Nations family.

Six Nations has spawned many artists, including actors such as Gary Farmer and Graham Greene, musicians like Robbie Robertson and Pappy Johns, dancer Santee Smith

Fresh fruit grown locally can be found throughout rural Ontario.

BELOW: First Nations Powwow, Brantford .

Map on page 194

and potter Steve Smith. You can check out original paintings, soapstone sculptures, and prints by the local artists at **Two Turtle Art Gallery** (tel: 519-751 2774; Middleport Plaza, Highway 54; Tues–Sat, plus Sun 1–4pm in Dec), which is run by Arnold Aron Jacobs, a local Iroquois artist whose own work is in public and private collections around the world.

Niagara Falls and Parkway

Two mighty cataracts on the Niagara River – the 52-metre (170-ft) high **Horseshoe Falls** and the smaller **American Falls**, between 21 and 35 metres (70 and 110 ft) high, have enthralled millions of visitors since they were first described, as a "vast and prodigious Cadence of Water" by a Belgian priest, Father Louis Hennepin, back in 1678. More than 300 years later, the rugged wilderness may no longer exist, but the immense power of Niagara Falls ensures its place as one of Canada's iconic, not to be missed attractions.

Although the actual town of **Niagara Falls** ⑬ has been taken over by tacky attractions and honeymoon hotels, the stretch of road that runs alongside the actual falls is more pleasant – and, besides, nothing could detract from this awesome natural spectacle. To stand at the point where the water silently slithers over the edge is both compelling and breathtaking.

Two other Falls experiences are noteworthy. Both involve a lot of spray and both provide waterproofs. Within the first, you descend through 38 metres (125 ft) of rock on the **Journey Behind the Falls** (tel: 905-354 1551), emerging between the cliff face and the falling water of the Horseshoe Falls. Then, from here, head downstream and queue up for however long it takes to board the ***Maid of the Mist*** (5920 River Road, tel: 905-358 5781; Apr–Oct; admission charge). These sturdy boats (they all have the same name) venture upstream right into the churning waters and heavy spray at the base of the falls.

If you stick around until nightfall, you will witness the spectacular rainbow illuminations, in which 21

Large hotels and casinos overlook Niagara Falls.

BELOW: Niagara Falls.

powerful Xenon lights provide a symphony of colour on the water.

There's lots more to do around the Falls, including jet-boat rides, Marineland and other family attractions. You can also cross the Whirlpool, formed where the river takes a sharp bend, in a historic (but perfectly safe) cable car. However, if your time is limited, there are further delights awaiting along the **Niagara Parkway**.

The Niagara Parkway follows the river north to Niagara-on-the-Lake. Described by Sir Winston Churchill in 1943 as "the prettiest Sunday afternoon drive in the world", the route takes you through a 1,720-hectare (4,250-acre) sweep of beautiful parkland that is unforgettable in any season. A 56-km (35-mile) scenic paved trail, created specifically for pedestrians, cyclists and joggers, parallels the Niagara River and connects Fort Erie to Niagara-on-the-Lake.

Along the way, you can visit the **Niagara Parks Butterfly Conservatory** (2405 Niagara River Parkway; daily; admission charge), where more than 2,000 tropical butterflies fly freely, foraging for nectar, searching for mates or simply basking in the sun in a rain-forest-like environment. If one of these delicate creatures happens to land on you, remember a cardinal rule: do not touch.

Continuing towards Queenston, the **Sir Adam Beck Generating Station** (mid-Mar–early Dec; daily; admission charge) offers guided tours that explain how Ontario's largest hydroelectric facility extracts energy from the power of the Niagara River as it drops a steep 99 metres (325 ft).

The Niagara River marks the border between Canada and the United States, and was the scene of many bloody battles during the War of 1812 and the brief American invasion of Canada. In **Queenston Heights Park**, you can visit every major scene of the pivotal 1812 battle along the Battle of Queenston Heights walking trail, or climb to the top of the 60-metre (196-ft) Brock Monument, commemorating General Isaac Brock, the British

Butterflies flock to the flora.

BELOW:
the Falls in winter.

leader of the Canadian forces, who was killed in the conflict. It is worth the effort for the magnificent views of the Niagara escarpment alone.

Many of the historic homes in the area have connections with the War of 1812, too. On the Parkway itself, **McFarland House** (15927 Niagara River Parkway; tel: 905-468 3322; mid-May to mid-Sept Wed–Sun; admission charge) was used as a hospital in 1812, by both British and American forces. There are guided tours of the house – restored to the Empire Style period of the 1840s – and its heritage gardens, where home baking or even a glass of local wine is served.

In **Queenston ⑭**, a small village on the outskirts of Niagara-on-the-Lake, the **Laura Secord Homestead** (29 Queenston Street; tel: 905-262 4851; mid-May to mid-Sept Wed–Sun; admission charge) was once the home of a female Canadian equivalent of Paul Revere, who undertook a treacherous 32-km (20-mile) journey to alert the British forces of an impending attack by American forces in June 1813.

At the end of the street, the **Mackenzie Heritage Printery & Newspaper Museum** (1 Queenston Street, tel: 905-262 5676; mid-May to mid-Sept Wed–Sun; admission charge) is appropriately housed in the restored limestone home of rebel publisher William Lyon Mackenzie.

Niagara-on-the-Lake

The lovely little town of **Niagara-on-the-Lake ⑮**, one of the prettiest places in Canada, was an early Loyalist settlement, an Underground Railroad destination, the first capital of Upper Canada (then known as Newark) and an elegant 19th-century summer resort. Only 20 minutes from Niagara Falls, it is light years away in ambience, and as well known for its theatre, for dining out, and for shopping for antiques, collectables, art, rare books and theatre memorabilia. It's one of Ontario's oldest settlements, and a visit to the **Niagara Historical Museum** (43 Castlereagh Street; tel: 905-468 3912; daily; small admission charge) interprets its heritage through its rich collection of early Canadian artefacts and archives.

During the War of 1812, **Fort George** (tel: 905-468 4257; Apr–Oct daily) was the major British post on the frontier with the US. It was occupied by the American forces for seven months in 1813, until it was retaken and kept in British hands for the remainder of the war. It is now restored to its War of 1812 appearance, but the only original building is the magazine.

Niagara-on-the-Lake is a magnet for theatre-lovers during the **Shaw Festival** (tel: 1-800-511 7429; Apr–Nov Tues–Sun; www.shaw fest.com), run by a repertory company renowned for its productions of plays by George Bernard Shaw and his contemporaries, including Oscar Wilde, Noel Coward, Chekhov, Ibsen and Brecht. Up to 10 produc-

BELOW: tasting local produce at a winery

tions are staged each year in the town's three theatres.

The Wine Route

If you are travelling by car and have plenty of time, there is a more leisurely approach to the Niagara Peninsula than the Queen Elizabeth Highway. From the QEW out of Toronto, take Highway 403 to Hamilton, then the Lincoln Alexander Parkway turnoff. This eventually becomes Mud Road, then Fly Road – a route that will take you past small villages, tidy farms, and sprawling fruit orchards and vineyards. Turn left on Country Road 24 and enjoy the glorious lake view as you descend into **Vineland**. From here, Country Road 81 follows the escarpment, a windy, hilly stretch, with woods rising steeply to the right.

By now, you will be on the **Wine Route** (www.winesof ontario.org), which leads, eventually, around St Catharines, over the Welland Canal and to Niagara Falls, Queenston, St David's and Niagara-on-the-Lake. Some of Canada's best wines are produced on the Niagara Peninsula,

and wine tourism is becoming big business. The area's 50 wineries are easily accessed by following the Wine Route signs; most offer tours and tastings, and several have acclaimed restaurants.

East of Toronto

A little over an hour's drive from Toronto, **Port Hope** sits beside the Ganaraska River, on Lake Ontario. Originally a native village called Cochingomink, it was "settled" by 40 United Empire Loyalist families after the American Revolution in the 1790s, and went on to become a prosperous port. Its small-town ambience has been beautifully preserved, with around 200 historically designated buildings and a main street that is considered Ontario's best-preserved Victorian street-scape.

The **Capitol Theatre** (20 Queen Street, tel: 905-885 1071), which opened in 1930, was the first theatre built in Canada specifically for the screening of talking pictures. An extensive restoration has transformed it into a performing arts centre.

Map on page 194

One of the Canadian wine industry's most unique products is icewine, made from grapes that have been left to freeze on the vines, hand picked and then pressed while still frozen. The intensely sweet juice is then fermented slowly. One of the largest producers, Hillebrand Estates Wineries (1249 Niagara Stone Road, tel: 905- 468 7123) offers tours and an Icewine Fest.

BELOW:
on the wine route.

BELOW: Port Hope has many antique shops.

Continue east along Highway 2 for 16 km (10 miles) and you come to **Cobourg**. The pride of the town is its **Victoria Hall**, an enormous building fronted by Corinthian columns, which was opened by the then Prince of Wales in 1860. Its Courtroom – still in use – was modelled on London's Old Bailey. It also houses a concert hall with a 10-metre (35-ft) high ceiling and splendid acoustics, plus the Art Gallery of Northumberland.

From Cobourg, Highway 2 becomes the **Apple Route** and winds through a 200-year agrarian heritage of gently rolling hills, pick-your-own apple orchards, tiny hamlets, small towns and sprawling farms.

Prince Edward County

Highway 33 leads south to **Prince Edward County**, which locals simply call "the County". A peninsula that juts into Lake Ontario, south of Belleville, it was settled by Loyalists in the 1780s. Though more and more people are discovering its charms, there is still an island-like sense of remoteness to this area. The highway becomes the Loyalist Parkway, the County's main east–west artery, with lovely vistas of New England-style clapboard houses, brick homes with gingerbread trim and of Wellington Bay.

The first town you will come to is **Wellington** ⓱, where many older homes have been converted into restaurants and bed-and-breakfast places. The **Wellington Historical Community Museum** (290 Main Street; tel: 613-399 5015; Victoria Day–1 July and Labour Day–Thanksgiving Fri, Sat and Mon; 2 July–Labour Day Mon–Sat; small admission charge) is housed in a former 1895 Quaker meeting house and focuses mainly on the area's Quaker history.

Antiques are big business along the main street of **Bloomfield** ⓲, as are gift and craft stores, artist galleries, and bed-and-breakfasts, mostly housed in historic buildings. The County is ideal for exploring by bike – and you can rent one at the Bloomfield Bicycle Company (225 Main Street, tel: 613-393 1060). You could reward your efforts later

with a visit to Slickers County Ice Cream (271 Main Street), where all-natural ice cream is made daily by hand, using fresh County products. The rhubarb-ginger is divine.

Picton ⓳ is the County's main town, with several historic buildings, including the County Courthouse and Jail on Union Street, where Sir John A. Macdonald, Canada's first prime minister, began practising law. **Prince Edward County Museum** (Church and Union streets; tel: 613-476 3833; Victoria Day–Thanksgiving; small admission charge) is housed in the old St Mary Magdelene Church – part of the **Macaulay Heritage Park** complex – and provides an excellent overview of the County's bygone days, including a fascinating presentation on Sir John and detailed exhibits on the town's Loyalist connection.

Restored theatre

When the **Regent Theatre** (224 Main Street, tel: 1-877-411 4761) opened in Picton in 1922, it was a rare example of an Edwardian opera house with a stage equal in size to that of Toronto's Royal Alexandra Theatre. Barely surviving the whims of the entertainment industry during the 20th century, it too has been restored as close to its original state as possible, and is now the County's centre for the arts, with a year-round programme of theatre, first run movies and alternative films, as well as festivals for chamber music and jazz.

The County has been attracting artists and artisans for years, drawn by its inspiring surroundings (and, perhaps, by the lower than big city prices). Studios of photographers and woodcarvers, weavers, sculptors and painters are found down many a country backroad. Every year Picton hosts **Art in the County** (June–July), a juried art show and sale, the Prince Edward County Studio and Gallery Tour (end Sept) and the Marker's Hand (early Nov).

One of its most renowned attractions is **Sandbanks Provincial Park ⓴**. Formed by a vast freshwater sand dune system, it's a laid-back, family-orientated park, with giant sand dunes, three wide golden sandy beaches – Outlet Beach, Sandbanks Beach and Dunes Beach – and shallow waters that are perfect for windsurfing, sailing and canoeing, as well as swimming in warm weather. Every spring, birdwatchers arrive in droves. The County's sandy shoreline, limestone outcrops, lakes, forests and wetlands attract over 300 species of birds.

Just east of Picton, there are over 20 km (12 miles) of hiking trails in **Macaulay Mountain Conservation Area**, through both lowland and wooded escarpment. Birdwatchers come to see the likes of great crested flycatchers and winter wrens, others to see the quirky folk art of Macaulay's Birdhouse City, in which many of the 100 birdhouses are colourful reproductions of local historic buildings. ❑

Rural Ontario has park and woodland trails ideal for birdwatching and nature hikes.

BELOW: cycling in rural Niagara Parkway.

RESTAURANTS, BARS & CAFÉS

Restaurants

Kleinburg

Chartreuse

10512 Islington Avenue. Tel: 905-893 0475. Open: L & D daily. **$$$**

Specialises in steaks, fish, local lamb. Large selection of side vegetables. Liberal use of chartreuse.

Elora

Alex's Kitchen

14 Mill Street. Tel: 519-846 8247. Open: L & D Wed–Sun. **$$$**

A fusion of French and Italian cuisine in a hip, minimalist setting.

Dragonfly Café

15 Mill Street. Tel: 519-846 0866. Open: daily. **$**

Home-style cooking and a relaxed ambience. Deck overlooks the river.

Stratford

The Belfry Grill Room

70 Brunswick Street. Tel: 519-273 3424. Open: L & D Tues–Sat. **$$$**

An all-day menu that highlights all things Canadian, from Prince Edward Island mussels to Alberta bison. Reservations necessary.

Down The Street

30 Ontario Street. Tel: 519-273 5886. Open: L & D Tues–Sun; D only Mon. **$$$**

A busy bar and eatery that combines ethnic flavours with organic and locally grown produce. A great late-night spot.

The Sun Room

55 George Street West. Tel: 519-273 0331. Open: L & D Tues–Sat; D Sun in July and Aug. **$$**

Hugely popular for its innovative cooking and moderate prices. Book ahead if you're planning a pre-theatre dinner.

Hamilton

Baranga's on the Beach

380 Van Wagners Beach Road. Tel: 905-544 7122. Open: Apr–Dec L & D daily. **$$**

A happening, lakeside spot, specialising in Mediterranean food. Outdoor patio and solarium.

La Cantina

60 Walnut Street South. Tel: 905-521 8989. Open: D Tues–Sat, L Tues–Fri. **$$**

Top Italian restaurant favoured by locals. Casual room offers luscious pizza; formal room modern Italian. Excellent well priced vino.

Wildflower

219 Highway 20 East, Fonthill. Tel: 905-892 6167. Open: D Wed–Sun, L Tues–Sat, Br Sun. **$$**

Bright, airy space. To best fit local reds, red meat comes first here.

Wild Orchid Restaurant and Bar

286 James Street North. Tel: 905-528 7171. Open: L & D Tues–Sun. **$$**

A popular Portuguese restaurant. Its changing menu always includes plenty of fresh fish.

Six Nations/Brantford

Ged's

97 Brant Avenue, Brantford. Tel: 519-759 1125. Open: D only Mon–Thur and Sat; L on Fri; closed Sun. **$$$**

A 25-minute drive from Six Nations Reserve, Ged's can be relied on for traditional dishes with an innovate twist.

Niagara Falls and Parkway

17 Noir

Fallsview Casino, 6380 Fallsview Boulevard, Niagara Falls. Tel: 888-FALLSVUE. Open: L & D daily. **$$$$**

Among the top tables in the area. Canadian *à la mode*, plus a creative Asian food bar.

Casa Mia Ristorante

3518 Portage Road, Niagara Falls. Tel: 905-356 5410. Open: D daily, L Mon–Fri. **$$$**

Local favourite with authentic old-style Italian food in a warm setting.

Casa D'Oro

5875 Victoria Avenue, Niagara Falls. Tel: 905-356 5646. Open: L & D Sun–Fri, D only Sat. **$$$**

Upmarket Italian cuisine, with second generation at the helm.

Queenston Heights Restaurant

14184 Niagara Parkway, Queenston. Tel: 905-262 4274. Open: L & D daily. **$$**

Tasty sandwiches at lunchtime. Dinner features decent cuisine and spectacular view.

Niagara-on-the-Lake and Wine Route

Escabeche

Prince of Wales Hotel, Niagara-on-the-Lake. 6 Picton Street. Tel: 905-468 3246. Open: L & D daily. **$$$$**

Continental fare delicately cooked. Outstanding wine list, at a price.

Epicurean

84 Queen Street, Niagara-on-the-Lake. Tel: 905-468 0288. Open: L & D daily. **$$**

Informal, in the heart of town. Pre-theatre a speciality. Picnics.

Hillebrand Winery Restaurant

1249 Niagara Stone Road, Niagara-on-the-Lake. Tel: 905-468 7123. Open: L & D daily. **$$$$**

One of the area's top restaurants, with lovely vineyard views. Superb à la carte and five-course tasting menus.

Lake House

3100 North Service Road, Vineland. Tel: 905-562 6777. Open: L & D daily. **$$$**

A long, Mediterranean-inspired menu in an 1867 lakeside house.

Lawrenceville Restaurant

1502 Niagara Stone Road, Virgil. Tel: 905-468 4333. Open: B, L & D Tues–Sun. **$$**

Loved by locals for prime rib and country cooking.

Niagara Culinary Institute

135 Taylor Road, RR4, Welland. Tel: 905-641 2252, ext 4619. Open: D Wed–Sat, L Tues–Sun. **$$**

A unique experience – students cook and wait on tables. Some wines from college winery.

On the 20

Cave Springs Winery, 3845 Main Street, Jordan Tel: 905-562 7313. Open: L & D daily. **$$$$**
Serious dining opposite a splendid Inn (on the Twenty). Inventive menu from top kitchen features local produce, Cave Springs wines and a few others.

Peller Estates Winery Restaurant
290 John Street East, Niagara-on-the-Lake. Tel: 905- 468 4678. Open: L & D daily. **$$$$**
Refined dining in an impressive setting, with views over miles of vineyards.

Peninsula Ridge Restaurant
5600 King Street, Beamsville. Tel: 905-563 0900. Open: L & D Wed–Sun. **$$$**
One of the top wine country eateries. Local ingredients, great wines, wonderful atmosphere, top-notch service and great vineyard views.

Stone Road Grill
238 Mary Street, Niagara-on-the-Lake. Tel: 905-468 3474. Open: L & D Tues–Fri, D only Sat–Sun. **$$**
Warmth inside belies strip-mall site. Superb Niagara list and ambitious bistro fare make this a local favourite.

Terroir La Cachette
Strewn Winery, 1339 Lake-shore Road, Niagara-on-the-Lake. Tel: 905-468 1229.

Open: L & D daily. **$$**
French country cooking, Niagara style.

The View
East Dell Estates, 4041 Locust Lane, Beamsville. Tel: 905-563 9463. Open: Br Sun, L & D Mon–Sat. **$$**
Huge windows give great view of lake and skyline.

Vineland Estates Winery Restaurant
3620 Moyer Road, Vineland. Tel: 1-888-846-3526, ext 15. Open: L & D daily. **$$$$**
Eclectic dishes with Tuscan pizazz. Best patio dining offers lake views.

Wellington Court
11 Wellington Street, St Catharines. Tel: 905-682 5518. Open: L & D Tues–Sat. **$$$**
Fresh Niagara cuisine, offering the best quality and price in the area. Pork tenderloin slices are anointed with a maple-mustard balsamic glaze, accompanied with scallop potatoes. Wine list is strong on regional labels.

Zee's Patio and Grill
92 Picton Street, Niagara-on-the-Lake. Tel: 905-468 5711. Open: L & D daily. **$**
Well-prepared grills, close to festival theatre.

Prince Edward County

Garden Dining Room
The Waring House, Highway 33 & Country Road 1, Picton. Tel: 613-476 7492. Open: L & D daily. **$$$$**
Renowned for superb County cuisine and its cooking school. Adjoining Barley Room Pub, with quirky carvings by local folk artist Robert

Danielis, offers good budget-price menu.

Bars & Cafes

Elora

Chat Room Café
90 Metcalfe Street. Tel: 519-846 5883
Speciality coffee and tea, sandwiches.

Kleinburg

Mr McGregor's House
10502 Islington Avenue. Tel: 905-893 2508. Open: daily in summer; Wed–Sun in winter.
A cosy tearoom that serves delicious home-made food, including a mouth-watering buffet of desserts. In warmer months, eat outside in the delightful tree-filled garden, surrounded by an eclectic mixture of sculptures.

Stratford

Tango Café Bistro
104 Ontario Street. Tel: 519 271-9202
A unique combination of warm atmosphere, art, delicious food and great coffee.

St Jacobs

Stone Crock Bakery & Bakery Café
1402 King Street North. Tel: 519-664 3612
Fresh baked treats using homegrown ingredients.

Niagara Falls

Hard Rock Café
5701 Falls Avenue. Tel: 905-356-7625.
Popular bar and nightspot. Guitars of

famous musicians line the walls .

Niagara-on -the -Lake & Wine Country

Coach House Café and Cheese Shoppe
Henry of Pelham Winery, 1469 Pelham Road, St Catharines. Tel: 905-684 8423.
Soups, salads and out-standing cheeses. Picnic baskets available.

De Luca's Cheese Market & Deli
2017 Niagara Stone Road. Tel: 905-468-2555.
Take-aways, great for cheese and paninis with local ingredients.

The Grill at the Epicurian
84 Queen Street. Tel: 905-468 0288.
A beautiful garden patio and sophisticated menu highlight this bistro.

The Pie Plate
1516 Niagara Stone Road, Virgil. Tel: 905-468 9743.
Great sandwiches and home-made pies over-filled with fruit.

Prince Edward County

Bean Counter Café
14 Elizabeth Street, Picton. Tel: 613-476 1718.
Perfect for a light bite – great coffee, soups, sal-ads, pastries and freshly made gelato.

PRICE CATEGORIES

Prices for three-course dinner per person with a half-bottle of house wine:
$ = under $25
$$ = $25–50
$$$ = $50–70
$$$$ = more than $70

TRANSPORT

GETTING THERE AND GETTING AROUND

GETTING THERE

By Air

Toronto is served by **Pearson International Airport** (YYZ), which lies 27 km (16 miles) west of the downtown core. It can be reached by highways 401, 427 and 409. Allow 90 minutes travel time by car from downtown before flight check-in, and as much as an extra hour at rush hour or in bad weather. The much smaller **Toronto City Centre Airport** (YTZ) lies on an island about 15 minutes from the downtown core. A passenger and vehicle ferry makes the round trip across the 121-metre (400-ft) channel every 15 minutes.

Airlines

Toronto Pearson is served by all the major international airlines, including national carrier Air Canada.

Air Canada, tel: 888-247 2262; www.aircanada.ca

CanJet Airlines, tel: 800-809 7777; www.canjet.com. A low-cost airline serving various destinations in Canada and Florida.

First Air, tel: 800-267 1247; www.firstair.ca. The Inuit-owned airline serving Canada's Arctic.

Harmony Airways, tel: 866-868 6789; www.harmonyairways.com. A Vancouver-based airline with services within Canada and to Hawaii and California.

WestJet, tel: 800-538 5696; www.westjet.com. Low-cost domestic flights.

ZOOM Airlines, tel: 1-866-359 9666; www.flyzoom.com. A young, Ottawa-based, company with flights within Canada, to the UK, France and the Caribbean.

By Rail

The terminal for **VIA Rail** and **AMTRAK** passenger trains is **Union Station**, located in the heart of the downtown business district on Front Street between Bay and University. Rail passengers can connect directly with subways and commuter trains without leaving the station.

By Road

Central Canada's major east–west route, **Highway 401**, passes right through the north end of Toronto, with numerous exits heading south towards the downtown core, including the **Don Valley Parkway** (central/east), **Allen Expressway** (central/west, ending at Eglinton Avenue) and **Highway 427** (west). The closest Canada/US border crossings are at **Niagara Falls**, **Fort Erie** and **Windsor**, all west of the city. Motorists heading into Toronto from the west can connect with the **Queen Elizabeth Way** (QEW) to drive directly into the downtown core. The Greater Toronto Area (GTA) has only one toll road: **Highway 407**, in suburban Vaughan.

The downtown **Bus Terminal** (610 Bay Street, tel: 416-393 7911; www.greyhound.ca) connects with numerous towns and cities in Canada and the US.

GETTING AROUND

On Arrival

Orientation

Toronto lies on the north shore of the huge freshwater **Lake Ontario**, and its contours gradually slope upwards away from the waterfront. The streets were laid out in a sensible grid system by British surveyors, but an underlying network of rivers and ravines breaks up the uniformity of the plan in places.

Yonge Street is the central north–south artery, so addresses on east–west streets are numbered from Yonge Street outward, and street names are designated as "East" or "West" of Yonge.

(Streets parallel to Yonge are generally numbered from south to north.) One of the two north–south subway lines follows Yonge (the other follows University Avenue and the Allen Express-way). The major downtown cross-streets are served by streetcars and by subway stations on both of these lines. Heading north from the lakeshore, these are King, Queen, Dundas and College/Carlton. The next major street is Bloor/Danforth, which is served by a subway line instead of a streetcar. Many Toronto streets, including some of the largest in the downtown core, are one-way.

Airport/City Transportation

Airport limousines use a standard, fixed fee schedule, set at about $50 between the airport and the downtown core, with staged fees as low as $20 for west-end suburbs, and as high as $80 for the far northeast. Additional charges apply for excess baggage and extra passenger drop-offs.

Taxis use a similar rate schedule, but prices are lower. Most limousines and taxis accept major credit cards, but not debit cards. Don't expect the driver to know the way. Unless you are headed for a prominent downtown location, you need to know the locality and/or near-est major intersection in addition to the actual address.

Toronto Airport Express buses shuttle between the air-port and most major downtown hotels every 20 to 30 minutes between 5am and midnight. The trip takes 60 to 90 minutes depending on traffic conditions. Buses depart from Terminal 1 (Arrivals Level and Ground Level), Terminal 2 (Area 18) and Termi-nal 3 (Area 27).

One-way fares: $15.50 (adult), $14 (student/senior). Round trip: $26.75. Up to two children under 11 with an adult ride free. Tel: 800-387 6787,

905-564 3232; www.torontoairport express.com

GO Transit buses run between the airport and the York Mills and Yorkdale subway stations every 60 minutes, between 6am and 1am (from 9am on Sunday). Buses depart from Terminal 1 (Ground Level) and Terminal 2 (Arrivals Level). Travel time is 30 to 35 minutes (to/from Yorkdale), or 40 to 45 minutes (to/from York Mills). One-way: $4.65 (adult), $2.35 (senior/ child). Transfer to the subway costs extra (see TTC opposite). Tel: 888-GET ON GO, 416-869 3200; www.gotransit.com.

TTC (public transit) buses are the least expensive option, run-ning between 1–5am when other bus services are off-duty. The "Airport Rocket" connects with the Kipling subway station between 5.30am and 2am. Travel time is about 20 minutes. The 58A Malton bus connects with Lawrence West subway sta-tion from about 5am to 1am. Travel time is about 45 minutes.

There are two late-night choices: the 300A Bloor-Danforth bus, which connects with the Yonge/Bloor subway station from 2–5am (about 45 minutes), and the 307 Eglinton West bus, which connects with Eglinton subway station from about 1.30–5am (about 45 min-utes). All TTC buses depart from Terminal 1 (Ground Level),

Terminal 2 (Arrivals Level) and Terminal 3 (Departures Level). One way: $2.50 (adult), $1.70 (student/senior), $0.60 (child). Tel: 416-393 INFO; www.ttc.com.

Public Transport

Subways, Buses and Commuter Trains

The **Toronto Transit Commission (TTC)** is Toronto's public trans-port authority. TTC tickets, tokens and passes are available at sub-way stations, and over 1,200 authorised ticket agents (usually small neighbourhood shops). Be warned: bus drivers do not carry change, so you need the exact amount to drop into the recepta-cle as you get on. If a trip requires changing between two or more bus or subway routes, one payment will cover the jour-ney, but a paper transfer must be obtained from the bus driver or subway station where the fare is first paid. Single fares: $2.50 (adult); $1.70 (student aged 13–19 and senior aged 65+ with proof of age); $0.60 (children under 12). Discounts apply for bulk purchases of five or ten tickets/tokens. Tel: 416-393 4636 (press 7 for multilingual assistance); www.ttc.ca.

TTC day passes are a bargain at $8. The **Single Day Pass** offers one person unlimited travel on any single day. The

BELOW: subway trains serve metropolitan Toronto.

Family Day Pass is good for unlimited travel on one weekend day or one statutory holiday for a group of up to six people. This group may be made up of two adults with up to four young people under the age of 19, or one adult with up to five young people (who need not be family members). A **Monthly Metropass** is also available.

GO Transit is Ontario's regional bus and train system, used by suburban commuters to get in and out of Toronto. Fares are modest, and vary according to distance and passenger category (adult, student, senior, child). Tickets good for multiple rides (two or 10) must be validated in an automated ticket booth before boarding. It is not necessary to show a pass or ticket before boarding a train, but passengers must carry their proof of purchase with them for the duration of the trip in case a conductor asks to see it. Tel: 888-GET ON GO, 416-869 3200; www.gotransit.com.

For public transport information within suburban and outlying areas, contact the following transit authorities:
Ajax/Pickering Transit: tel: 905-683 4111; www.townofajax.com/apta
Brampton Transit: tel: 905-874 2999; www.city.brampton.on.ca/transit/home.tml
Mississauga Transit: tel: 905-615 4636; www.mississauga.ca/portal/residents/publictransit
York Region Transit: tel: 905-762 2100; www.yorkregiontransit.com

Taxis

Several taxi companies operate in Toronto, but their fares are standard and metered (do not hire a cab with a broken meter). A minimum "drop charge" of about $3 applies as soon as the ride starts, and the price increases with distance and waiting time. A very small additional charge applies for baggage handling, and it is normal to tip 10–15 percent of the total fare. An average trip within the downtown area will cost between $8 and $20. Receipts are available upon demand. According to the Passengers' Bill of Rights, the passenger may choose the route, and the cab should be clean and in good repair. Four passengers is the normal maximum. Some major cab companies are:
Beck Taxi: tel: 416-751 5555
Co-op Cabs: tel: 416-504 2667
Crown Taxi: tel: 416-750 7878
Diamond Taxi: tel: 416-366 6868
Metro Cab: tel: 416-504 8294
Royal Taxi: tel: 416-777 9222

Ferries

A year-round ferry operated by the City's Parks and Recreation Department runs to the Toronto Islands. **Toronto Islands Ferry** service runs from 7am until 11pm, depending on the day of the week and the season. During peak summer service, ferries run every 30 minutes, but hourly in the winter. The adult return fare is around $6. Ferries for Centre Island and Ward's Island depart from the terminal at the foot of Bay Street, while Hanlan's Point ferries (for the city airport) leave from the foot of Bathurst Street, further west. The crossing usually takes 15 minutes, but at non-peak times one vessel may pick up passengers at two docks, doubling the length of the trip. For current fares and schedules, contact Metro Ferry Docks, tel: 416-392 8193; www.city.toronto.on.ca/parks/island/index.htm

A **Water Taxi** is also available for trips between the mainland and the Islands. The one-way fare is $7.50 per person ($8 after midnight). A minimum of four fares is required to make a trip, so a lone passenger would have to pay $30. Call 416-203 8294 to arrange a pickup from a variety of locations on the Islands or lakeshore.

A fast ferry runs between Toronto and Rochester, New York out of the International Marine Passenger Terminal at the base of Cherry Street in the eastern downtown. *The Cat* crosses Lake Ontario in about 2 hours 15 minutes. It can accommodate 750 walk-on passengers, 220 cars and ten trucks or buses. Peak-season, one-way fees vary: $32 (adult); $25 (senior); $12 (youth aged 6–13); $47 (business class). Bicycles cost $10 extra ($15 with a trailer). Motor vehicle fares range from $35 for a vehicle up to 6 metres/20 ft) to $255 for a vehicle up to 15 metres (50 ft) long. Motorcycle fare is $20. A special blanket rate ($131) covers a car with up to six passengers. Tel: 877-283 7327; www.catfastferry.com

Car Services

Getaway Limousine Services: Limousine service for individuals or groups. Tel: 866-281 LIMO, 416-281 5466; www.getawaylimo.com
Global Alliance Worldwide Chauffeured Services: Luxury transport for major events. Tel: 416-410 3555; www.global-alliance.ca
Global Transportation Network: Specialising in meetings and events. Tel: 877-872 6772, 416-441 3409; www.gtn-events.com
Luxury Coach: Vehicles accommodating six to 47 passengers for airport, in-town and tour services. Tel: 416-746 5466; www.luxury-coach.com
Park Lane Livery: Vehicles accommodating six to 47 passengers for airport, in-town and tour services. Tel: 888-263 3302; www.livery.com

Car Rental

All the major international car rental companies have a presence in Toronto, at the airport or in downtown locations.
Avis: tel: 800-TRY-AVIS; www.avis.com
Budget: tel: 800-561-5212, 905-673-3322; www.budgettoronto.com
Dollar/Thrifty: tel: 800-667-2925; www.dollar.com or www.thrifty.com
Hertz: tel: 800-263-0600; www.hertz.com
National/Alamo: tel: 800-CAR-RENT or 1-800-GO-ALAMO; www.nationalcar.com or www.alamo.com

Private Transport

By Car

Toronto is not a difficult city to drive in, but the streets are congested throughout the day, and traffic can be slow during morning and evening rush hours (about 7–9am and 4–6pm). Routes out of the city are crowded on summer Fridays, with corresponding hold-ups in the other direction on Sundays when the weekenders are returning to the city. Congestion is especially bad on holiday weekends, when people leave work as early as 2pm on Friday to beat the rush.

Parking spaces are scarce downtown, and the search for one may add up to 15 minutes to a trip. Many smaller streets are reserved for residential permit holders. Larger ones are generally governed by coin-operated machines that issue receipts to be displayed inside the front windscreen. Commercial car parks can be very expensive; the most reasonable prices are found in public parking places marked by a green "P". Illegally parked cars are towed to remote areas of the city, and reclaiming them is both time-consuming and expensive, so it is important to read the posted parking rules carefully in every location.

The rule of the road in Canada, as in the US, is to drive on the right, and maximum speed limits are posted everywhere. The complete rules of Ontario's roads are summarised in *The Official Driver's Handbook*, published by the provincial Ministry of Transportation. It is available for under $15 at retail stores and government outlets, or online at: www.mto.gov.on.ca.

It is worth noting that severe legal penalties are applied for driving under the influence of alcohol. During holiday seasons, police carry out roadside spot-checks, known as the "R.I.D.E. Program", to catch drivers who are over the limit.

By Bicycle

Although local motorists are rather aggressive compared to those in other cities where cycling is commonplace, Toronto is a cycling city, and City Hall has taken steps to make the streets more hospitable to bikes. An ever-increasing network of roadways is marked with bicycle lanes next to the curb. Many downtown pavements are equipped with Post-and-Ring bike parking stands. Standard blue Bikeway Network Route signs identify recommended bikeways, and the *Toronto Cycling Map*, available from many bicycle shops and public buildings, provides further details about routes and resources. For more information about Toronto's cycling programmes, call 416-392 7592 or visit www.toronto.ca/cycling.

Under normal circumstances, bicycles are allowed on TTC vehicles and GO Trains, except from 6.30–9.30am and 3.30–6.30pm. They are not allowed on board GO buses, but they are permitted on the Toronto Island Ferries, except for Centre Island runs on Saturdays, Sundays and statutory holidays.

By law, bicycles must have a bell or horn. From dusk to dawn they also need a white front light and a red rear light or reflector. Riders under the age of 18 must wear helmets, which are also recommended for adults. Theft is common, so bicycles should never be left unlocked.

Bicycles are available for rent in many places around town, including Centre Island (near the beach). For an annual fee of $25, **Bikeshare** (101–761 Queen Street West, tel: 416-504 2918; www.bikeshare.org) lends sturdy bicycles to riders. They may be picked up and dropped off at a number of downtown locations.

On Foot

Toronto is an immensely walkable city, and many areas – particularly the neighbourhoods – are best explored on foot.

ABOVE: a city bike exchange.

Pedestrian crosswalks are marked by signs bearing a large "X". These are usually hung above a roadway with corresponding pavement markings. Pedestrians who wish to cross the street may push a button to activate a flashing light that warns approaching vehicles to stop. If there is no light, the pedestrian simply holds out one arm and points into the intersection to show that they wish to cross. Although this works most of the time, the wise walker will adopt a degree of mistrust and wait for vehicles to stop before crossing. It is important to be alert at all times, even if there's a traffic light in your favour.

As an added bonus to pedestrians, many of the major office buildings, hotels, shopping centres and points of interest in the downtown core are linked by a 27-km (16-mile) underground pedestrian network known as the PATH System, especially useful for avoiding winter wind and snow, and quite a relief from the heat of summer, too. Always busy with locals on the move, PATH can be rather confusing, but it is marked with standardised signage, and handy maps are available at Toronto City Hall (100 Queen Street West) and Metro Hall (55 John Street).

ACCOMMODATION

SOME THINGS TO CONSIDER BEFORE YOU BOOK THE ROOM

Hotels

Toronto has a good range of hotels, from luxurious modern glass palaces on the lake shore to downtown suite hotels and the iconic, historic Fairmont Royal York, opposite Union Station. There's even a hotel built into one side of the Rogers Centre, with rooms overlooking the stadium. The majority of downtown hotels lie within a few blocks of Yonge Street or University Avenue, between Front and Bloor streets. Expect to pay about $150–250 per night for an average room in establishments listed in the "Expensive" category, depending upon amenities, with "Luxury" accommodation starting in the $200 range and moving up to hundreds – or even thousands – of dollars per night.

Toronto does not really have the cheap, run-down hotels that you find in some North American cities. "Inexpensive" rooms are around $90–150 per night, with many options at about $100 (most chain motels fall into this range). "Budget" options – and there are not many of these – have rooms for less than $100.

In all hotel/motel categories except "Budget", it is normal to expect a private bath, double bed and television in every room.

Complimentary continental breakfast, exercise facilities and some form of Internet access are so common that they have not been noted in most cases.

Accommodation prices spike and availability drops during major events such as Pride Week (June), the Toronto Grand Prix (July) and the Toronto International Film Festival (September). In particular, hotel room availability can be scarce during the Caribana Festival (late July/early August).

For assistance contact Tourism Toronto (tel: 1-800-363 1990, 416-203 2500; www.toronto tourism.com). For general information and crisis assistance, contact the Travellers' Aid Society of Toronto (tel: 416-366 7788, www.travellersaid.ca). They operate information desks in all terminals at Pearson International Airport, as well as at the Toronto Coach Terminal and Union Station.

B&Bs

There are a great number of B&Bs in Toronto, many located in Victorian or Edwardian homes, and you'll find a cluster of them to the east of Yonge Street, between Dundas and Bloor (many of these are gay/lesbian-friendly). There is also a good selection around the Annex

neighbourhood, where Victorian brick homes lend themselves to hospitality. Bed-and-breakfast is not always an inexpensive choice in North America. To find out more, contact one of the following associations:
A Bed & Breakfast Association of Downtown Toronto, tel: 1-888-559 5515, 416-410 3938; www.torontobedandbreakfast.com
Bed & Breakfast Homes of Toronto, tel: 416-363 6362; www.bbcanada.com/toronto2.html
Toronto Guild of Bed and Breakfasts, tel: 416-925 3061; www.torontoguild.com
Bed & Breakfast Canada: www.bbcanada.com
Federation of Ontario Bed & Breakfast Accommodation: www.fobba.com
Ontario's Finest Inns: tel: 1-800-340 INNS; www.ontario'sfinestinns.com

Hostels

All Toronto hostels fall into the "Budget" category, with some room prices as low as $24, and few higher than $60–80. Linen is generally included, and most offer coin-operated laundry facilities. These may be booked through www.hostelworld.com and www.hostels.com. Many offer discounts to members of international hostelling associations.

Residences

Toronto does not really have pension-style accommodation. However, universities and colleges house travellers during the academic summer break (May–August), and these spaces are ideal for longer stays; in fact, several require at least a week's booking. Some are appropriate for family groups. This selection includes the most central locations; other establishments (York University, Centennial College, Humber College, Seneca College) offer rooms in suburban areas. Rates fall into the "Budget" category, but are a little more costly than hostels, typically in the $40–80 range.

Campsites

Toronto has just one campsite, the Glen Rouge Campground, in a lovely wooded parkland setting, just off Highway 2, north of the 401, not far from Toronto Zoo. The pitches are level and spacious, and there are comprehensive facilities, including electric hook-ups. Buses connect to Rouge Hill GO station. The camping season is from mid-May to early October. Contact **Ontario Parks** for information: www.ontarioparks.com

House, Apartment and Condo Rentals

There is scope for renting a self-catering holiday home in Toronto, including apartment hotels, suite hotels and serviced condominiums. Prices vary, but a stylish one-bedroom apartment in a downtown high-rise block would cost $1,500 or more for a week, or $2,500–$3,500 for a month. You may be able to find an apartment within one of Toronto's historic homes, but these are privately owned and operated, and you would need to do a bit of research to find them. Try:

Apartments International Inc.: Furnished apartments with full kitchens and housekeeping services (tel: 1-888-410 2400; www.apts-intl.com)

Bay Bloor Executive Suites: Furnished apartments with full kitchens and housekeeping services (tel: 1-800-263 2811, 416-968 3878; www.bayblooexec.com)

Corporate Housing Locators: Assistance in finding residential quarters for business or leisure travellers (tel: 416-502 9909, 1-877-502 9909; www.chlocators.com)

Cosmopolitan Furnished Suites: Furnished condominium suites (tel: 1-888-566 8566; www.cosmopolitansuites.com)

Delsuites: One- and two-bedroom furnished condominium suites with kitchens. Minimum 30-day booking. (tel: 1-877-228 7688, 416-296 8838; www.delsuites.com)

Suite Toronto: One- and two-bedroom furnished suites (tel: 416-595-5599; www.suitetoronto.com)

Other Ontario Destinations

Ontario's tourism authority offers a free Ontario trip planning and accommodation reservation service. From Canada and the US, call toll-free to 1-800 ONTARIO.

For a French language service within Canada, call 1-800-268 3736 toll-free or 1-888-908 8825 for TTD.

From Toronto call 905-282 1721 (English); 905-612 8776 (French), and 905-612 0870 (TTY and TTD).

Ontario's tourism website is www.ontariotravel.net.

PRICE CATEGORIES

Price categories are for a double room without breakfast:

Luxury = more than $200
Expensive = $150–200
Inexpensive = $100–150
Budget = under $100

ACCOMMODATION LISTINGS

DOWNTOWN WATERFRONT

HOTELS

Expensive

Westin Harbour Castle
1 Harbour Sq
Tel: 1-800-WESTIN-1,
416-869 1600
www.westin.com
With 977 rooms, this is much the grander of the two waterfront options,

built right above the ferry docks and priced at the upper end of its category. The Harbour Castle has two good dining rooms: Mizzen and the well regarded Toula, which serves fine Italian cuisine on the rooftop level. A rapid transit station lies virtually at the door, providing quick access to Union Station.

Radisson Admiral – Toronto Harbourfront
249 Queen's Quay W
Tel: 1-800-333 3333,
416-203 3333
www.radissonadmiral.com
A few blocks west of the Westin (and also served by rapid transit), this boutique-style hotel is perfect for sailing fans. It lies on the waterfront, and is close to a sailing school and the docking

facilities for several graceful tall ships. It has two dining spots, the Commodore's Restaurant and Bosun's Bar.

FINANCIAL DISTRICT/OLD TOWN TORONTO

HOTELS

Luxury

Cosmopolitan
8 Colborne St
Tel: 416-350-2000
www.cosmotoronto.com
This is a sister hotel of the equally new-age Pantages Suites. Incense sticks are offered upon check-in, semi-precious stones (for "vibrational healing") replace the chocolate on the pillow, and there's an aromatherapy spa. Doku15 serves Asian fusion cuisine. Catering to long-term guests, suites have full kitchenettes and laundry facilities, wood floors, live bamboo and plenty of feng-shui. Upper suites have superb harbour views.

Fairmont Royal York
100 Front St W
Tel: 1-800-866 5577,
416-368 2511
www.fairmont.ca
The 1,365-room Royal York is the quintessential grand old Toronto hotel, built opposite

BELOW: a Royal welcome.

Union Station as one of the chain of Canadian Pacific Railway hotels. It offers every comfort, and there are several bars and restaurants, including the esteemed Epic, serving French cuisine, with organic fruit, vegetables and herbs from the roof garden.

Pantages Suites Hotel and Spa
200 Victoria St
Tel: 1-866-852 1777,
416-945 5444
www.pantageshotel.com
Like its sister, the Cosmopolitan, this 111-suite boutique hotel offers not only full kitchenettes and laundry, but also a similar new-age theme: the Zen-inspired, ocean-scented Serenity Floor suites have whirlpool baths, air purifiers, fountains and yoga mats. Fran's, a classic Toronto diner, is open 24 hours.

Le Royal Meridien King Edward Hotel
37 King St E
Tel: 1-800-543 4300,
416-863 9700
www.toronto.lemeridien.com
This 294-room Edwardian beauty is one of the city's great old hotels. Built in 1903 by E.J. Lennox (of Old City Hall fame), it was renovated and restored in the 1990s. The lobby rooms are an opulent delight, where traditional English high tea is an exquisite treat.

Sheraton Centre Toronto Hotel
123 Queen St W
Tel: 1-800-325 3535,
416-361 1000
www.sheraton.com/centretoronto
The only Canadian

recipient of the Gold Key Hall of Fame Award, this fine 1,377-room hotel is less ostentatious than others in the area – just down the block from the Four Seasons Centre and opposite City Hall. There's a waterfall garden in its lobby, and dining options include Bistro On Two, Traders and modestly-priced Le Biftheque steakhouse.

Suites at 1 King West
1 King St W
Tel: 1-866-470 KING,
416-363 7399
www.onekingwest.com
Another of Toronto high-rise boutique hotel, currently with 300 suites and studios, but expanding. Located near the Toronto Stock Exchange, it's aimed at business travellers, with deluxe amenities including fine dining in the Dominion Club.

Expensive

Cambridge Suites Hotel
15 Richmond St E
Tel: 416-601 3750
www.cambridgesuitestoronto.com
In the heart of the business district, the Cambridge has 229 well-appointed two-room suites that are set up for business travellers. Prices include breakfast, and high-speed Internet is available.

Hilton Toronto
145 Richmond St W
Tel: 1-800-267 2281,
416-869 3456
www.hilton.com
Towards the upper end of its price category, the 601-room Hilton is luxurious with noteworthy restaurants, especially

the minimalist Tundra, highlighting native game, where diners are given a weathered oval stone. The hotel has business facilities, and an excellent location on busy University Avenue.

Intercontinental Toronto Centre
225 Front St W
Tel: 1-800-422 7969,
416-597 1400
www.torontocentre.intercontinental.com
Like the Hilton, the 586-room downtown branch of the Intercontinental chain straddles the "Luxury" category. It has indoor connections with the Convention Centre, Union Station and the Rogers Centre. There are two restaurants and a large spa.

Novotel Toronto Centre
45 The Esplanade
Tel: 1-800 NOVOTEL,
416-367 8900
www.novotel.com
Part of a French chain, this 262-room boutique-style hotel has European flair. It's the closest hotel to the Air Canada Centre, and is in a quiet corner of old downtown, near St Lawrence Market.

Toronto Marriott Eaton Centre Hotel
525 Bay St
Tel: 1-800-228-9290,
416-597-9200
www.marriotteatoncentre.com
Towering above (and

connected to) the Eaton Centre complex, this contemporary giant has 459 suites and 282 rooms. Business clients are the main focus, with efficient service and lots of amenities for all guests.

Inexpensive

Hotel Victoria Downtown
56 Yonge St
Tel: 1-800-363 8228,
416-363 1666
www.hotelvictoria-toronto.com
This 56-room hotel is a relative bargain in such a central location, although rooms are rather small. It is close to most of the big theatres and Union Station, and would be a top choice for its charm and affordability.

ABOVE: check-in at the Sutton Place Hotel.

Holiday Inn Express Toronto Downtown
111 Lombard St
Tel: 1-800-465 4329,
416-367 5555
www.ichotelsgroup.com
Good value, modest chain motel with 196 rooms with wireless high speed internet.

Budget

The Strathcona Hotel
60 York St
Tel: 1-800-268 8304,
416-363 3321
www.thestrathconahotel.com
Cheerful, cosy and centrally located boutique-style hotel. Rates include guest privileges at a nearby fitness club.

DOWNTOWN EAST

HOTELS

Luxury

Metropolitan Hotel
108 Chestnut St
Tel: 1-800-668 6600,
416-977 5000
www.metropolitan.com
Tucked away behind City Hall, the Met is a lavish contemporary hotel with 366 rooms, and 56 suites. It is renowned for the cuisine in its two restaurants: Lai Wah Heen (great dim sum) and Hemispheres.

The Sutton Place Hotel
955 Bay St
Tel: 1-800-268 3790,
416-924 9221
www.suttonplace.com
With 294 extra-large rooms, this high-rise hotel gleams with glamour and luxury. It's a favourite with visiting Hollywood celebrities, and its Stillwater Spa is highly regarded. Floors 19–32 are La Grande Résidence, where long-term residential guests enjoy full concierge and housekeeping services, pool, health club and other perks.

Windsor Arms
18 St. Thomas St
Tel: 1-877-999 2767,
416-9711 9666
www.windsorarmshotel.com
A romantic 1927 Gothic Revival style building, the Windsor houses 26 suites and two luxurious rooms just off the ritziest section of Bloor Street. Its Courtyard Café and Tea Room are Toronto icons. Rooms feature Frette linens, limestone bathrooms, mahogany or birch fittings and a butler's cupboard from which shoes and laundry are discreetly dealt with.

Expensive

Delta Chelsea
33 Gerrard St W
Tel: 1-800 CHELSEA,
416-595 1975
www.deltachelsea.com
A big (1,590 rooms), busy, cheerful downtown hotel, with tourist class, but good-sized rooms, a large busy foyer and a choice of restaurants. The Delta Chelsea can be counted on to be abreast of any-

thing that may be happening in town, and its handy Yonge Street location makes it feel connected to the city itself. An indoor waterslide is its most offbeat benefit.

PRICE CATEGORIES

Price categories are for a double room without breakfast:
Luxury = more than $200
Expensive = $150–200
Inexpensive = $100–150
Budget = under $100

ABOVE: choose a room with a view Downtown.

Ramada Hotel and Suites Downtown
300 Jarvis St
Tel: 1-800-567 2233,
416-977 4823
www.ramadahotelandsuites.com
This dependable chain motel is comfortably old-fashioned but renovated, with 102 rooms and suites. Its Bistro Lounge and Dining Room offer a European/American menu, and a squash court and table tennis facilities are among the unusual extras.

Town Inn Suites
620 Church St
Tel: 416-964-3311
www.towninn.com
This all-suite hotel has rooms with kitchens, but at relatively modest prices; short- and long-term stays are encouraged. It's close to Yonge/Bloor, and many entertainment companies accommo-date visiting musicians and actors here while they're in town.

Inexpensive

Best Western Primrose
111 Carlton St
Tel: 1-800-268 8082,
416-977 8000
www.torontoprimrosehotel.com
With 338 rooms and four suites, the Primrose is a busy chain motel that's much used by tour bus operators; perhaps only slightly less so than when the city's beloved Maple Leafs played their home games right next door at Maple Leaf Gardens.

Clarion Hotel & Suites Selby
592 Sherbourne St
Tel: 1-800-387 4788;
416-921 3142
www.hotelselby.com
The Selby is an 1882 Victorian brick home across the street from a subway station, and its 82 rooms are a bargain in their category, with lots of little extras like free breakfast, local calls and newspaper. Ernest Hemingway and his wife resided here in the 1920s.

Days Hotel and Conference Centre Toronto Downtown
30 Carlton St
Tel: 1-800-329 7466,
416-977 6655
www.dayshoteltoronto.ca
With 538 renovated rooms on 23 floors, this modestly priced chain motel, like the nearby Primrose, it does a brisk business. Its Windows Restaurant and the Beer Cellar are usually abuzz.

Grand Hotel & Suites Toronto
225 Jarvis St
Tel: 1-877-324 7763,
416-863 9000
www.grandhoteltoronto.com
Offering 177 attractive suites with kitchenettes, appropriate for long stays or overnight, this concrete high-rise was once a Royal Canadian Mounted Police head-quarters. The intimate and elegant Citrus Restaurant offers a good European menu.

Budget

Bond Place Hotel
65 Dundas St E
Tel: 1-800-268 9390,
416-362 6061
www.bondplacehoteltoronto.com
Just a block from Yonge Dundas Square, this red high-rise overlooks the downtown core. It has two dining options: the modestly priced Garden Café and Monika's Bar/Lounge, with a billiard table.

Isabella Hotel and Suites
556 Sherbourne St
Tel: 416-922 2203
www.isabellahotel.com
The main part of the hotel, including the eight suites, is in a Victorian mansion, while the standard rooms are in an adjacent seven-storey building. Rooms are small and the immediate neighbourhood is seamy, but the central downtown location makes the Isabella's low rates very good value.

B&Bs

Expensive

Cawthra Square Inn
(10 Cawthra Sq) and
Gloucester Square Inn
(512 and 514 Jarvis St)
Tel: 1-800-259 5474,
416-966 3074
www.sleepwithfriends.com
Two sister properties with gracious Victorian style , which includes high tea. They offer gay-positive accommoda-tion near Church and Wellesley streets.

Inexpensive

Banting House Inn Bed & Breakfast
73 Homewood Ave
Tel: 416-924-1458
www.bantinghouse.com
An Edwardian home with a delightful back garden, located between Church and Wellesley and Cabbage-town. Most bathrooms are shared; parking is free. It's within easy reach of a lovely park, with a free-admission greenhouse.

Budget

Ainsley House
19 Elm Ave
Tel: 1-888-423 3337,
416-972 0533
www.ainsleyhouse.com
Rooms and fresh baked goods, on a tranquil street tucked away in the heart of downtown.

The House on McGill
110 McGill St
Tel: 416-351 1503
www.mcgillbb.ca
On a quiet downtown side street, rooms in a lovely Victorian house with a garden.

The Toronto Townhouse
213 Carlton St
Tel: 1-877-500 0466
www.torontotownhouse.com
A lovely Edwardian home in Cabbagetown, with wrought-iron fences, a garden and fish pond. Private decks are available.

HOSTELS

HI-Toronto
56 Church St
Tel: 1-877-848 8737,
416-971 4440
www.hi-hostels.ca
Activities, a kitchen and family rooms. Credit cards accepted; reservations essential.

Toronto Budget Hostel
233 Church St
Tel: 416-703 3939
www.torontohostel.com
Bike rental and an on-site restaurant and bar.

RESIDENCES

Neill-Wycik Co-op
96 Gerrard St E
Tel: 1-800-268 4258,
416-977 2320
www.neill-wycik.com

Close to Ryerson University and a short walk from the subway system, this place offers single, twin and quad rooms (May–Aug), with linens (but not crockery), and continental breakfast included. There's a café, barbecues, saunas and laundry facilities. Good view from 23rd-floor patio.

Ryerson University: Pitman Hall Residence
160 Mutual St
Tel: 1-866-592 8882,
416-979 5296
www.ryerson.ca/conference
A 550-room residence for student travellers only, with dorms and suites with shared washrooms. Free local calls. Ryerson is close to Yonge-Dundas Square, the Eaton Centre and the subway.

University of St Michael's College
81 St Mary St
Tel: 416-926 7296
www.utoronto.ca/stmike's
In an older corner of the campus and associated with adjacent St Basil's church. No kitchen, but an on-site cafeteria. Minimum one week stay.

University of Toronto: 89 Chestnut Residence
89 Chestnut St
Tel: 416-977 0707
www.89chestnut.com
Behind City Hall, on a side street. Rates include breakfast and laundry facilities.

Victoria University
140 Charles St W
Tel: 416-585 4524
www.vicu.utoronto.ca
Single "study rooms" with shared bathrooms. Full breakfast included; meal plans are available. Free local calls.

DOWNTOWN WEST

HOTELS

Luxury

Hotel Le Germain
30 Mercer St
Tel: 1-866-345 9501,
416-345 9500
www.germaintoronto.com
In keeping with the area's focus on art and design, this is a fresh, upmarket and stylish, but friendly place. The delightful library has complimentary capuccino and internet, a fireplace and a collection of books on art and design. The 122 rooms are stocked with Aveda bath products, and all windows above the sixth

floor can be opened. The Luce restaurant has Italian cuisine, and breakfast in the penthouse bar is included in the rates.

Soho Metropolitan
318 Wellington St W
Tel: 1-800-668 6600,
416-599 0555
www.soho.metropolitan.com
A boutique hotel, with 89 rooms on four floors (there are condominiums above). The Dale Chihuly light fixture above the entrance, like a bouquet of 80 multi-coloured Venetian glass flowers, sets the tone. Smooth, luxurious surfaces, Frette linens, Dornbracht bath fixtures, and the likelihood of bumping into an A-list

celebrity are among the attractions. The Sen5es restaurant has an Asian-European menu that features tapas, and there's a bar and café.

Expensive

Drake Hotel
1150 Queen St W
Tel: 1-866-DRAKE TO,
416-531 5042
www.thedrakehotel.ca
A bold experiment that seems to be working. The Drake is the rebirth of a seedy, crumbling vintage hotel that is now a cultural hotspot in the West Queen West arts district. The Drake's 19 small rooms have gadgets and high-speed internet, windows that

open, hardwood floors, vintage furniture and aromatherapy room sprays. The dining room has a raw bar, lounge and café.

PRICE CATEGORIES

Price categories are for a double room without breakfast:
Luxury = more than $200
Expensive = $150–200
Inexpensive = $100–150
Budget = under $100

Holiday Inn on King
370 King St W
Tel: 1-800-263 6364,
416-599 4000
www.hiok.com

A Holiday Inn it may be, but it's a very desirable spot, with good services and a high profile locally. Rooms close to lifts are provided for lone female guests. The Canadian Bar and Grill serves a hearty meat, fish and pasta menu. There's also a lounge, deli and The Laugh Resort comedy club.

Renaissance Toronto Hotel at the Rogers Centre
1 Blue Jays Way
Tel: 1-800-2371512,
416-3417100
www.renaissancehotel.com

Perfect for baseball fans, this hotel has views over the sports stadium from 70 of its 348 rooms. It's also right next door to the Convention Centre and CN Tower.

Inexpensive

Gladstone Hotel
1214 Queen St W
Tel: 416-531 4635
www.gladstonehotel.com

One of the last remaining 19th-century hotel buildings still being put to its original use. A one-time rundown pied-à-terre for local artists and eccentrics, it is transforming into a classy hotel, and artist-designed suites and eclectic public activities in three bars keep it true to its funky past.

Travelodge Toronto Downtown West
621 King St W
Tel: 416-504 7441
www.travelodgetorontodowntown.com

With 85 rooms and one of the few secure car parks in a downtown hotel, this Travelodge is a bit of a throwback to the 50s, but it's clean and comfortable, and close to the theatres.

Budget

Grange Hotel
165 Grange Ave
Tel: 1-888-232 0002,
416-603 7700
www.grangehotel.com

Alexandra Apartment Hotel
77 Ryerson Ave
Tel: 1-800-567 1893,
416-504 2121
www.alexandrahotel.com

These two properties, both on out-of-the-way residential streets, offer modest studio suites with kitchenettes for as little as $75 per night, perfectly placed for bohemian Queen Street West and Kensington Market.

HOSTELS

Canadiana Backpackers
42 Widmer St
Tel: 416-215 1225
www.canadianalodging.com

A row of Victorian town-houses. Child-friendly; breakfast is included.

College Hostel & Guesthouse
280 Augusta Ave
Tel: 416-929 4777
www.collegehostel.com

A hostel with a street-level sushi bar, internet access and a kitchen.

Global Village Backpackers
460 King St W
Tel: 416-703 8540
www.globalbackpackers.com

This cheerful, high-profile hostel that has some private rooms, a kitchen and Internet.

Kensington Castle
75 Bellevue Ave
Tel: 416-594 1818
www.kencastle.com

A friendly, intimate hostel, with a full kitchen (reservations vital).

Planet Travelers Hostel
175 Augusta Ave
Tel: 416-599 6789
www.theplanettraveler.com

Breakfast and Internet service are included.

ANNEX/YORKVILLE

HOTELS

Luxury

Four Seasons
21 Avenue Rd
Tel: 1-800-268 6282 (Canada),
1-800-332 3442 (US),
416-964 0411

PRICE CATEGORIES

Price categories are for a double room without breakfast:

Luxury = more than $200
Expensive = $150–200
Inexpensive = $100–150
Budget = under $100

www.fourseasons.com

An air of contemporary elegance with a traditional flair prevails at this choice of the stars at Film Festival time. Truffles, its stylish restaurant, has a great reputation, and its location – foot in Yorkville head in the clouds – is unbeatable. Some rooms suitable for travellers with disabilities.

Intercontinental
220 Bloor St W
Tel: 1-800-267 0010,
416-960 5200
www.toronto.intercontinental.com

One of the big Bloor/Avenue Road trio, the Intercontinental has fully established itself as a luxury destination, and is as mobbed by autograph seekers as the Four Seasons during the Film Festival. It has 209 rooms, and most services are available round the clock. Some are adapted to suit the needs of travellers with disabilities. Signatures Restaurant is highly regarded.

Park Hyatt Toronto
4 Avenue Rd
Tel: 1-800-977 4197,
416-925 1234
www.parktoronto.hyatt.com

The Park Hyatt has 346

rooms and 45 suites. This fabulous old hotel has a misleadingly cramped foyer, but its rooms are gracious and its rooftop bar is a legend, for its view as well as its old-school style and service. The Annona is a fine restaurant and there's a full-service spa.

TRANSPORT

Expensive

Toronto Marriott Bloor Yorkville
90 Bloor St E
Tel: 1-800-859 7180,
416-961 8000
www.marriott.com/yyzmc
With 222 rooms and 36 suites, this hotel lies just east of Yonge Street, at the east end of the "Mink Mile", Toronto's most expensive shopping strip, and its direct access to the PATH underground network is an important perk in winter. Wall-to-wall windows are a nice feature and the bright Matisse restaurant and bar is a visual treat.

Inexpensive

Crawford House
40 Dundonald St
Tel: 416-968 0117
There's a three-day minimum stay at this guesthouse with only two suites. Its location, on a tree-lined side street off Church and Wellesley, puts it in high demand for Pride Week.

Howard Johnson Hotel Downtown Yorkville
89 Avenue Rd
Tel: 1-877-967 5845,
416-964 1220
www.hojo.com
A comfortable chain motel offering a great location, close to the subway, the University and Yorkville, at a bargain price.

Madison Manor Boutique Hotel
20 Madison Ave
Tel: 1-877-561 7048
www.madisonavenuepub.com
A quirky 23-room boutique hotel, run by the owners of two of the city's best-loved pubs – Paupers and the Madison (the latter right next door). Rooms are mostly furnished with Victorian antiques.

Budget

Annex Quest House
83 Spadina Rd
Tel: 416-922 1934
www.annexquesthouse.com
Laid out according to *vastu* (think: Indian feng shui), the decor here is tranquil, simple and

colourful. Weekly rates are inexpensive. It's adjacent to a subway, steps from the university, and close to a strip of Bloor Street packed with good food and intriguing shops.

Residence College Hotel
90 Gerrard St W
Tel: 416-351 1010
www.theresidence.net
A block from the subway and close to the bus terminal, this simple place has single beds with shared bathrooms, communal TV, kitchen and laundry. Rates are among the lowest in town. Guests can use the nearby fitness club.

B&Bs

Expensive

Terrace House Bed & Breakfast
52 Austin Terrace
Tel: 416-535 1493
www.terracehouse.com
A heritage home with unusual Italian and

North African decor in the Bathurst/Davenport neighbourhood, a little out of downtown, but close to Dupont subway station and a bus line. Gourmet breakfast.

Inexpensive

Lowther House Bed & Breakfast
72 Lowther Ave
Tel: 1-800-265 4158
www.lowtherhouse.ca
Private baths and cable TV are on offer in this quiet home near the university and the St George subway station.

ACCOMMODATION

RESIDENCE

University of Toronto: New College
40 Willcocks St
Tel: 416-946 0529
www.torontores.com
A modern building on a quiet street at the western edge of the campus, near Kensington Market. Inexpensive rates include an "all-you-can-eat" hot breakfast.

ACTIVITIES

THE BEACHES & TORONTO ISLANDS

There are some chain motels in the vicinity of The Beaches, but the best way to experience the friendly, laid-back hospitality would be to stay at a B&B.

B&Bs

Inexpensive

At Kew Beach
83 Elmer Ave
Tel: 416-690 3675

Beaches Bed & Breakfast
174 Waverley Rd, at Queen Street East
Tel: 416-699 0818
But-A-Dream Island Cottage
2A Nottawa Ave, Algonquin Island
Tel: 416-203 9946
www.torontoisland.org
Fourth Street Bed & Breakfast
22 Fourth St, Ward's Island
Tel: 416-203 0771
www.torontoisland.org

Smiley's B&B
4 Dacotah Ave, Algonquin Island
Tel: 416-203 8599
www.torontoisland.org
Toronto Island Getaway Cabin Bed & Breakfast
9 Dacotah Ave, Algonquin Island
Tel: 416-203 7695
www.torontoisland.org

Budget

The Belvedere
4 Dacotah Ave, Algonquin Island

Tel: 416-203 8599
www.torontoisland.org
Toronto Island Bed & Breakfast
8 Lakeshore Ave, Ward's Island
Tel: 416-203 0935
www.torontoisland.org

A – Z

OUTSIDE THE DOWNTOWN CORE

HOTELS

Luxury

Old Mill Inn
21 Old Mill Rd
Tel: 1-866-653 6455,
416-236 2641
www.oldmilltoronto.com
A converted mill on the
Humber River features
picturesque stone hall-
ways, an extensive buf-
fet lunch, a fine spa and
lovely wooded surround-
ings. It's a short walk to
Old Mill subway station.

AIRPORT HOTELS

Among the chains that
serve the airport are
Holiday Inn, Ramada
Inn, Days Inn, Best
Western, Quality Inn,
Comfort Inn and
Marriott. Most provide
complimentary airport
shuttles. Room rates
tend to cluster in the
$125–200 range.

Luxury

**Courtyard by Marriott
Toronto Airport**
231 Carlingwood Dr
Tel: 416-675 0411
www.courtyard.com
With its 168 rooms and
one suite, this hotel is a
reliable refuge very
close to the airport. It
offers free 24-hour shut-
tle service, in-room cof-
fee/tea and high-speed
internet access. Some
rooms are equipped
with features for busi-
ness travellers, and the
café offers a daily hot
breakfast buffet; the

Library Lounge opens in
the evenings. There are
exercise facilities and a
heated pool.

Expensive

**Park Plaza Toronto
Airport**
33 Carlson Court
Tel: 1-800-528 1234,
416- 675 1234
www.parkplaza.com
A gigantic 505-room
hotel very close to the
airport. Some of the
rooms include duvets
and windows that open.
Many are equipped as
business rooms with
desks and ergonomic
chairs. The Capri
restaurant and lounge,
has a lunchtime pasta
bar. Airport shuttle.
**Sheraton Gateway
Hotel**
Terminal 3, Pearson International Airport
Tel: 1-800-325 3535,
905-672 7000
www.sheraton.com/torontoairport
Distinguished by having
a direct link to the air-
port via a pedestrian
bridge, this is the only
hotel that travellers can
walk to. Its casual
Mahogany Grill is open
until 11pm; the bar
closes at 2am. Besides
the usual amenities,
dog beds can be pro-
vided. Some rooms are
accessible for travellers
with disabilities.

Inexpensive

**Doubletree Inter-
national Plaza Hotel
Toronto Airport**
655 Dixon Rd
Tel: 1-800-222 TREE,
416-244 1711
www.doubletree.com

Big, bright and comfy,
this hotel has plenty of
little extras (especially
for business travellers).
Executive rooms are fur-
nished in Edwardian
style. There are accessi-
ble rooms for travellers
with disabilities, and a
babysitting service.
Dining choices include
Alfredo's (Italian), Ginko
Japanese Restaurant
and Orchid Café. The
airport shuttle is free.
Quality Toronto Airport
262 Carlingview Dr
Tel: 1-877-755 4900,
416-674 8442
www.choicehotels.ca/cn309
This hotel has 254 two-
room suites with large
rooms, and some have
kitchenettes. Graffiti's
Italian Eatery and
Saloon features a pizza
bar. Free extras include
high-speed internet,
weekday newspapers
and an airport shuttle
service. Pets welcome.
Valhalla Inn
1 Valhalla Inn Rd
Tel: 1-800-268 2500,
416- 239 2391
www.valhalla-inn.com
Popular with locals as a
wedding, office party
and conference
location, this is a
sprawling 240-room
complex with 30 func-
tion rooms, very close
to the airport. There's
free coffee and tea, as
well as a free airport
shuttle.

Budget

Belaire Toronto Airport
240 Belfield Rd
Tel: 1-866-823-5247,
416-241-8513
Off Highway 27
between Dixon and

Rexdale, this is a no-
frills alternative to
some of the fancier
airport hotels. Airport
shuttle and continental
breakfast incur an
extra charge.
**Toronto Airport/Dixon
Road Travelodge Hotel**
925 Dixon Rd
Tel: 1-888-483 6887,
416-674 2222
www.travelodge.com
A chain motel with 283
rooms towering high
above the airport strip.
Breakfast, lunch and
dinner are available,
and there are fitness
facilities and a
conference centre.

CAMPSITES

**Glen Rouge
Campground**
Off Kingston Rd, east of
Sheppard Ave
Tel: 416-338 2267
www.city.toronto.on.ca/parks
The only campground
within city limits is run
by the City of Toronto.
**Indian Line
Campground**
7625 Finch Ave W
Tel: 905-678 1233
www.trcacamping.ca
This site, just outside
the city, is run by the
Toronto Region Conser-
vation Authority, and is
accessible by GO bus,
and by Brampton and
Mississauga Transit .

EXCURSIONS FROM TORONTO

HOTELS

Luxury

Inn on the Twenty
3845 Main St, Jordan
Tel: 1-800-701 8074,
905-562-5336
www.innonthetwenty.com
About 20 minutes by
car from Niagara Falls,
an inn that epitomizes
the spirit of Niagara's
bountiful farms and
vineyards. It partners
the pioneering restaurant On the Twenty, one
of the first to specialise
in matching local wines
and produce.

**Queen's Landing Inn and
Conference Resort**
155 Byron St, Niagara-on-the
Lake
Tel: 1-888-669 5566
www.vintageinns.com
One of a small group of
upscale properties
known as Vintage Inns,

Queen's Landing is a
Georgian mansion with
144 rooms near the
Niagara River, a short
drive north of Niagara
Falls. Fine dining in the
Tiara restaurant.

Expensive

Elora Mill
77 Mill Street West, Elora
Tel: 1-866-713 5672,
519-846 9911
www.eloramill.com
The pretty little town of
Elora is an easy day trip
from Toronto, but it's
worth lingering overnight just to stay in this
lovely old stone mill
beside the Grand River
rapids. Beautifully furnished with antiques
and Canadian art, and
the restaurant has fine
dining and a wine list
that features the best
Ontario wines.

Mercer Hall Inn
108 Ontario St, Stratford
Tel: 1-888-816 4011,
519-271 1888
www.mercerhallinn.com
Local artists artisans
were consulted over the
decor of the stylish
rooms at this beautiful,
inn in the heart of
Stratford. Each of the 14
rooms has fresh fruit,
cookies and feather
duvets and pillows.

**Niagara Fallsview
Casino Resort Hotel**
6380 Fallsview Blvd
Niagara Falls
Tel: 1-888-FALLSVUE
This deluxe casino is
right next to the Falls,
and offers lavish dining,
entertainment and, of
course, the casino
atmosphere. Prices
tend towards the upper
end of the range.

**Radisson Hotel &
Suites Fallsview**
6733 Fallsview Blvd,
Niagara Falls
Tel: 1-877-325-5784
www.niagarafallsview.com
The Radisson offers a
view of the Falls and
two restaurants, with
prices at the lower end
of the expensive range.

**White Oaks Conference
Resort and Spa**
253 Taylor Rd,
Niagara-on-the-Lake
Tel: 1-800-263 5766,
905-688-2550
www.whiteoaksresort.com
This well situated resort
hotel, a short drive from
Niagara Falls, offers a
tranquil spa and pleasant restaurant focusing
on local produce.

Inexpensive

**Carriage House
Motor Lodge**
8004 Lundy's Lane, Niagara
Falls
Tel: 1-800-267 9887
www.chfalls.com
Swimming pools, free
parking, a seasonal
shuttle to local sights
and whirlpool suites are
among the amenities.

B&Bs

Inexpensive

Century House
192 Main St, Bloomfield
Tel: 613-393 5577
www.bbcanada.com/centuryhouse
An elegant bed-and-breakfast in a Victorian
house in Prince Edward
County. It's three rooms
are in keeping with its
era, and a gourmet
breakfast is included.

Cornelius White House
8 Wellington St, Bloomfield
Tel: 1-866-854 2282
www.bbcanada.com/588.html
This is an architectural
gem dating from 1862,
with friendly hospitality
and great breakfast.

Budget

Bridie's B&B
307 Main St, Wellington
Tel: 613-399 2376
A cosy little Prince
Edward County spot.
Great value with its
comfortable rooms and
a full home-style
breakfast.

CAMPSITE

**King Waldorf's Tent
and Trailer Park**
9015 Stanley Ave,
Niagara Falls
Tel: 1-877-700-0477,
905-295-8191
www.marinelandcanada.com
A beautiful site close to
Marineland (discounted
admission for campsite
guests), with a large
swimming pool.

PRICE CATEGORIES

Price categories are for
a double room without
breakfast:
Luxury = more than $200
Expensive = $150–200
Inexpensive = $100–150
Budget = under $100

STRATFORD

Since the 1950s, this
pretty town has been
known for its Shakespeare Festival, which
has welcomed thespians such as Christopher Plummer, Alec
Guinness and Maggie
Smith, alongside the
finest Canadian actors.
The festival produces
an annual *Visitors'
Guide* with copious
accommodation listings
as well as details of the
season's plays. It handles bookings through a
general information
line, tel: 1-800-567-
1600 and website:
www.stratfordfestival.ca

ACTIVITIES

THE ARTS, NIGHTLIFE, FESTIVALS, SHOPPING AND SPECTATOR SPORTS

THE ARTS

Toronto is the cultural capital of English-speaking Canada and the third largest theatre-producing city in the English-speaking world, after New York and London. Art galleries, book shops and live music venues abound. Toronto is also a city of festivals, with year round celebrations of every kind.

Theatre

Audiences flock to Toronto's big productions, including local and touring hits from Broadway and London's West End, along with homegrown productions such as *Kiss of the Spider Woman*; *2 Pianos, 4 Hands*; *Sunset Boulevard* and *Lord of the Rings*. Most are staged at the **Elgin and Winter Garden Theatres** (189 Yonge St); the **Canon Theatre** (244 Victoria St); the elegant old **Royal Alexandra** (260 King St W); and the modern **Princess of Wales** (300 King St W). For information about all four, call 1-800-461 3333 or 416-872 1212.

Dependable productions of original Canadian drama, classics and experimental work can be seen from October to May on the stages of the city's mid-size, non-profit theatres, all in the downtown core. The biggest is **CanStage** (tel: 416-367 8243; www.canstage.com), which produces broad-appeal work at the **St Lawrence Centre for the Arts** (27 Front St E), and a riskier season at the **Berkeley Street Theatre** (26 Berkeley St). Others include **Factory Theatre** (125 Bathurst St, tel: 416-504 9971; www.factorytheatre.ca); the **Tarragon Theatre** (30 Bridgman St, tel: 416-531 1827; www.tarragontheatre.com); **Theatre Passe Muraille** (16 Ryerson Ave, tel: 416-504 7529; www.passemuraille.on.ca), and the gay/lesbian-focused **Buddies in Bad Times Theatre** (12 Alexander St, tel: 416-975 8555; www.buddiesinbadtimestheatre.com).

Scores of excellent smaller theatre groups produce work on the stages of the larger companies, or in independent venues like the tiny **Poor Alex Theatre** (296 Brunswick St, tel: 416-923 1644; www.pooralextheatre.com); and **Artword Theatre** (75 Portland St, tel: 416-366 7723, ext 290; www.artword.net). Summer highlights include the classic repertory season of **Soulpepper Theatre** in the Distillery Historic District (tel: 416-203 6264; www.soulpepper.ca), and outdoor Shakespeare productions such as **Dream in High Park** (tel: 416-367 8243; www.canstage.com), **Shakespeare in the Rough** (tel: 647-438 6742; www.sitr.ca) and **Shakespeare Works by the Lake** (tel: 416-463 4869; www.shakespeareworks.com). The **Fringe of Toronto Theatre Festival** in July (tel: 416-966 1062; www.fringetoronto.com) has a huge following: it's an unpredictable extravaganza of small shows in theatres all over the Annex neighbourhood.

There are theatre festivals across southern Ontario all summer and into the fall. The biggest are the **Stratford Shakespearean Festival** (tel: 1-800-567 1600; www.stratfordfestival.ca), and Niagara-on-the-Lake's **Shaw Festival** (tel: 1-800-511 SHAW; www.shawfest.com). Although both specialise in the work of a particular playwright, they offer a range of other productions. Also notable is the **Blyth Festival** (tel: 1-877-TO BLYTH; www.blythfestival.com), which commissions new Canadian work inspired by its rural setting. The **Association of Summer Theatres Around Ontario** (ASTRO, tel: 416-408 4556; www.summertheatre.org) offers information about these and other theatre getaways in many charming small towns.

Dance

Toronto has a lively dance scene, with contemporary dance companies, classical and world folklore traditions, and a creative

TRANSPORT

ACCOMMODATION

ACTIVITIES

A – Z

array of independent choreo-graphers. From October to May, Harbourfront Centre presents a dance series of international-calibre at **Premiere Dance Theatre** (tel: 416-973 4000; www.harbourfront.on.ca). The annual **fFIDA International Dance Festival** in early August (tel: 416-214 5854; www.ffida.org) features the world's foremost independent choreo-graphers and emerging talent at the Distillery Historic District.

Other dance stages include: **Betty Oliphant Theatre** (404 Jarvis St, tel: 416-964 3780; www.nbs-enb.ca), a locus for smaller dance companies; **Dancemakers Studio** (Distillery Historic District, tel: 416-535 8880; www.dancemakers.org), show-casing important independent work; **Hummingbird Centre for the Performing Arts** (1 Front St E, tel: 416-393 7474; www.humming birdcentre.com), hosting important touring dance troupes; **Winchester Street Theatre** (80 Winchester St, tel: 416-967 1365; www.tdt.org), home of acclaimed Toronto Dance Theatre, and rented by many cutting-edge independents.

Ballet and Opera

One of the biggest developments on the Toronto performing arts scene has been the 2006 open-ing of a long-awaited ballet and opera house, the 2,000-seat **Four Seasons Centre for the Per-forming Arts** (southwest corner of Queen St and University Ave; www.fourseasonscentre.ca), home of the internationally acclaimed **Canadian Opera Company** (tel: 416-363 6671; www.coc.ca), and the **National Ballet of Canada** (tel: tel: 416-345 9686; www.national.ballet.ca). There is one other true ballet company in Toronto: **Ballet Jörgen** (tel: 416-961 4725; www.balletjorgen.ca), and many small opera companies, notably the baroque **Opera Atelier** (tel: 416-703 3767; www.operaatelier.com), which per-forms at the Elgin Theatre.

Concert Venues

Besides the major locations below, check local listings publi-cations for concerts in churches and other small venues. **Air Canada Centre** (40 Bay St, tel: 416-815 5500; www.theair canadacentre.com): stadium venue for large-scale concerts; **Glenn Gould Studio** (250 Front St W, tel: 416-205 5555; www.glenn gouldstudio.cbc.ca): the concert recording studio of CBC; **Harbourfront Centre** (tel: 416-973 4000; www.harbourfront.on.ca): performances of all types and big-name outdoor summer concerts; **Massey Hall** (178 Vic-toria St, tel: 416-872 4255; www.masseyhall.com): Toronto's old-est concert hall, with local and touring classical, jazz, world, pop and rock; **Molson Amphitheatre** (909 Lakeshore Blvd W, tel: 416-260 5600; www.molsonamp.com): open-air venue with a summer series of popular touring per-formers; **Hummingbird Centre for the Performing Arts** (1 Front St E, tel: 416-363 7474; www.hummingbirdcentre.com): major touring classical and jazz acts; **Rogers Centre** (1 Blue Jays Way, tel: 416-341 3663): stadium hosting the largest rock concerts; **Roy Thomson Hall** (60 Simcoe St, tel: 416-872 4255; www.roythomson.com): premier clas-sical music venue; home of the Toronto Symphony Orchestra (tel: 416-593 4828; www.tso.on.ca).

Cinema

In Toronto, you can not only see films in the theatre, but also watch them being made on the street. The city is a major film and TV production centre, and you might bump into a film star on any corner. You can combine star-gazing with film viewing every September at the **Toronto International Film Festival** (tel: 416-967 7371; www.bell.ca/filmfest), which has become one of the world's most important movie events. The city hosts

numerous smaller film festivals; some of the most popular are **Hot Docs, the Canadian Interna-tional Documentary Festival** (tel: 416-516 3320; www.hotdocs.ca) and the **InsideOut Lesbian and Gay Film and Video Festival** (tel: 416-977 6847; www.insideout.ca), both in May; the **Toronto World-wide Short Film Festival** (tel: 416-445 1446, ext. 815; www.worldwideshortfilmfest.com) in June; the **Images Festival** (tel: 416-971 8405; www.imagesfestival.com) of independent and experimental film in April, and **Toronto Jewish Film Festival** (tel: 416-324 9121; www.tjff.com) in March. **Cinema-theque Ontario** (www.bell.ca/cinema theque) shows films for serious movie buffs at the Art Gallery of Ontario, 317 Dundas St W; the **National Film Board** (150 John St, tel: 416-973 3012; www.nfb.ca) makes 1,700 of its award-winning animations and documentaries available via touch-screen for free.

NIGHTLIFE

At heart, Toronto is a beer-drink-ing town with an appreciation for live rock and R&B. That said, the

BELOW: enjoy a night at the opera.

city's nightlife is extremely varied. In one night on the town a visitor can sample entertainment (and cuisine) from almost any corner of the globe. Most live shows begin between 9 and 10pm. Last call at establishments that serve liquor is 2am.

Brew Pubs

Amsterdam Brewing Co. (600 King St W, tel: 416-504 1040) is Toronto's original brew pub, with a shop, intimate bar and a patio. **C'est What** (19 Church St, tel: 416-867 9499; www.cestwhat.com) has one of the best international beer lists and house brews. **The Feathers** (962 Kingston Rd, tel: 416-694 0443; www.home. primus.ca/~eastleaf/). An excellent list of fine whiskeys plus a few house beers in a British-style pub. **Granite Brewery** (245 Eglinton Ave E, tel: 416-322 0723; www.granitebrewery.ca). Good house beer and a high-end pub menu.

Comedy Clubs

Canada is famous for producing some of the best comedy talent in the world, and many started out in Toronto comedy clubs.

Laugh Resort Comedy Club (370 King St W, tel: 416-863 6231; www.laughresort.com), specialising in stand-up; **The Second City** (99 Mercer St, tel: 416-343 0011; www.secondcity.com), fertile ground for improv and sketch comedians, where stars such as John Candy and Dan Aykroyd started. **Yuk Yuk's Comedy Cabaret** (224 Richmond St W, tel: 416-967 6425; www.yukyuks.com), Canada's premiere chain of stand-up clubs.

Dance Clubs

Toronto's lively nightclub district is on and around Richmond Street West, between University and Peter. Clubs cater mainly to those in their 20s and 30s, but embrace diverse musical tastes. Cover charge: up to $10; some are free. **Easy & The Fifth** (225 Richmond St W, tel: 416-979 3000; www.easyandthefifth.com) draws a stylish, affluent professional crowd. The Fifth is one of the city's best restaurants; **Fluid Lounge** (217 Richmond St W, tel: 416-593 6116): the liquid theme includes a fish tank; **Joker** (318 Richmond St W, tel: 416-598 1313; www.joker nightclub.ca): enormous, with different music on each floor.

Places outside the club zone, include: **Berlin** (2335 Yonge St, tel: 416-489 7777; www.berlin nightclub.com): upmarket, with a Latin flair, drawing a young single crowd; the **Big Bop Concert Hall & Nightclub** (651 Queen St W, tel: 416-504 0744; www.thebig bop.com): sensationally rundown, post-punk party palace, containing three eclectic venues; the **Docks Entertainment Complex** (11 Polson St, tel: 416-461 3657; www.thedocks.com): a massive waterfront club; the **Guvernment/Kool Haus** (132 Queen's Quay E, tel: 416-869 0045; www.theguvernment.com): a mammoth venue, with an eclectic range of music; **Phoenix Concert Theatre** (410 Sherbourne St, tel: 416-323 1251; www.libertygroup. com): themed DJ nights are a staple, but big-name touring bands also play.

Jazz and Blues Venues

The Cameron House (408 Queen St W, tel: 416-703 0811; www.the cameron.com): an arty bohemian hangout hosting local musicians; **Chicago's Diner** (335 Queen St W, tel: 416-977 2904; www. chicagosdiner.ca): a genuine R&B

GETTING TICKETS

Expect to pay $50 and up for tickets to large-scale theatre, dance and music productions. However, many excellent smaller theatres have seats in the $12–25 range, and the majority of musical performances – in genres from classical to hip-hop to country to jazz – charge extremely modest fees (free right up to $25).

Most theatre and concert venues are "dark" (closed) on Monday. Prices are generally lowest on Tuesday and Wednesday, highest on Friday and Saturday. There are often discounts for students, seniors and others. Many theatre productions and some dance or

music events offer "Pay What You Can" tickets on Sunday matinees or other designated days, with a suggested minimum of about $10. Most theatre/dance shows start at 8pm Tuesday to Saturday and 2.30pm on Sunday. To purchase tickets, call the venue directly, or use one of the following services:

Arts box office: A relatively new service offering tickets to exciting independent theatre and dance performances. Tel: 416-504 PLAY; www.artsboxoffice.ca
TicketKing: Agents for Princess of Wales, Royal Alexandra and Canon Theatres, plus some other performances. Major

credit cards accepted, including Visa, MasterCard and American Express. Tel: 1-800-461 3333, 416-872 1212
TicketMaster: Canada's largest ticket agent, handling most major online events, by telephone and through some 240 ticket kiosks around town. Major credit cards accepted. Tel: 416-870 8000; www.ticketmaster.ca
TO TIX: Offers half-price tickets for a variety of shows on the day of performance, plus a selection of full-price advance tickets (no phone sales; in person or online only). Kiosk at Yonge Dundas Sq, tel: 1-800-541 0499 ext. 40, 416-536 6468; www.totix.ca

spot with a sturdy pub menu; **Chick'n Deli** (744 Mt Pleasant Ave, tel: 416-489 3363; www.chickndeli.com): an uptown BBQ restaurant with a long-standing reputation for live music; **Grossman's** (379 Spadina Ave, tel: 416-977 7000; www.grossmans tavern.com): a legendary dive where the cream of the local music scene comes to jam; **Healy's** (178 Bathurst St, tel: 416-703 5882; www.jeffhealys.com): outstanding music at a club founded by world-famous blind guitarist Jeff Healy; **Montreal Bistro** (65 Sherbourne St, tel: 416-363 0179; www.montreal bistro.com), one of the city's few dedicated jazz venues; **N'Awlins** (299 King St W, tel: 416-595 1958; www.nawlins.ca), an upmarket Cajun restaurant with nightly live jazz or blues; **Reservoir Lounge** (52 Wellington St E, tel: 416-955 0887; www.reservoir lounge.com), an elegant place, with swing jazz and jump blues; **Rex Hotel** (194 Queen St W, tel: 416-598 2495; www.therex.ca): an unpretentious jazz bar. You never know who'll turn up; **Trane Studio** (964 Bathurst St, tel: 416-913 8197; www.tranestudio.com), a hidden gem featuring high-calibre soul, Latin and jazz.

Folk, Roots and World Music Venues

The **Cadillac Lounge** (1296 Queen St W, tel: 416-536 7717; www.cadillaclounge.com): local and touring Western-flavoured acts, from urban country to rockabilly; **Dominion on Queen** (500 Queen St E, tel: 416-368 6893; www.dominiononqueen.com), a bright neighbourhood pub featuring everything from urban bluegrass to gypsy jazz; **Free Times Café** (320 College, tel: 416-967 1078; www.thefreetimescafe.com): cosy folk and blues venue in the university area. Vegetarian menu; **Hugh's Room** (2261 Dundas St W, tel: 416-531 6604; www.hughsroom. com): city's top folk venue, showcasing local and international per-

formers; **Lula Lounge** (1585 Dundas St W, tel: 416-588 0307; www.lula.ca): exciting Latin/fusion music, with food to match; **Tranzac Club** (292 Brunswick Ave, tel: 416-923 8137; www.tranzac.org): home of the Flying Cloud Folk Club also hosts other styles of music.

Indie and Classic Rock Venues

At one time, popular music clubs were clustered around Queen and Spadina, but now much of the action has moved west on Queen, and north to College.

The laid-back Queen/Spadina block still includes the **Horseshoe Tavern** (370 Queen St W, tel: 416-598 4753; www.horseshoe tavern.com): 50 years of excellent Canadian and international alternative rock and country; the **Rivoli** (332–4 Queen St W, tel: 416-596 1908; www.rivoli.ca): comedy early in the week; music at weekends; The **Velvet Underground** (510 Queen St W, tel: 416-504 6688; www.libertygroup.com): caters to the alternative rock crowd; **Drake Hotel** (1150 Queen St W, tel: 416-531 5042; www.the drakehotel.ca): stylish, eclectic arts hot-spot; **Underground Room** is a key venue for live music and record label showcases; **Gladstone Hotel** (1214 Queen St W, tel: 416-531 4635; www.gladstone hotel.com) is a hangout for the arts crowd, hosting music, comedy and spoken word; **Mitzi's Sister** (1554 Queen St W, tel: 416-532 2570): local singer/songwriters.

West on College Street from Spadina is **Rancho Relaxo** (300 College St, tel: 416-920 0366; www.ranchorelaxo.biz), a Mexican restaurant with nightly live music; **Sneaky Dee's** (431 College St, tel: 416-603 3090; www.sneaky-dees.com) has loud, raunchy rock music, with a few big names, upstairs from a Mexican restaurant; **Mod Club Theatre** (722 College St, tel: 416-588 4MOD; www.themodclub.com): Brit indie, pop and electronic music; **Revival** (783 College St, tel: 416-

ABOVE: Steam Whistle Brewery.

535 7888; www.revivalbar.com): an eclectic mix of rock, world, jazz and even the odd fashion show; **El Mocambo** (464 Spadina Ave, tel: 416-777 1777; www.elmo cambo.ca): a renowned bar with an awesome reputation (including an incognito Rolling Stones concert); **Lee's Palace/Dance Cave** (529 Bloor St W, tel: 416-532 1598; www.leespalace.com): a big, well-worn, well-loved home to alternative rock.

WHAT'S ON?

The most comprehensive listings sources are found in the appropriately named "What's On" section in the Thursday edition of the *Toronto Star* (www.thestar.ca). For theatre, dance, comedy and music, the best source is the free weekly *NOW Magazine* (www.nowtoronto.com). For classical and new music, jazz and opera, get the free monthly *The Whole Note* magazine (www.thewholenote.com).

The best overall website is www.toronto.com, but theatre is best on the Toronto Alliance for the Performing Arts site www.torontoperforms.com. For club notes, see www.martiniboys.com.

EVENTS

January
Toronto Winterfest, tel: 416-338 0338; www.city.toronto.on.ca/winterfest
February
Black History Month
Lunar New Year
International Auto Show, tel: 905-940 2800; www.autoshow.ca
March
St Patrick's Day Parade, tel: 416-487 1566; www.topatrick.com
Canada Blooms, tel: 416-447 8655; www.canadablooms.com
One of a Kind Craft Show and Sale, tel: 416-960 3680; www.oneofakindshow.com
May
Asian Heritage Month
Victoria Day fireworks
Doors Open Toronto, tel: 416-338 3888; www.doorsopen.org
Summer theatre season begins
June
Taste of Little Italy, tel: 416-240 9338; www.tasteoflittleitaly.com
Pride Week, tel: 416-92 PRIDE; www.pridetoronto.com
Toronto Downtown Jazz, tel: 416-928 2033; www.torontojazz.com
Toronto International Dragon Boat Race Festival, tel: 416-598 8945; www.dragonboats.com
CHIN International Picnic, tel: 416-531 7838; www.chinpicnic.com
Queen's Plate Horse Racing, tel: 416-675 RACE; www.woodbine entertainment.com
July
Canada Day fireworks, tel: 416-395 0490; www.city.toronto.on.ca/special_events
Celebrate Toronto Street Festival, tel: 416-395 0490; www.city.toronto.on.ca/special_events
Toronto Outdoor Art Exhibition, tel: 416-408 2754; www.toronto outdoorart.org
Grand Prix of Toronto, tel: 1-877-865 RACE (7223); www.grandprixtoronto.com
Beaches International Jazz Festival, tel: 416-698 2152; www.beachesjazz.com

Fringe of Toronto Theatre Festival, tel: 416-966 1062; www.fringetoronto.com
Caribana Festival, tel: 416-466 0321; www.caribanafestival.com
August
Bloor West Ukrainian Festival, tel: 416-410 9965; www.ukrainian festival.org
fFIDA Dance Festival, tel: 416-214 5854; www.ffida.org
Taste of the Danforth, tel: 416-469 5634; www.tasteofthedanforth.com
Canadian National Exhibition (CNE, "The Ex"), tel: 416-393 6000; www.theex.com
September
Toronto International Film Festival, tel: 416-968 FILM; www.bell.ca/filmfest
Toronto ArtsWeek, tel: 416-392 6800; www.artsweek.ca
Word on the Street, tel: 416-504 7241; www.thewordonthe street.ca
October
Canadian International Marathon, tel: 416-972 1062; www.runtoronto.com
International Festival of Authors, tel: 416-973 3000; www.readings.org
Mainstage theatre and dance seasons begin
November
Royal Agricultural Winter Fair, tel: 416-263 3400; www.royalfair.org
Santa Claus Parade, tel: 416-249 7833; www.thesantaclaus parade.org
One of a Kind Craft Show and Sale, tel: 416-393 6000; www.oneofakindshow.com
December
Cavalcade of Lights, tel: 416-395 0490; www.city.toronto.on.ca/special_events
Kensington Festival of Lights, tel: 416-598 3729; www.torfree.net
First Night Toronto, tel: 416-362 3692; www.firstnighttoronto.com
Boxing Day sales.
New Year's Eve at City Hall, tel: 416-395 0490; www.city.toronto.on.ca/special_events

Gambling

Under Ontario law, a person must be at least 19 to gamble. There are no casinos within the city limits, but a few are within easy reach, with public transport links.

About one hour's drive north of the city is **Casino Rama** (5899 Rama Rd, Rama, tel: 1-800-832 7529; www.casinorama.com; open 24 hrs; Greyhound bus from Bay Street Bus Terminal, tel: 1-800-661 TRIP, 416-367 8747), Ontario's First Nations-owned commercial casino. With more than 2,400 slot machines, 110 gaming tables, restaurants and other entertainment.

Niagara Falls has two casinos operated by the same company. **Casino Niagara** (Falls Ave, tel: 1-888-946 3255; www.casino niagara.com) is comfortable and friendly and has 77 tables and over 2,400 slot machines.

Niagara Fallsview Casino Resort (Fallsview Blvd, tel: 1-888-946 3255; www.fallsviewcasinoresort.com) is bigger and more extravagant, with 150 tables and over 3,000 slots, plus fine dining, Las Vegas-style entertainment, a hotel, a spa and a view of the Falls. Both are open 24 hours a day.

(See also Sports, page 232, for **Woodbine Racetrack**.)

SHOPPING

Canadian art, fashion, music, literature, industrial design, jewellery and other craft items are held in high esteem around the world, and they are easy to track down in Toronto. The city also has plenty of shops with luxury items and electronics.

Canadian price tags usually give the cost before taxes, so the purchase price will be 15 percent higher. Visitors are eligible for certain rebates (see page 237).

There are seasonal sales, and on 26 December most shops have extremely low prices, which may continue for a week. Winter merchandise is generally reduced from January to April and summer goods may be reduced from June to early August.

Shopping malls

The Shopping feature *(see page 61)* highlights some of the best areas for shopping and goods to look out for. Most follow the same general plan: a mixture of clothing and speciality shops at various price points, with a food court offering fast food. Often the mall is anchored by a department store.

Find a directory of all the malls in the Toronto area at www.torontomalls.com.

Dixie Outlet Mall (1250 South Service Rd, Mississauga, 905-278 7492; www.dixieoutletmall.com) is made up entirely of discount outlets, and includes the aptly named Fantastic Flea Market.

Dragon City Mall (Chinatown, corner of Dundas and Spadina) has a fine array of anime videos, Japanese manga comics and Hello Kitty merchandise.

Eaton Centre (Yonge Street, *see page 61*) is a huge, multi-level downtown shopping paradise. Nearest subways: Dundas or Queen.

Hazelton Lanes (Avenue Road) is a spectacular upmarket galleria.

Pacific Mall (4300 Steeles Ave E, 905-470 8785; www.pacificmall toronto.com) is North America's largest Asian mall, with food, electronics, fashion and more.

Queen's Quay Terminal *(see page 63)* provides a selection of up-market waterfront, glass enclosed shops.

Scarborough Town Centre, McCowan Rd at Hwy 401, Scarborough, tel: 416-296 0296; www.scarboroughtowncentre.com

Sherway Gardens, Hwy 427 at Queensway, tel: 416-621 1070; www.sherwaygardens.ca

Vaughan Mills 1 Bass Pro Mills at Hwy 400 and Rutherford Rd, Vaughan, 905-879-2110, www.vaughanmills.com. A mall specialising in big US retailers.

What to Buy

Art & crafts

Elegant, upmarket art, craft and jewellery galleries abound in **Yorkville** and the **Distillery Historic District**. A lively scene has also sprung up on **West Queen West**, between Ossington and Dunn, where art galleries range from tiny, avant-garde spots to the **Stephen Bulger Gallery** (1026 Queen West, tel: 416-504 0575; www.bulgergallery.com), for high-end photography. It's worth continuing west to **Made You Look** (1338 Queen St W, tel: 416-463 2136; www.made youlook.ca), a good jewellery studio.

Another key spot is the area around the Art Gallery of Ontario and Ontario College of Art, near Dundas West and McCaul, with such favourites as **Prime Gallery** (52 McCaul St, 416-593 5750; www.primegallery.ca) and **Bau-Xi Gallery** (340 Dundas St W, tel: 416-977 0600; www.bau-xi.com).

In the Spadina-Richmond area, are two buildings dedicated to small and non-profit galleries (not all exhibits are for sale): **80 Spadina** and **401 Richmond** (tel: 416-595 5900; www.401richmond.net).

Books

Toronto is the publishing and book selling centre of English Canada, and Chapters/Indigo (www.chapters.indigo.ca) is its largest bookshop chain *(see page 65)*. Others of note are: **Bakka-Phoenix Science Fiction Bookstore** (697 Queen St W, tel: 416-963 9993; www.bakkaphoenix books.com); **Book City (**501 Bloor St W, tel: 416-961 4496 and four other locations; www.bookcity.ca). A small local chain with an excellent selection; **David Mirvish Books on Art** (596 Markham St, tel: 416-531 9975); **A Different Booklist** (746 Bathurst St, tel: 416-538 0889). African and Caribbean works and gender studies; **Glad Day Bookshop** (598-A Yonge St, tel: 416-961 4161; www.gladdaybook shop.com);

Gay/lesbian literature; **Nicholas Hoare Books** (45 Front St E, tel: 416-777 BOOK; www.nicholashoare.com) *(see page 65)*; **Pages Books and Magazines** (256 Queen St W, tel: 416-598 1447; www.pages books.ca), for art, design, culture and new fiction; **Silver Snail Comic Shop** (367 Queen St W, tel: 416-593 0889; www.silver snail.com); **TheatreBooks** (11 St Thomas St, tel: 1-800-361 3414, 416-922 7175; www.theatre books.com); **This Ain't the Rosedale Library** (483 Church St, tel: 416-929 9912): gay/lesbian works; **Toronto Women's Bookstore** (73 Harbord St, tel: 416-922 8744; www.womensbook store.com) for feminist literature; and the **World's Biggest Bookstore** (20 Edward St, tel: 416-977 7009; www.chapters.indigo.ca), with kilometres of shelving.

Cameras and electronics

Black's and **MotoPhoto** photo finishing chains have branches all over town. The professionals head to **Steichenlab** (500 Richmond St E, tel: 416-3668745; www.steichen lab.com), **Chas Abel** (5 lower

BELOW: Canadian home style.

CLOTHING CHART

Be warned: because of the diversity of Toronto shops, garment sizing varies widely. Clothes may be tagged according to North American or European sizes, or a combination of these. Some shops use only approximations: XS (extra small), S (small), M (medium), L (large), XL (extra large), XXL (extra-extra large) and XXXL (extra-extra-extra large). Also, high-end shops catering to more mature and moneyed customers tend to size more generously than inexpensive boutiques catering to slender teens, so always try on clothes before you buy it.

Women's Garments

NA	EU	UK
6	38/34N	8/30
8	40/36N	10/32
10	42/38N	12/34
12	44/40N	14/36
14	46/42N	16/38
16	48/44N	18/40

Men's Suits

NA	EU	UK
34	44	34
—	46	36
38	48	38
—	50	40
42	52	42
—	54	44
46	56	46

Men's Shirts (collars)

NA	EU	UK
14	36	14
14½	37	14½
15	38	15
15½	39	15½
16	40	16
16½	41	16½
17	42	17

Women's Shoes

NA	EU	UK
4½	36	3
5½	37	4
6½	38	5
7½	39	6
8½	40	7

Sherbourne St, tel: 416-364 2391; www.chasabel.com) or **West Camera** (514 Queen St W, tel: 416-504 9432). Professional quality cameras and equipment are available at **Henry's** (119 Church St, tel: 416-868 0872; www.henrys.com) and **Vistek** (496 Queen St E, tel: 416-365 1777; www.vistek.ca).

There's also a cluster of inexpensive **computer shops** along College Street from Spadina to Augusta. A broad range of **electronics** are available along Yonge Street from Dundas to Gerrard.

Toys and kids' stuff

All the shopping centres feature a range of children's clothing and toy shops, but these listed below are special:

Collectors Lane Hobbies (1220 Markham Rd, Unit 1, tel: 416-264 4941; www.collectorslanehobbies.com). New and vintage model cars, trains, airplanes and so on.
George's Trains (510 Mt Pleasant Rd, tel: 416-489 9783; www.georgestrains.com). A shop for model railway enthusiasts.
Kidding Awound (91 Cumberland St, tel: 416-926 8996). Every imaginable type of wind-up toy.
Kol Kid (670 Queen St W, tel: 416-681 0368). Lovely children's furniture, toys and clothing.
Mabel's Fables (662 Mount Pleasant Rd, tel: 416-322 0438; www.mabelsfables.com). Toronto's premiere bookstore for children.
Little Dollhouse Company (617 Mount Pleasant Rd, tel: 416-489 7180; www.thelittledollhousecompany. com.) Everything for the dollhouse collector.
Treasure Island Toys (311 Danforth Ave, tel: 416-778 4913). A well-stocked toy shop.

Fashion

A leaisurely stroll along funky Queen Street West, from University west to Strachan, leads past numerous designer boutiques and trendy one-off stores, while Bloor-Yorkville specialises in high-end clothing.

Annie Thompson Studio (674 Queen St W, tel: 416-703 3843; www.anniethompson.ca). Creatively original women's streetwear.
Boudoir (990 Queen St W, tel: 416-535 6600). Vintage cocktail frocks and chic chapeaux.
Brian Bailey (878 Queen St W, tel: 416-221 3355; Bayview Village, 2901 Bayview Ave, tel: 416-516 7188; www.brianbailey fashion.com). Sophisticated women's wear from a noted local designer.
Comrags (654 Queen St W, tel: 416-360 7249; 3362 Yonge St, tel: 416-485 6260; www.comrags. com). Women's designs that range from edgy to comfortable, most often produced in easy-textured knits.
Courage My Love (14 Kensington Ave, tel: 416-979 1902). The Market's signature vintage shop.
Elegant Expectations (2 Toronto St, tel: 416-368 5581; www.elegant expectations.com). Unusual maternity clothes, both stylish and funky.
Fashion Crimes and Misdemeanours (322 Queen St W, tel: 416-351 8758). Frou-frou prom dresses and gorgeous girly sparkles with a humorous edge .
Hoax Couture (114 Cumberland, tel: 416-929 4629; www.hoax couture.com). Men's and women's original designs.
John Fluevog (242 Queen St W, tel: 416-581 1420; www.fluevog. com). Outrageous original footwear from a Vancouver designer.
Lilliput Hats (462 College St, tel: 416-536 5933; www.lilliputhats. com). Straw and fabric hats.
Lowon Pope (779 Queen St W, tel: 416-504 8150; www.lowon pope.com). Vintage-inspired gowns from Lana Lowon and Jim Pope.
Rubenesque (1751 Avenue Rd, tel: 416-787 8893; www.rubenesque. net). Women's wear in Canadian sizes 14 and up.
Sim & Jones (388 College St, tel: 416-920 2573; www.simandjones. com). Local designers exhibit contemporary flair in men's and women's lines.

Music and DVDs

There's a concentration of music stores around Yonge and Dundas. These include Toronto icon **Sam the Record Man** (347 Yonge St, tel: 416-646 2775; www.samtherecordman.com) with its large classical section, the **Sunrise Records Flagship Store** (336 Yonge St, tel: 416-595 5848; www.sunrise records.com), and **Play de Record** (357A Yonge St, tel: 416-586 0380; www.playde record.com) The Queen Street West area has vintage vinyl and second-hand CDs at **Neurotica** (642 Queen St W, tel: 416-603 7796; www.neurotica.ca) and **Rotate This** (620 Queen St W, tel: 416-504 8447; www.rotate.com).

Speciality foods

Pure maple sugar and syrup are available in many souvenir shops and the better grocers. All the ethnic neighbourhoods have foods from the home countries. **The Spice Trader** (805 Queen W, tel: 416-430 7085) sells exotic and organic spices. Downstairs, the **Olive Pit** carries only olive oils and balsamic vinegars.

Handmade chocolate truffles from a sixth-generation German chocolatier at **Stubbe Chocolate & Pastry Ltd** (253 Davenport Rd, tel: 416-923 0956; www.stubbechoco lates.com). Smoked salmon from the Canadian Pacific is the speciality of **Kristapson's** (3248 Yonge St, tel: 416-489 3474 and 1095 Queen St E, tel: 416-466 5152).

Cooks can also check out **Williams-Sonoma** for stylish cookware and ingredients (100 Bloor St W, tel: 416-962 9455 and Eaton Centre, tel: 416-260 1255; www.williams-sonoma.ca).

Sports shops

Centresports (Air Canada Centre, tel: 416-815 5746; www.centresports.ca) sells official Maple Leafs and Raptors team clothing and souvenirs.
Duke's Cycle (625 Queen St W, tel: 416-504 6138; www.dukeson queen.com) is an excellent source of cycling gear and for hockey sticks.

ABOVE: big city bookstore chain.

Europe Bound (383 King St W, tel: 416-205 9992; 47 Front St E, tel: 416-601 1990; www.europe bound.com) is a reputable outdoor gear retailer.
Jays Shop (Rogers Centre, tel: 416-341 2904; Sears, Eaton Centre, tel: 416-349 7111; www.bluejays.com) sells official Blue Jays clothing and souvenirs.
Just Hockey (900 Don Mills Rd, North York, tel: 416-445 5700; www.justhockeysfs.com) supplies every kind of hockey equipment.
Mountain Equipment Co-op (400 King St W, tel: 416-340 2667; www.mec.ca) is the largest, best-staffed shop for outdoor gear.
Spirit of Hockey (30 Yonge St, tel: 416-933 8228; www.hhof.com), the shop at Hockey Hall of Fame.
Sporting Life (2265 Yonge St, tel: 416-485 1611, plus four other locations; www.sportinglife.ca) is a large, well-stocked general-sporting equipment store.

SIGHTSEEING TOURS

By Bus

City tours cost about $30–35 for adults and $15–16 for children. Day trips to Niagara are around $90–125 for adults, $75 for children. "Hop-on, hop-off" tours are an easy way to explore Toronto.
Gray Line Sightseeing Tours (tel: 1-800-594 3310, 416-594 3310; www.grayline.ca).
Niagara Bound Tours (tel: 905-685 5375; www.niagaraboundtours. com).
Niagara Tours (tel: 416-868 0400; www.torontotours.com).
Niagara Wine Tours International (tel: 1-800-680 7006, 905-468 1300; www.niagaraworldwinetours.com).
Shop Dine Tour Toronto (tel: 416-463 7467; www.shopdinetour.com).

By Boat

Short harbour tours cost about $10–20 and are usually available without advance booking. Just stroll along the lake shore at Harbourfront and choose a vessel you like the look of. Cruises with meals, dancing or special events (like a fireworks display) are priced around $40–80, and must be reserved. Don't count on the food being spectacular, but the views usually are.
Hippo Tours (boarding at 151 Front St W, tel: 416-703 4476; www.torontohippotours.com) gives unique tours of the city and harbour in an amphibious bus.
Kajama Tall Ship (boarding at Queen's Quay W at Lower Simcoe St, tel: 416-203 2322; www.great lakesschooner.com) is a three-masted schooner.
Mariposa Cruise Line (Queen's Quay W at foot of York St, tel: 1-800-976 2442, 416-203 0178; www.mariposacruises.com).
Nautical Adventures (boarding on Queen's Quay W at the foot of Spadina, tel: 416-364 3244; www.nauticaladventure.com) dinner cruises on a three-masted schooner and a motor vessel.
TorontoHarbour.com (various locations along the waterfront, tel: 416-777 5777; www.toronto harbour.com).
Toronto Harbour Tours (145 Queen's Quay W, foot of York St, tel: 416-868 0400; www.harbour tours.com).

TRANSPORT

ACCOMMODATION

ACTIVITIES

A – Z

Toronto Kayak and Canoe Adventures (tel: 416-536 2067; www.torontoadventures.ca).
Voyageur Quest (tel: 1-800-794 9660, 416-486 3605; www.voyageurquest.com).

By Bicycle

The cost of bicycle touring varies widely, from as low as $15 for a two-hour junket around town to several thousand dollars for a multi-day ride with luxury accommodation and dining. Most operators can provide advice on bicycle rentals and Niagara Wine Tours International actually provides bikes.
Niagara Wine Tours International (see under "By bus", *page 231*).
Steve Bauer Bike Tours (tel: 905-563 8687; www.stevebauer.com).
A Taste of the World (tel: 416-923 6813; http://torontowalksbikes.com).
Urban Expeditions (tel: 416-606 7227; www.urbanexpeditions.com).

On Foot

Discovery Walks (tel: 416-338 0338; www.toronto.ca). Self-guided walks around the city landmarks.
Haunted Toronto (tel: 416-449 0356; www.ontarioghosts.org/walkingtours). Walks operated by the Ghosts and Haunting Research Society.
Historic Paths (tel: 416-338 3886; www.heritagetoronto.org). Free architecture and history tours.
Lost River Walks (tel: 416-781 7663; www.lostrivers.ca). Free tours retracing watercourses that are now buried under the modern city streets.
Nature walks (tel: 416-593 2656). Low price rambles run by Toronto Field Naturalists.
ROM Walks (tel: 416-488 5061; www.rom.on.ca). Free tours of local points of interest conducted by guides from the Royal Ontario Museum.
Toronto Bay Initiative (tel: 416-598 2277; www.torontobay.net). Free tours of waterfront areas, focusing on ecological restoration.

SPORTS

Spectator Sports

Toronto is a sports fan's city, and Torontonians are dedicated to their teams.
Baseball Toronto Blue Jays, are two-time World Series champs. Season: Apr–early Oct (Rogers Centre. Tel: 1-888-OK GO JAY, 416-341 1234; www.bluejays.com).
Basketball Toronto's professional team are the Raptors, in the National Basketball Association (NBA). Season: Nov–Apr (Air Canada Centre. Tel: 416-872 5000; www.raptors.com).
Canadian football Similar, but not the same as American football. The Toronto Argonauts compete in the Canadian Football League (CFL). Season: June–Oct (Rogers Centre. Tel: 416-341 1234; www.argonauts.ca).
Hockey The essential Canadian sport. The Toronto Maple Leafs compete in the National Hockey League (NHL). Season: Oct– Apr (Air Canada Centre. Tel: 416-872 5000; www.mapleleafs.com). The Toronto Marlies play in the American Hockey League (AHL; Ricoh Coliseum. Tel: 416-263 FANS; www.torontoroadrunners.com).
Horseracing Woodbine Racetrack, in the northwest outskirts, hosts some of Canada's top standard and thoroughbred events (555 Rexdale Blvd, tel: 1-888-675 RACE; www.woodbine entertainment.com/woodbine).
Lacrosse Canada's national game, played by the Iroquois some 350 years ago. The Toronto Rock team play in the National Lacrosse League games. Season: Jan–Apr (Air Canada Centre. Tel: 416-596 3075; www.torontorock.com).

Participatory Sports

Canoeing and kayaking: The harbour and island lagoon system are friendly waters for novice and expert paddlers. Mountain

Equipment Co-op (400 King St, tel: 416-340 2667; www.mec.ca) and Harbourfront Canoe and Kayak Centre (283A Queen's Quay W, tel: 1-800-960 8886, 416-203 2277; www.paddle toronto.com) rent kayaks and canoes for as little as $20 per day, including equipment and map; the latter also have lessons.
Cycling: There are many park trails around the city, including the Don Trail in the Don Valley, which winds north through a network of parks (access from Lakeshore Boulevard at Cherry Street, Don Valley bridge at Queen Street, pedestrian bridge in Riverdale Park). Tommy Thompson Park (tel: 416-661 6600), an artificial peninsula that juts 5 km (3 miles) out into Lake Ontario, is open to the public at weekends and most holidays. The Toronto Islands are also good for cycling, and bikes can be rented on the south shore of Centre Island. Wheel Excitement (249 Queen's Quay W, tel: 416-260 9000; www.wheelexcitement.ca) is a dependable rental outlet for bicycles and in-line skates. Serious cyclists should contact the Ontario Cycling Association (tel: 416-426 7242; www.ontariocycling.org) for more challenging rides.
Golf: There are many golf clubs in the Toronto area. The most famous is Glen Abbey (1333 Dorval Dr, in Oakville, tel: 905-844 1800; www.clublink.ca), designed by Jack Nicklaus, about 45 minutes west of downtown. Other notable courses within about an hour's drive include Royal Woodbine (195 Galaxy Blvd, tel: 416-674 7773; www. royalwoodbine.com); St Andrew's Valley (368 St John's Sideroad E, Aurora, tel: 905-707 7888; www. standrewsvalley.com); Hockley Valley Resort, (Rural Route #1 in Orangeville, tel: 416-363 5490, 519-942 0754; www.hockley.com); Wooden Sticks, (40 Elgin Park Dr, Uxbridge, tel: 905-852 4379; www.wooden sticks.com); Lionhead (8525 Mississauga Rd, Brampton, tel: 905-455 8400;

www.golflionhead.com), and Angus Glen (10080 Kennedy Rd, Markham, tel: 905-887 0090; www.angusglen.com). Some 2½ hrs north lies Taboo Golf Club (Muskoka Beach Rd, near Gravenhurst, tel: 866-982 2669; www.tabooresort.com), the home course of Canadian PGA star Mike Weir. There are about 30 courses in the Niagara region, about 2 hours southwest of the city (tel: 1-800-56 FALLS; www.discoverniagara.com/golf/main)

Hiking: The trails mentioned in the cycling section are all good places to walk in a natural environment. The Toronto and Region Conservation Area (tel: 416-661 6600; www.trca.on.ca) can provide information about more extensive hikes in a variety of beautiful municipal parks. Enthusiasts can tackle the 200-km (120-mile) Oak Ridges Moraine Trail (Oak Ridges Trail Association, tel: 1-877-314 0285; www.orta.on.ca) and the 50-sq. km (30-sq. mile) Rouge Park (tel: 905-713 7426; www.rougepark. com). Most challenging of all is the Bruce Trail, a 800-km (480-mile) hiking trail that winds through a variety of wild and rural landscapes from the Niagara escarpment to Tobermory, on Georgian Bay, passing just west of Toronto. The Bruce Trail Association (tel: 1-800-665 HIKE, 905-529 6821; www.brucetrail.org) can connect hikers with guides, and provide advice and supply a comprehensive trail guidebook.

Ice skating: The most popular outdoor skating rinks are at Nathan Phillips Square and at Harbourfront Centre (tel: 416-973 4886; www.harbourfront.on.ca). Inexpensive skate rental is available at both locations. .

Rock climbing: Joe Rockhead's Climbing Gym (29 Fraser Ave, tel: 416-538 7670; www.joerockheads. com) offers lessons at all levels. Some of the closest rises are Rattlesnake Point (about 45 minutes away) and Mount Nemo (about an hour). About 3½ hours north, Lion's Head in Tobermory is highly recommended. The

Alpine Club of Canada (tel: 905-277 5287; www.climbers.org/section/toronto) is the best source for information; Mountain Equipment Co-op (400 King St W, tel: 416-340 2667; www.mec.ca) rents gear.

Skiing and snowboarding: For a taster, go to the Centennial Park Snow Centre (256 Centennial Rd, Etobicoke) or North York Ski Centre (4169 Bathurst St, in Earl Bales Park). For both, tel: 416-33 TO SKI; www.city.toronto.on. ca). Ontario's premiere ski hills are at Blue Mountain, about 2 hours north in Collingwood (tel: 416-869 3799, 705-445 0231; www.bluemountain.ca). Closer to town are Snow Valley (tel: 416-366 7669, 705-721 SNOW; www.skisnowvalley.com) and Horseshoe Valley (tel: 416-283 2988, 705-835 2790; www.horseshoe resort.com), both about an hour north at Barrie. Just a little further up Highway 400, Mount St Louis/Moonstone in Coldwater (tel: 705-835 2112; www.mslm. on.ca). Hidden Valley Highlands, about 90 minutes north near Huntsville (tel: 1-800-398 9555; www.skihiddenvalley.on.ca) specialises in family and beginner skiing. Toronto and Region Conservation Area (tel: 416-661 6600; www.trca.on.ca) can advise on cross-country skiing trails.

CHILDREN

Black Creek Pioneer Village (see page 191).
Centreville (see page 94).
Harbourfront Centre (tel: 416-973 4000; www.harbourfrontcentre.com). Music and storytelling events.
High Park (see page 167).
Lorraine Kimsa Theatre for Young People (165 Front St E, tel: 416-862 2222; www.lktyp.ca). Award-winning professional company producing drama for children.
Milk International Children's Festival (Harbourfront Centre, tel: 416-973 4000; www.harbourfront centre.com/milk. International showcase of the world's best theatre

for young audiences (late May).
National Film Board (150 John St, tel: 416-973 3012; www.nfb.ca). Free film viewings for all ages, and animation workshops.
Ontario Place (see page 83).
Ontario Science Centre (see page 192).
Riverdale Farm (see page 183).
Sprockets International Film Festival for Children (tel: 416-968 FILM; www.bell.ca/sprockets; late Apr).
Toronto Zoo (see page 193).

SPAS

A spa day is a perfect antidote to sightseeing overload. Prices vary, but as a rough guide a manicure may cost $15–35, a pedicure $30–50 and a massage from about $75–95 per hour. It is customary to tip at least 10 percent, plus a little for a junior assistant.

Civello (887 Yonge St, tel: 416-924 9244; 2620 Yonge St, tel: 416-487 3535; 269 Queen St W, tel: 416-977 7755; 145 Lakeshore Rd E, tel: 905-842 4222; www.civello.com).
Clear Day Spa (300 York Mills Rd, tel: 416-386 0300; www.clearday spa.com).
Elizabeth Milan Day Spa (100 Front St W, tel: 416-350 7500; www.elizabthmilanspa.com).
The Elmwood Spa (18 Elm St, tel: 1-877-284 6348, 416-977 6751; www.elmwoodspa.com).
Healthwinds (2402 Yonge St, Suite LL01, tel: 416-488 9545; www.healthwindsspas.com).
Ici Paris (370 Danforth Ave, tel: 416-461 1774; www.iciparis.ca).
Jean Pierre Aesthetics & Spa (350 Yonge St, tel: 416-964 2505; www.jp_obsidian.com).
The Old Mill Inn & Spa (21 Old Mill Rd, tel: 416-232 3700; www.oldmilltoronto.com).
Pure + Simple (2375 Yonge St, tel: 416-481 2081; 27 Bellair St, tel: 416-924 6555; www.pureand simple.ca).
Uptown Spa (801 York Mills Rd, Suite 311, tel: 416-449 4044; www.uptownspa.com).

A - Z

A HANDY SUMMARY OF PRACTICAL INFORMATION, ARRANGED ALPHABETICALLY

Admission

See *Getting Tickets, page 226*.

Budgeting for your trip

An average traveller should be able to spend one day in Toronto very comfortably for about $200 ($125 for hotel, $10 for breakfast, $20 for lunch, $35 for dinner and $10 for public transport. A thrifty traveller might even get away with about $80–115 per day ($50–75 for accommodation, $30 for restaurant food, or as little as $20 self-catering and $10 for fares). For extravagant luxury, expect to pay at least $700–800 per day ($300–500 for accommodation, $25 for breakfast, $75 for lunch, as much as $200 for dinner and $100 for taxi fares).

Business Hours

Most offices open at 8 or 9am, and close at 4.30 or 5pm, Monday to Friday. Most banks are open between 10am and 3pm, Monday to Friday, with some keeping later hours and/or opening on weekends. Most downtown shops are open from 10am to 6pm Monday to Friday, and at least noon to 5pm on weekends. Some stay open until 9pm (especially on Fridays).

Climate

When to visit

Weather ranges from extreme heat and humidity in summer, with temperatures in the high 20°s–30°s Celsius (80°s–90°s Fahrenheit) to icy winters. Summer is lovely, but

the most comfortable months for sightseeing are May–June and September–October. From early November to April, snow and extreme cold are possible (a certainty mid-Dec to mid-Mar).

What to wear

Toronto is both fashion-conscious and informal. In business, men wear a seasonal suit and tie; women a suit or conservative dress. Jeans and T-shirts are generally accepted elsewhere, even at theatre, opera and symphony concerts, and in all but the most formal restaurants. Most people do dress up for nightlife.

In summer (June–Aug) you'll only need light clothing, with a jacket or sweater for cooler evenings (and air-conditioned buildings) and waterproofs in case of a shower. Add a layer or

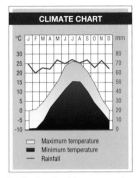

CLIMATE CHART

- Maximum temperature
- Minimum temperature
- Rainfall

two for the shoulder seasons. In winter (Nov–Apr) you need serious outer wear – a wind- and water-proof coat (over a warm fleece in severe weather), plus a scarf, warm hat and gloves. Carry these even on short car trips in case of the unexpected.

Crime and Safety

Toronto is a safe city at any time of day or night, but exercise common sense and no special precautions need be taken. Subway cars have emergency strips that alert authorities in the case of emergencies. All platforms have designated waiting areas (DWAs) with video surveillance and two-way speaker systems. From 9pm–5am, women travelling alone on buses can ask to disembark between regular stops.

Customs Regulations

There are strict restrictions on items that can be taken into Canada. These include living vegetation and firearms. Full details are available from Revenue Canada, Customs and Excise (tel: 204-983 3500 or 506-636 5064; www.ccraadrc.gc.ca). Check regulations about what you can bring back into your home country.

D isabled Travellers

Ontario has introduced legislation that will eventually require all public buildings and services to

be completely accessible. Until this takes full effect, it is wise to call ahead – especially to restaurants, clubs and theatres in older buildings – to confirm accessibility. Almost all pavements have dips at the curb, and most public buildings have ramps and accessible washrooms. Most car parks have spaces for people with disabilities. Some traffic lights have audio for the visually impaired.

Public Transit

Some subway stations have lifts, and all platform edges have textured strips for the safety of people with impaired vision. The TTC operates **Wheel-Trans** for people with disabilities (tel: 416-393 4181, TTY: 416-393 4555). A route map and information are available at www.city.toronto.on.ca

Important TTY numbers

Access Toronto (tourism advice): 416-338 0889
Bell Relay Service: Assistance in using TTY/teletypewriters, VCO (Voice Carry Over) and HCO (Hearing Carry Over) calls: 1-800-855 0511 (TTY only: 711)
Operator assistance for TTY users: 1-800-855 1155

E mbassies & Consulates

Foreign consulates

Australian Consulate-General: 175 Bloor St, tel: 416-323 1155
British Consulate-General: 777 Bay St, tel: 416-593 1290
Consulate General of Ireland: 20 Toronto St, tel: 416-366 9300
New Zealand Consulate: 225 MacPherson Ave, tel: 416-947 9696
South African Consulate General: 110 Sheppard Ave E, tel: 416-944 8825
United States Consulate General: 360 University Ave, tel: 416-595 1700

Canadian embassies and consulates abroad

Australia: Commonwealth Avenue, Canberra ACT 2600,

tel: 02-6270-4000 or 01-613-944 9136 (TTY)
New Zealand: Canadian High Commission, P.O. Box 8047, Level 11, 125 The Terrace, Wellington, tel: 64-4-473 9577
UK: Canadian High Commission, MacDonald House, 1 Grosvenor Sq, London, tel: 020-7258 6600
US: Consulate General of Canada, 1251 Ave of the Americas, New York, tel: 212-596 1628

Emergency Numbers

Police, fire, ambulance (emergencies only): 911
Police (non-emergency): 416-808 2222 (TTY only: 416-467 0493)
Poison information: 416-813 5900 (TTY only: 416-597 0215)
Crime Stoppers: 1-800-222 8477
Assaulted Women's Helpline: 416-863 0511 (TTY only: 1-866-863 7868); Elle écoute (for French speakers): 416-657 2229

Entry Requirements

US citizens born in the US should carry a passport or birth certificate plus photo ID. Naturalised US citizens need a naturalisation certificate plus photo ID. Permanent residents of the US who are not citizens need an alien-registration card. Residents of other countries must carry a passport. In some cases a visa is also required. For more information, call 1-800-992 7037 (outside Canada); 1-888-242 2100 (within Canada), 416-973 4444 (in Toronto), or visit www.cic.gc.ca.

Etiquette

Toronto is an informal but courteous city. To really fit in: hold doors open for people following

ELECTRICITY

Canada operates on **110 volts**. Electrical adaptors are commonly available at stores that sell electrical appliances.

TRANSPORT
ACCOMMODATION
ACTIVITIES
A – Z

you through; don't jump ahead in a queue; let people get off public transport before you get on; offer your seat to older passengers or pregnant women, offer assistance to other travellers struggling with luggage; on escalators, stand on the right, walk past on the left; say "Excuse me" if you accidentally nudge someone or need to walk in front of them. If you are a smoker, ask the people around you if it's OK to light up.

G ay & Lesbian Travellers

Toronto has large and politically active gay, lesbian, bisexual, transgendered and transsexual communities. The Church and Wellesley area is the main community hub, but gay and lesbian travellers should feel at home in most places. The free newspaper *Xtra!* (www.xtra.ca), for news and listings, is distributed every second week to pink boxes around downtown. Same-sex marriage is legal in Toronto, for more information call 416-392 7036, or visit www.toronto.ca/divisions/legserv_marriage.htm. Pride Week (tel: 416-92-PRIDE; www.pridetoronto.com), in late June, attracts hundreds of thousands of people with its parade.

BELOW: Union Station.

H ealth & Medical Care

Emergencies: Dial 911 (24 hrs). Non-emergencies: Call **Telehealth Ontario** (1-866-797 0000) for free consultation by phone. Non-Canadians must pay for most medical services at the time of treatment, then claim through their medical insurance.

24-hour hospital emergency rooms

The Hospital for Sick Children: 555 University Ave (at College)
St Michael's Hospital: 30 Bond St (Yonge & Queen)
Women's College Hospital: 76 Grenville St (near Bay & College)

Dental emergencies

Dental Emergency Service: 1650 Yonge St (north of St Clair), tel: 416-485 7121. Payment must be made in full by cash, VISA, MasterCard or Interac.

24-hour pharmacies

Shoppers Drug Mart have 24-hour opening at: 700 Bay St (at Gerrard), tel: 416-979 2424; 523 St Clair Ave W (at Bathurst), tel: 416-538 1155; 2345 Yonge St (north of Eglinton), tel: 416-487 5411.

Clinics

CanHealth Medical Clinic: 595 Bay St, tel: 416-598 1703.
Hassle Free Clinic: 556 Church St, tel: 416-922 0566 (women), 416-922 0603 (men). Free medical services relating to sexual and reproductive health matters.
Queen-Spadina Medical Centre: 455 Queen St W (at Spadina), 416-869 3627.

I nternet

Most hotels offer Internet access to guests. **Toronto Public Libraries** (tel: 416-393 7131; TTY: 416-393 7100; www.tpl.toronto.on.ca) offer free Internet access, but you will need to book ahead. Many inexpensive Internet cafés are listed in the telephone directory.

L anguage

In the 2001 Census, more than half of Torontonians reported that they speak English at home. About 8 percent usually speak Chinese and almost 5 percent speak Italian. Then come Punjabi (49,180), Portuguese (37,055), Tamil (36,225), Spanish (27,520) and Polish (25,535).

Left/Lost Luggage

Pearson International Airport Left luggage/lost-and-found: Terminal 1 (tel: 416-776 7749); Terminal 3 (tel: 416-776 7751). Items left in Terminal 2 are sent to Terminal 1.
VIA Rail baggage office is on the upper level of Union Station (tel: 416-956 7632).
GO Transit Lower level, Union Station (tel: 416-869 3600 ext 7273).
Toronto Transit Commission Bay station (tel: 416-393 4100).
Toronto Police Service report lost or stolen property on tel: 416-808 2222.

M aps

Most bookshops and hotels sell good local maps. **TTC Ride Guide** maps are free from subway stations. Other useful free maps are available from community and civic centres: *Toronto Regional Parks and Trails*; *Toronto Cycling Map* (from bike shops); *The Other Map of Toronto* (Green Tourism Association, tel: 416-392 1288; www.greentourism.on.ca).

Media

Print

Canada's national newspapers are the *Globe and Mail* and the *National Post*. Toronto's dailies are the *Toronto Star* and the tabloid *Toronto Sun*. The best free listings and entertainment coverage appears weekly (on Thursday) in *NOW Magazine* and *Eye Weekly*. *Maclean's* is Canada's weekly news magazine.

Television

More than 50 channels are broadcast in Toronto. CBC Television (channel 5; cable 6) is the national broadcaster, with a French-language sister station at (channel 25; cable 12).

Radio

There are many popular stations, including CBC One (99.1FM) and Two (94.1FM); CJBC Radio Canada (French; 90.3 FM), and specialist music between 88.1 and 107FM.

Money

The currency is the Canadian dollar. Coins are the penny (1 cent), nickel (5 cents), dime (10 cents), quarter (25 cents), loonie (1 dollar) and toonie (2 dollars). Notes (bills) come in 5, 10, 20, 50 and 100-dollar denominations. Some shops won't take a $50 or $100.

There are plenty of banks and bureaux de change downtown. US dollars are accepted in most places, but change will be given in Canadian dollars. Cash can be withdrawn in Canadian funds from cashpoints (ATMs) with shared banking systems. Traveller's cheques, major credit cards and debit cards are widely accepted.

P ostal Services

The standard rate for cards and letters within Canada is 50 cents; to the US it is 85 cents and to other countries $1.45. Canada Postal locations are listed in the business section of the telephone directory; drugstores and malls have a postal kiosk. Red mail boxes are located on street corners. The general information line is 1-800-267 1111.

Public Toilets

Toronto does not have a public washroom system, so try any handy establishment. Best bets are shopping malls and stations. Small places regulate users by holding washroom keys at the till or posting a customers only sign.

PUBLIC HOLIDAYS

Banks and government offices are generally closed on the following statutory holidays, but many shops remain open (except on Christmas Day).
January 1: New Year's Day
July 1: Canada Day
November 11: Remembrance Day
December 25: Christmas Day
December 26: Boxing Day

Movable Dates
Easter: Easter Sunday may fall anywhere from 22 March to 25 April. The preceding Friday (Good Friday) and following Monday are also holidays.
Victoria Day (Mon closest to 24 May)
Simcoe Day (Mon closest to 1 Aug)
Labour Day (first Mon in Sept)
Thanksgiving Day (second Mon in October)

R eligious Services

Roman Catholics are by far the largest religious group, with Protestants in second place. Muslims, Sikhs, Hindus, Buddhists and Jews are also represented. Any hotel concierge will direct you to the nearest place of worship.

S tudent Travellers

Students with a valid international student card are eligible for discounts on transit passes, theatre tickets and museum admission.

T axes

Canada's 7 percent Goods and Services Tax (GST) and Ontario's 8 percent Provincial Sales Tax (PST) apply to most purchases except essential services. However, visitors to Canada can apply for a rebate on GST paid on goods to be taken home and on up to 30 nights accommodation. Keep all receipts and get a form at any tourist office, shops or hotel. Call

800-668 4748 (in Canada) or 902-432 5608; www.pcra.gc.ca/visitors.

Telephones

Local calls from private telephones are free. The area codes **416** or **647** must be dialled within the city, in the GTA dial **905**. Numbers starting 1-800, 1-866, 1-877 and 1-888 are toll-free. To call long distance within North America dial 1; for international calls dial 011.

Public phones may be found in subway stations, restaurants and shopping malls. The charge for a local call is 25 cents; phone cards are widely available.
Directory assistance: 411
Operator assistance: 0

Tourist Information Offices

Access Toronto (tel: 416-338 0338, (TTY: 416-338 0889) runs an information kiosk inside City Hall (100 Queen St W). **Ontario Tourism** (www.ontariotravel.net) has a booth at the Eaton Centre, Level 1. **Tourism Toronto** (tel: 1-800-499 2514, 416-203 2600; www.torontotourism.com).

W eights and Measures

Canada uses the metric system.
1 centimetre (cm) = 0.394 in
1 kilometre (km) = 0.621 miles
1 litre = 0.22 UK gallon
1 litre = 0.26 US gallon
1 gram (g) = 0.035 oz
1 kilogram = 2.2 lbs

TIME ZONE

Toronto is in the **Eastern Standard Time Zone**. This is the same time as New York, five hours behind London and three hours ahead of Vancouver, San Francisco and Los Angeles. On the first Sunday in April, the clocks move ahead by one hour for Daylight Savings Time. They are set back again by one hour on the last Sunday in October.

TRANSPORT

ACCOMMODATION

ACTIVITIES

A – Z

FURTHER READING

Studies and Stories

Accidental City: The Transformation of Toronto by Robert Fulford. An insightful look at the evolution of the postwar city (Macfarlane Walter & Ross, 1996).

The City Man by Howard Akler. A dark, funny romance set in 1930s Toronto. (Coach House Books, 2005).

The Discovery of Insulin by Michael Bliss. The definitive account by a distinguished Toronto historian. (University of Chicago Press, 1984).

The Essential Toronto Island Guide by Linda Rosenbaum & Peter Dean. History, nature, architecture and anecdotes

Haunted Toronto by John Robert Colombo. True ghost stories (Dundurn Press, 1996)

I Brought the Ages Home by Charles Trick Currelly. The founding of the Royal Ontario Museum (Ryerson Press, 1967)

In the Skin of A Lion by Michael Ondaatje. An internationally acclaimed novel set in an imaginary Toronto of the early 1900s. (McClelland & Stewart, 1988)

Kensington by Jean Cochrane. Photos by Vincenzo Pietropaulo. An informative picture book about a fascinating city neighbourhood (The Boston Mills Press, 2000)

Old Toronto Houses by Tom Cruickshank. Photos by John de Visser. A beautiful and informative coffee-table book (Firefly Books, 2004)

Spadina Avenue by Rosemary Donegan. Introduction by Rick Salutin. Pictorial history of a street associated with many waves of immigration (Douglas & McIntyre, 1986).

Streets of Attitude: Toronto Stories edited by Cary Fagan & Robert MacDonald. A small-press collection of short stories (Yonge and Bloor Publishing, 1991).

Toronto – A Literary Guide by Greg Gatenby. Literary connections (McArthur & Co., 2000)

Toronto, No Mean City by Eric Arthur. A classic architectural study. (University of Toronto Press, 1964)

Toronto, The Unknown City by Howard Akler & Sarah B. Hood. Little-known facts (Arsenal Pulp Press, 2003).

Other Insight Guides

Insight Guides

The 190-title Insight Guides series is the main series in the Insight stable, known for its superb pictures, detailed maps excellent coverage of sights and comprehensive listings section. *Insight Guide: Canada* makes an excellent companion to this *City Guide: Toronto*, especially if you are planning to travel beyond the Greater Toronto Area.

Insight City Guides

Other cities included in Insight's highly successful City Guide series include Amsterdam, Barcelona, Beijing, Boston, Brussels, Cape Town, Hong Kong, Las Vegas, London, Madrid, Miami, New York, Paris, Prague, Rome, Singapore, Tokyo, Vancouver and Washington DC.

Insight Pocket Guide: Toronto has recommendations from a local host and a pull-out map. **Berlitz Pocket** guides to **Toronto** and **Canada** are on-the-spot reference guides. **Insight FlexiMap: Toronto** has a rainproof finish making it ideal for heavy use on the ground.

FEEDBACK

We do our best to ensure the information in our books is as accurate and up-to-date as possible. The books are updated on a regular basis, using local contacts, who painstakingly add, amend and correct as required. However, some mistakes and omissions are inevitable and we are ultimately reliant on our readers to put us in the picture.

We would welcome your feedback on any details related to your experiences using the book "on the road". Maybe we recommended a hotel that you liked (or another that you did not), as well as interesting new attractions, or facts and figures you have found out about the country itself. The more details you can give us (particularly with regard to addresses, e-mails and telephone numbers), the better.

We will acknowledge all contributions, and we'll offer an Insight Guide to the best letters received.

Please write to us at:
Insight Guides
PO Box 7910
London SE1 1WE
United Kingdom
Or send e-mail to:
insight@apaguide.co.uk

TORONTO STREET ATLAS

The key map shows the area of Toronto covered by the atlas section. An index of street names and places of interest shown on the maps can be found on the following pages. For each entry there is a page number and grid reference.

Map Legend

Freeway with Junction	✈ Airport	Freeway
Freeway (under construction)	✝ Church (ruins)	Divided Highway
Divided Highway	✝ Monastery	Main Roads
Main Road	🏰 Castle (ruins)	
Secondary Road	∴ Archaeological Site	Minor Roads
Minor Road	∩ Cave	
International Boundary	★ Place of Interest	Footpath
Province/State Boundary	🏠 Mansion/Stately Home	Railway
National Park/Reserve	※ Viewpoint	Pedestrian Area
Ferry Route	⚑ Beach	Important Building
		Park

Ⓜ Subway	
🚌 Bus Station	
❶ Tourist Information	
✉ Post Office	
✝ Cathedral/Church	
☾ Mosque	
✡ Synagogue	
⚲ Statue/Monument	
⌷ Tower	
⌖ Lighthouse	

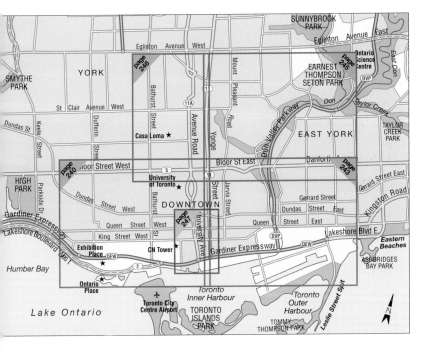

A B

Sterling Rd
Perth Ave

Herman Ave
Ritchie Ave
Golden Ave
St Johns Rd
Morrow Ave

Dundas St West

Lynd Ave
Parkway Ave
Columbus Ave

St Helens Avenue
Lansdowne Avenue
St Clarens Avenue
Marguerita Street

Brock Cr.
Croatia St

Gladstone Ave
Havelick St
Road
Road
Avenue
Avenue
Ossington Ave

Dufferin Park Ave

DUFFERIN GROVE

Hepbourne
Street

Dovercourt
Delaware
Concord

Harbord St

Roxton

Crawford

Whytock Ave

Chesley Ave
Muir Ave
Lindsey Ave
Bonar Pl.

Sylvan Ave
Lindsay Ave

Dewson
Avenue
Dewson St

College St

Lumbervale Ave

College St

1

Geoffrey Street
Westminster Avenue
Fermanagh Avenue
Wright Avenue
Fern Avenue
Garden Avenue
Galley Avenue
Pearson Avenue
Marion Avenue
Harvard Ave
Grafton Ave

Wabash Ave

Lansdowne

Shirley St
Kohenn Pl.
Rideau Ave
Wyndham St
Delaney Ave
Mechanic Ave

Hickson St
Brockton Ave
Norfolk St
Marshall St
Frankish Ave
Bank St
Middleton St
Gordon St
Florence St

Brock Ave

Moutray Street
Atkins Ave
Fisher St
Sheridan

Markle
Parr St
St Annes

Gladstone Ave
Rushholme Rd

Dufferin St

Heydon
Shannon St
Pk Rd
Churchill Ave
Ossington Ave
Harrison St
Baden

Dovercourt Rd
Coolmine Rd

Ossington Ave

HAMILTON PARK
Shaw St
Crawford

Dundas St West

Collahie St
MacKenzie
Beaconsfield Ave
Cross St

Stonehouse Cr.

Harrison St
Roxton Rd
Rolyat St

Grove Ave
Halton St
Givins St
Argyle St

Ossington Ave

West Lodge Avenue
Sorauren Avenue

Lansdowne Avenue

Seaforth Ave
Cunningham Ave
Margaret Ave

Waterloo Ave
Afton Ave
Alma Ave

Argyle St
Gladstone

Foxley St
Foxley Pl.

Humbert St

Peel Ave

Virtue St
Saunders Ave
Fuller Ave

MacDonell
West Lodge
O'Hara Ave
Abbs St
Noble St

Maple Grove Ave
Cambridge Ave
Strickland

Lisgar St

Beaconsfield
Northcote
Dovercourt Road

Fennings St
Brookfield St
Pridham Pl.
Rebecca St

Argyle St
Givins St
Lobb Ave

Museu Contem Canadia

2

Queen St West

Tiller
Wilson Park Road
Beaty Avenue
Dowling Avenue
Laxton Ave
Leopold St
Maynard Avenue

Gwynne Ave
Elm Grove

Cowan Ave

Melbourne Pl.
Melbourne Ave

Gladstone
Drake
Queen St West

Ontario Hospital

Gladstone

Lisgar St

Shaw St
Adelaide St

PARKDALE

King St West

Jameson Avenue

Glen Avon Rd
Dowling Ave
Springhurst Ave

Close
Dunn
Cowan Ave
Spencer Ave

Dufferin St

Avenue
Liberty
Street

Lamport Stadium

Avenue
Avenue
Avenue

King St West

Sudbury St

Shank

Douro St

East Liberty

3

Gardiner Expressway
Lake Shore Blvd West

Nel Dr.
Oasment Dr.

Queen Elizabeth Hospital

Tyndall
R. Route St
Springhurst

Trenton Terr.

Temple Ave
Thorburn Ave

Tyndall
Mowat
Fraser
Pardee Ave
Jefferson
Atlantic
Hanna

Liberty Grand

MARILYN BELL PARK

Aquatic Drive

British Columbia Dr.

Scadding Cabin

Dufferin St

Dufferin Gates

Saskatchewan Rd
Quebec St

Manitoba

Newfoundland Dr.
Ontario Dr.

Princess Blvd

Strachan Ave
Newfoundland Dr
Princess Blvd

National Trade Centre

Princess Blvd

Prince Gate

Autom Buildi

Exhibition Place

4

N

0 ──── 600 m

0 ──── 600 yards

Lake Shore Blvd West

Remembrance Dr.

Inukshuk

Ontario Place

Cinesphere

A B

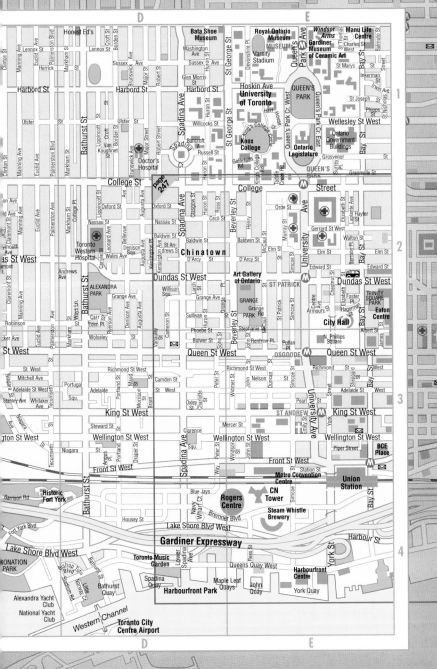

Map Labels

Top / Danforth area

Danforth Ave

Hampton Ave
Garnock Ave
Wolfrey Ave
garth Ave
Grandview Ave
Hampton Ave
Albemarle Ave
Bain
Withrow
riverdale

Logan Ave
Fenwick Ave
Gough Ave
McConnell Ave
Harcourt
Cavell Ave
Strath- cona Ave
Wroxeter Ave
Frizzell Ave
Dingwall Ave

WITHROW PARK

Hazelwood Ave
Avenue

Eustolia Ave
Chatham Ave
Ravina Ct
Baird Ave
Barley Grey Rd
Dawson Ave
Shudell Ave
Hunter St
Boothroyd Ave
Crystal Arts Stan
Boultbee Ave
Bain Ave

Chatham Ave
Byron Ave
Phin Ave
Queen Victoria St
Seymour Ave
Condor Ave
Boultbee Ave

Langley Ave
Victor Ave
Simpson Ave

Chatham Ave
Oakvale Ave
Mountalan Ave

Lagysmith Ave
Mountjoy Ave
Lamb Ave
Gillard Ave
Monarch
Parkmount Rd
Craven Rd
Rhodes Ave

Mountnoel Ave
Felstead Ave
Felstead Ave
Hanson St

MONARCH PARK

Quarry Ct
Torbrick Rd
Lount St
Walpole Ave
Hiawatha Rd
Ashdale Ave
Craven Rd
Rhodes Ave

Fairford Ave

Wagstaff Dr.

Pape Ave

Carlaw Ave
Blake Street
Kiswick St

Avenue
Avenue
Avenue
Withrow
Avenue

Boultbee Ave

Myrtle Ave
Bushell Ave
Leslie St
Harriett St
Hastings Ave
Ivy Ave
Prust Ave
Bloomfield Ave
Sandford Ave

Ivy Ave
Redwood Ave
Glenside Ave
Highfield Rd
Woodfield Rd

Greenwood Ave

Pouchert St
Galt Ave
Jones Ave
Margon St

Gerrard St East

Gerrard St East

Richard Ave
Athletic Ave
Billings Ave
Herlie
Highfield Rd
Hiawatha Rd
Ashdale Ave
Rhodes Ave

First Ave
Boston Ave
Badgerow Ave
Dickens St
Thackeray St

Austin Ave
Badgerow Ave
Dagmar Ave

Endean Ave
Sproat Ave
Curzon St
Stanton Ave
Parkfield Ave
Sawden Ave
Hastings Ave
Alton Ave

GREENWOOD PARK

Dundas St East

West Ave
Iverton Ave
Paisley Ave
Logan Ave
Booth Ave

Boston
Audley Ave
Brighton Ave
Blong Ave
Mallon Ave
Brookfin Ave
Coady Ave
Bertmount Ave

Hiltz Ave
Dorothy St
Cherry Nook Gdns
Kerr Rd
Vancouver Ave
Kent Rd
Woodfield Rd
Ashdale Ave
Craven Rd
Rhodes Ave
Wood Ward Ave

Cummings St
De Grassi St
Bruton Ave

Colgate Ave
Busy St
Bisley St
Verrall Ave
Louvain Ave

Jones Ave
Curzon St
Leslie St
Hastings Ave
Alton Ave
Greenwood Ave

Queen St East

Graham Pl
Doble St
McGee St
Empire Ave
Morse St
Logan Ave

Heward Ave
Carlaw Ave
Winnifred Ave
Caroline Ave
Larchmount Ave
Berkshire Ave
Rushbrooke Ave

Sears
Laing St
Knox Ave
Minto St
Connaught Ave

Eastern Ave

Pape Ave

Mosley St
Leslie St
Woodfield Rd

Eastern Ave

Lake Shore Blvd East

Gardiner Expressway

Lake Shore Blvd. East

Logan Ave
Morse St
Carlaw Ave
Bouchette St

Commissioners St

Leslie St

Sewage Treatment

Basin St

Turning Basin

Unwin Ave

A

B

Manor Rd
West

Manor Rd East

Manor Rd East

Manor Rd East

Gresham Rd

Lola Ave

Glebe Rd
West

Colin Ave

Dinsdale

Ave

Yonge St

Imperial Ave

Chaplin Cr.

Tullis Dr

Belsize

Carey
Rd

Cuthbert Cr

Oswald Cr

Servington Cr

Wilfrid Ave

Acacia

Penrose Rd

Tudor

Gate

Cleveland St

Tilson Rd

Hadley Rd

Harwood Rd

Bayon Rd

Belsize Rd

Belsize Dr.

Thurston Rd

Belcourt Rd

Cheston Rd

Belsize Dr.

Whitehood

Millwood Rd

Drive

Davisville Avenue

Mount Pleasant Rd

Millwood Rd

Davisville

Belle
Blvd

McCord
Rd

Forsyth

Fulman Ave

Lerway Rd

Ave

Millwood Rd

Bayview Ave

Berney Rd

Rolland

1

DAVISVILLE

Balliol St

Dalton Cr.

Balliol St

Cleveland St

Balliol St

St Cuthberts Rd

Mc Rae Dr.

Merton Street

Merton Street

Merton St.

Lawton Blvd

Airdrie Rd

Leaside Ave

Astor Ave

Bessborough Dr.

Southlea Ave

MOUNT   PLEASANT   CEMETERY

Sutherland Dr.

Leadale Ave

Mallory
Gdns

Glen Elm Ave

Moore Ave

Moore Ave

Moore Ave

Airlie St

Bessborough

Maton Cr.

Leacrest Rd

Heath St East

Ferndale
Ave

Cornish
Rd

Inglewood

Moore Ave

Wildwood Rd

Hudson Dr.

Brendan Rd

Burnham Rd

Ever-green

Orchard green Gdns

Heath Bridge
Pk Rd

2

Heath St East

Rose Pk. Cr.

Heath St E.

Hudson Dr.

Heath Dr.

Ridley

Heath St

East

ST CLAIR

Heath
Rose

Rose Park Dr.

Clifton Rd

Rose   Park   Dr.

Noel Ave

Bayview Hts.

St Clair Ave East

Inglewood Dr.

St Clair Ave E.

Welland Ave

Harper

Harper
Gdns

Bennington Heights Dr.

Red Oaks Cr.

Pleasant Blvd

Avoca Ave

Glenrose Ave

Valleyview

Nesbitt Dr.

Rosehill Ave

Clifton Rd

Inglewood Dr.

Inglewood Dr.

Douglas Cr

Yonge St

Jackes Ave

Reservoir

Sigmthill Ave

Garfield Ave

Rosedale Hights Rd.

Astley Ave

Governor's Rd

Woodlawn Ave East

Summerhill Gdns

Ridge Dr.

Ridge Dr.

Rosedale Heights Dr.

Old Bridle Path

Standish Ave

Edgewood Cr.

Glen Rd

Summerhill
Ave

Tacoma
Ave

Ottawa
St

BALFOUR
PARK

Carstowe Rd

Summerhill Ave

Jean St

Douglas Dr.

CHORLEY
PARK

3

SUMMERHILL

Shaftesbury Ave

Highland
Cr.

Whitehall Rd

Gregory
Ave

Summerhill Ave

St Andrews
Gdns

Glen Rd

Douglas Dr.

Pricefield Rd

Douglas

MacLennan Ave

Douglas Dr.

Price St

Cluny
Ave

Thornwood Rd

Highland
Gdns

ROSEDALE
PARK

Edgar Ave

Roxborough Dr.

Whitney Ave

Rowanwood

Chestnut Pk.

Highland
Ave

Schofield
Ave

Scarth   Rd

Roxborough

Cluny
Dr

St East

Roxborough Dr.

Old George Pl.

Highland Ave

Bin

Beaumont Rd

Bayview Ave

Don

TODM
M

Crescent Rd

Wrentham

Park Dr.

ROSEDALE

Crescent Rd

Crescent Rd

Lamport
Ave

May St

Reservation St.

Chester

Thorncliffe Ave

4

ROSEDALE

Cluny
Ave

Rosedale Dr.

South Dr

Ancroft Pl.

South Dr.

Meredith
Cr.

South Dr.

Sherbourne St

Crescent Rd

Dunbar Rd

Milkman's Rd

CRAIGLEIGH
GARDENS

Eastmount
Ave

Ozark Cr.

Yonge St

Rathnelly Ave

Binscarth Rd

Park Rd

Mount Pleasant Rd

South Dr.

Elm Ave

Elm Ave

Castle

Powell

HAWTHORNE
GDNS

Nanton Ave

Hawthorne Ave

Frank Rd

Pretor

Severn St

Collier St

Church St

Rachael
St

Maple
Ave

Glen Rd

Dale Ave

Powell
Ave

Ave

Dale Ave

Almeridge

0   600 m

0   600 yards

McKenzie
Ave

SHERBOURNE

CASTLE FRANK

Bloor   St   East

BROADVIEW

A

B

MOORE   PARK   RAVINE

LEAS

Errington Ave

Hudson Dr.

Welland Ave

MacLennan Ave

Nanton Ave

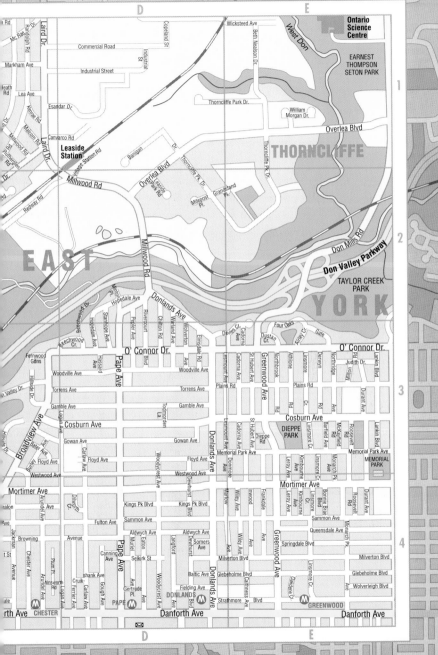

D

Mc Raeligh Rd
Mc Raeligh Dr.
Laird Dr.
Randolph Rd
Markham Ave
Heath Rd
Lea Ave
Kenrae Rd
Esandar Dr.
Milverton Rd
Malcolm Rd
Sutherland Dr.
Rumsey Rd
Canvarco Rd

Copeland St
Wicksteed Ave
Commercial Road
Industrial St
Industrial Street

West Don

**Ontario
Science
Centre**

**EARNEST
THOMPSON
SETON PARK**

Beth Nealson Dr.

Thorncliffe Park Dr.

William
Morgan Dr.

Overlea Blvd

THORNCLIFFE

1

**Leaside
Station**

Banigan
Leaside Village Station Rd

Millwood Rd
Overlea Blvd
Redway Rd

Thorncliffe Pk. Dr.
Leaside Park Rd
Milepost Pl.
Grandstand Pl.

Thorncliffe Pk. Dr.

Don Mills Rd

2

E A S T

Millwood Rd

Don Valley Parkway

**TAYLOR CREEK
PARK**

Y O R K

Beechwood Dr.
Donlands Ave
Minton Pl.
Hopedale Ave

Fernwood
Gdns
Beechwood
Cr.
Hogarth Ave
Stanhope Ave
Pepler Ave
Rivercourt
Blvd
Chilton Rd
Warland Ave
Wolverton
Ave
Elmsdale Rd
Davies Cr.
Cadorna Ave

Four Oaks

O' Connor Dr.
O' Connor Dr.

Woodville Ave
Hassard
Ave
Pape Ave
Woodville Ave
Cadorna Ave
St. Hubert Ave
Greenbrook
Northbrook
Athlone
Linsmore
Derwyn
Northridge
Judith Dr.
Lankin Blvd
Mann
Durant Ave

Torrens Ave
Logan Ave
Torrens Ave
Lesmount Ave
Plains Rd
Plains Rd

3

Hillside Dr.
Broadview Ave
Gamble Ave
Todmorden
La.
Gamble Ave
Lesmount Ave
Cadorna Ave
St. Hubert Ave
Linsmore
Cr.

Cosburn Ave
Cosburn Ave
**DIEPPE
PARK**
Linsmore Cr.
Barfield Ave
McKayfield
Ave
Roosevelt
Rd
Lankin Blvd

Gowan Ave
Carlaw Ave
Gowan Ave
Donmore
Dieppe
Rd
Kimbourne
Ave
Leroy Ave
Linsmore Cr.
Monarch
Ave
Memorial Park Ave

**MEMORIAL
PARK**

Bater Ave
Floyd Ave
Woodycrest Ave
Floyd Ave
Memorial Park Ave
Westwood Ave
Dewhurst
Westwood Ave
Mortimer Ave

Mortimer Ave
Arundel
Ave
Dillworth
Cr.
Kings Pk Blvd
Marrow
Wiley Ave
Inwood
Frandale
Leroy Ave
Kimbourne
Cr.
Linsmore
Cr.
Bonnie Brae
Blvd
Roosevelt
Rd
Durant Ave

4

Avalon
Jackman
St St
Avenue
Browning
Kings Pk Blvd
Sammon Ave
Fulton Ave
Aldwych Ave
Somers
Ave
Queensdale Ave
Sammon Ave
Springdale Blvd
Monarch
Ave
Milverton Blvd

Chester Ave
Plum Pl.
Ainsworth Rd
Logan Ave
Ferrier Ave
Cruikshank Ave
Carlaw Ave
Gough Ave
Avenue
Canning Ave
Muriel
Eaton
Selkirk St
Langford
Dewhurst
Somers
Aldwych Ave
Milverton Blvd
Glebeholme Blvd
Wolverleigh Blvd
Linsmore Cr.
Oakgene Cr.
Gertrude
Pl.
PAPE
Baltic Ave
Glebeholme Blvd
Fielding Ave
Strathmore
Blvd
Cathness Blvd
DONLANDS
GREENWOOD

CHESTER
Danforth Ave
Danforth Ave

✉

D

E

College St
Princess
Margaret
Hospital
Toronto General
Hospital
QUEEN'S
PARK
Maple Leaf
Gardens
Maple Leaf
Gardens
College St
Carlton St
COLLEGE
Stranby St
McGill St
Church St

Spadina Ave
Glasgow St
Ross St
Beverley St
Cecil St
Huron St
Henry St
Baldwin Street
University Ave
Orde St
Mt. Sinai
Hosp.
Murray St
Gerrard St West
Elizabeth St
Hayter St
Laplante Ave
Walton St
Gerrard St West
Delta
Chelsea
Inn
Bay St
O'Keefe
Gerrard St East
Ryerson
Polytechnic
University

Chinatown
McCaul St
Hospital for
Sick Children
Elm St
Barnaby Pl.
Elm St
Gould St
Victoria Lane
Bond St
Church St

D'Arcy Street
Larch St
Simcoe Street
Edward St
Edward St
Victoria St

Dundas St West
Art Gallery
of Ontario
ST PATRICK
Chestnut St
Dundas St West
DUNDAS
Dundas Sq.
Bond St

Grange Ave
Grange Pl.
Metropolitan
Holiday
Inn
Centre Ave
Elizabeth St
Foster Pl.
Marriott
TRINITY
SQ.
PK.
Eaton
Centre
Bond
Place

Sullivan St
Huron St
Soho St
GRANGE
PARK
Ontario College
of Art & Design
McCaul
St Patrick St
Armoury St
Hagerman
Simcoe St
Shuter St

Phoebe St
Stephanie St
City Hall
Massey
Hall
Salvation
Squ.
St Michael's
Hospital

Butwer St
Renfrew Pl.
Pullan Pl.
Beverley Street
Osgoode
Hall
N. Phillips
Square
Old City
Hall
Albert St
James St

Queen St West
OSGOODE
Four Seasons
Centre for the
Performing Arts
Queen St West
Queen St East
QUEEN

CITY-TV Museum
Bank of
Canada
Sheraton Centre
The Bay
Richmond St East
Berti St
Queen St East

Richmond St West
Hilton
Richmond St West
Sheppard St
Cambridge
Suites
The Arcade

Peter St
John St
Widmer St
Nelson St
Duncan St
Simcoe St
Richmond-
Adelaide Centre
Adelaide St West
Bay St
Temperance St
Adelaide St East
Court St

St West
Oxley St
Charlotte St
Holiday Inn
Royal
Alexandra
Theatre
Pearl St
Stock
Exchange
First Canadian
Place
Scotia
Plaza
KING
Toronto St
King St East

St West
Clarence Square
Princess of
Wales Theatre
Mercer St
ST ANDREW
Roy
Thomson
Hall
Emily St
King St West
Toronto
Dominion
Centre
York St
Jordan St
Melinda St
Bank of
Commerce
Hotel
Cosmopolitan
King
Edward

Wellington St West
St Andrew's
Presbyterian
University Ave
Wellington St West
Wellington St East

Peter St
Windsor St
CBC
Headquarter
Front St West
Piper St
Royal
Bank
Plaza
BCE
Place
Humm-
ingbird
Centre
Front St E.
Scott St
Church St

Way
Renaissance
Hotel
Station St
Fairmont
Royal York
UNION
STATION
The Esplanade
Novotel

Blue Jays Way
Navy Wharf Ct
Rogers
Centre
Bremner Blvd
CN
Tower
Simcoe St
Metro Convention
Centre
Union
Station
Bay St

Shore Blvd West
Steam Whistle
Brewery
Air Canada
Centre
Lake Shore Blvd East
Freeland St
Cooper St

Gardiner Expressway
York St
Harbour St
Conference
Centre
Queens Quay East
Harbour Castle
Westin

Spadina Ave
Rees St
Queens Quay West
Harbourfront
Centre
Radisson
Queen's
Quay
Terminal
Pier 6
Centre
0   400 m

to Music
n
Maple Leaf
Quays
John Quay
York Quay
Centre
York Quay
0   400 yards

ourfront Park

STREET INDEX

ART & PHOTO CREDITS

Alamy 177T
Shaun Best/Reuters/Corbis 37
Bettman/Corbis 25, 26, 123
Bridgeman Art Library 18
Bill Brooks/Alamy 172, 174T, 177
Mary Evans Picture Library 20
Jackie Garrow/APA back cover CR & BC, 7CL, 7BR, 9TR, 12/13, 27, 30/31, 35, 41, 43, 44, 48, 49L, 49R, 50L, 80T, 92T, 93, 102T, 104T, 109, 113T, 115T, 115BR, 119, 119T, 120T, 120, 121, 125, 131T, 131BL, 131BR, 132BR, 143, 145T, 148T, 153, 154, 179, 180, 181L, 181R, 183L, 188/189, 190, 192BL, 194T, 195T, 195, 196T, 196BL, 196BR, 197, 198T, 198, 199, 201T, 202, 205, 225, 231
Gehry International, Architects, Inc. 51
Getty Images 5BR
Hulton/Getty Images 16
Adam Hunger/Reuters/Corbis 116T
Image Ontario 102, 173, 191, 199T, 200T, 201, 202T, 202, 203T, 204, 206, 207T, 207
Britta Jaschinski 59
Keith Levitt/Alamy 34
Erling Mandelmann 199
JP Moczulski/AFP/Getty Images 7TR, 86
NBC-TV/The Kobal Collection 112
Peter Newark's American Pictures 19
Daniella Nowitz 3, 4, 6TR, 9BR, 54, 56, 57, 60, 63, 64, 66/67, 68/69, 76T, 78, 81, 82, 83, 87, 94, 95, 98T, 98, 99, 114T, 118, 121T, 122, 130T, 132T, 133, 134T, 150, 151, 156R, 157, 158L, 158R, 162, 162T, 164, 165, 166, 167BR, 167BL, 167T,

168T, 169T, 169, 170T, 170, 171, 178, 183R, 184T, 184, 185, 193T, 193, 229, 236
Richard Nowitz back cover CL, 1, 2/3, 4C, 5T, 6BR, 8TR, 8B, 9CL, 10/11, 14, 32, 33, 36, 40, 42, 50R, 55, 58, 61, 62, 65, 70, 74, 75, 79, 79T, 80, 82T, 85T, 88, 89, 92, 96T, 96, 97T, 97, 100, 101T, 101, 103T, 103, 104, 108, 110T, 111T, 113, 114, 115BL, 116, 117T, 118T, 122T, 128, 129, 132BL, 133T, 134, 135T, 135, 136, 142, 145, 146T, 146, 147, 156L, 157T, 159, 174, 175, 182, 192T, 192BR, 211, 213, 216, 217, 218, 227
Ontario Archive 17, 21, 22, 23, 29
Nicolas Sumner 117
Cylla von Tiedemann 47, 111
Tourism Toronto 6BL, 85, 91, 100T, 144T, 148, 155, 160R, 160L, 161, 203
Underwood & Underwood/Corbis 24
www.heritagemissussauga.com 28
Bruce Zinger 45

PICTURE SPREADS

Pages 38/39: Getty Images 38BR; David Hou 38BL; Toronto Tourism 38/39, 39TR, 39BC; RB/TS/Keystone/Rex 39CL

Pages 52/53: Canadian Museum of Civilization 52/53, 52CR, 52BR, 53CL, 53TR; Werner Forman Archive 52BL, 53BL, 53BR

Pages 106/107: Claus Anderson/Getty Images 108/109; Steve Babineau/NBAE via Getty

Images 109BC; Bruce Bennett Studios/Getty Images 109TR; Don Emmert/AFP/Getty Images 108BL; Peter Jones/Reuters/Corbis 109BR; Zoran Milich/Getty Images 108BR; J P Moczulski 109CL

Pages 126/127: Ronald Grant Archive 126/127, 126BL, 126BR, 127BL, 127TR, 127C; Andrew Wallace/Corbis 127BR

Pages 138/139: Courtesy of the Elgin and Winter Garden theatres 138/139, 138TL, 138BR, 139BL; Jackie Garrow/Apa139C

Pages 140/141: all pictures Courtesy of the Elgin and Winter Garden theatres.

Permissions
Every effort has been made to trace the copyright holders, and we apologise in advance for any unintentional omissions.

Works of art have been reproduced with the permission of the following copyright holders:

Tom Thomson (1877-1917), *Black Spruce in Autumn*, c. 1916, oil on panel, 21.7 x 26.8 cm, Gift of Mrs. W. Tweedale, McMichael Canadian Art Collection *p46*

Cartographic Editor: Zoë Goodwin
Map Production:
Dave Priestley, James Macdonald and Mike Adams
©2006 Apa Publications GmbH & Co. Verlag KG Singapore Branch

Book Production: Linton Donaldson

GENERAL INDEX

A page reference in **bold**
indicates the main entry
in the book. A page reference in *italics* indicates a
photograph.

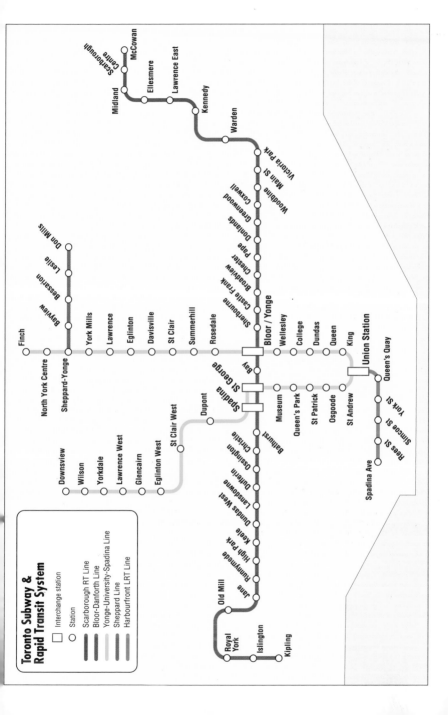

Toronto Subway & Rapid Transit System

Legend:
- □ Interchange station
- ○ Station
- Scarborough RT Line
- Bloor-Danforth Line
- Yonge-University-Spadina Line
- Sheppard Line
- Harbourfront LRT Line